Neil J. Anderson

ACTIVE

Skills for **Reading**: Book 4

HEINLE
CENGAGE Learning

Australia • Brazil • Japan • Korea • Mexico • Singapore • Spain • United Kingdom • United States

HEINLE
CENGAGE Learning

Active Skills for Reading,
2nd Edition Student Book 4
Neil J. Anderson

Editorial Director: Joe Dougherty
Director of Content Development:
Anita Raducanu
Director of Product Marketing: Amy Mabley
Editorial Manager: Sean Bermingham
Development Editor: Derek Mackrell
Content Project Manager: Tan Jin Hock
International Marketing Manager: Ian Martin
Sr. Print Buyer: Mary Beth Hennebury
Contributing Writers: Paul MacIntyre and
Tay Lesley
Compositor: CHROME Media Pte. Ltd.
Cover/Text Designer: CHROME Media Pte. Ltd.
Cover Images: All photos from Photos.com,
except amusement park (Index Open) and cyclist
(iStockphoto)
Photo Credits
Photos.com: pages 8, 9, 19, 39, 47, 54, 79,
81, 93 (all except bottom), 121, 127, 147, 149,
173, 175, 187 (top right and bottom right),
189; iStockphoto: pages 11, 27, 73, 119, 155,
195, 203; Landov: pages 13, 14, 87, 181, 201,
209; PhotoDisc/TYA Inc: pages 33, 65, 67;
Shutterstock: pages 41, 59, 62, 93 (bottom),
95, 108, 113, 162, 170, 217 (top), 224; Associated
Press: page 120; NASA/JPL-Caltech: pages 141,
167; Noemí Guil López: page 187 (top left);
Tjapukai Aboriginal Cultural Park: page 217
(bottom)

ISBN-13: 978-1-4240-0236-8

ISBN-10: 1-4240-0236-2

Heinle
25 Thomson Place
Boston, Massachusetts 02210
USA

Cengage Learning is a leading provider of customized learning solutions
with office locations around the globe, including Singapore, the United
Kingdom, Australia, Mexico, Brazil and Japan. Locate our local office at:
international.cengage.com/region

Cengage Learning products are represented in Canada by Nelson Education, Ltd.

Visit Heinle online at **elt.heinle.com**
Visit our corporate website at **cengage.com**

Printed in Canada
1 2 3 4 5 6 7 8 9 10 11 10 09 08 07

Dedication & Acknowledgments

This book is dedicated to Miranda Anderson. You will develop into a competent, fluent reader of good books as you read with your parents and family.

ACTIVE Skills for Reading has been a wonderful project to be involved with. I have enjoyed talking with teachers who use the series. I enjoy talking with students who have read passages from the book. When we published the first edition, I had no idea that we would be preparing the second edition so quickly. The success of the book is due to the teachers and students who have been engaged in ACTIVE reading. To the readers of ACTIVE Skills for Reading, I thank you.

I also express great appreciation to Paul MacIntyre for your significant contributions to this edition. It is a great pleasure to work with a committed professional like you. I also express appreciation to Derek Mackrell, Sean Bermingham, and Chris Wenger from Thomson. The support you provided me was unbelievable. I enjoy working with you. Special thanks to Maria O'Conor who played an essential role in the conception of the first edition of ACTIVE Skills for Reading.

Neil J. Anderson

Reviewers for this edition

Chiou-lan Chern National Taiwan Normal University; **Cheongsook Chin** English Campus Institute, Inje University; **Yang Hyun** Jung-Ang Girls' High School; **Li Junhe** Beijing No.4 High School; **Tim Knight** Gakushuin Women's College; **Ahmed M. Motala** University of Sharjah; **Gleides Ander Nonato** Colégio Arnaldo and Centro Universitário Newton Paiva; **Ethel Ogane** Tamagawa University; **Seung Ku Park** Sunmoon University; **Shu-chien, Sophia, Pan** College of Liberal Education, Shu-Te University; **Marlene Tavares de Allmeida** Wordshop Escola de Linguas; **Naowarat Tongkam** Silpakorn University; **Nobuo Tsuda** Konan University; **Hasan Hüseyin Zeyrek** Istanbul Kültür University Faculty of Economics and Administrative Sciences

Reviewers of the first edition

Penny Allan Languages Institute, Mount Royal College; **Jeremy Bishop** Ehwa Women's University; **William E. Brazda** Long Beach City College; **Michelle Buuck** Centennial College; **Chih-min Chou** National Chengchi University; **Karen Cronin** Shinjuku, Tokyo; **Marta O. Dmytrenko-Ahrabian** Wayne State University, English Language Institute; **James Goddard** Kwansei University; **Ann-Marie Hadzima** National Taiwan University; **Diane Hawley Nagatomo** Ochanomizu University; **Carolyn Ho** North Harris College; **Feng-Sheng Hung** National Kaohsiung First University of Science and Technology; **Yuko Iwata** Tokai University; **Johanna E. Katchen** National Tsing Hua University, Department of Foreign Languages; **Peter Kipp** Ehwa Women's University; **Julie Manning** Ritsumeikan Uji High School; **Gloria McPherson** English Language Institute, Seneca College; **Mary E. Meloy Lara** John F. Kennedy Primary School; **Young-in Moon** English Language and Literature Department, The University of Seoul; **Junil Oh** Pukyong National University; **Serdar Ozturk** Terraki Vakfı Okullarj; **Diana Pelyk** Ritsumeikan Asia Pacific University; **Stephen Russell** Meiji Gakuin University; **Consuelo Sañudo** Subsecretaria de Servicios Educativos para el Distrito Federal; **Robin Strickler** Kansai Gaidai University; **Liu Su-Fen** Mingchi Institute of Technology; **Cynthia Cheng-Fang** Tsui National Chengchi University; **Beatrice Vanni** University of Bahcesehir; **Kerry Vrabel** LaGuardia Community College; **Aysen Yurdakul** Buyuk Kolej

Contents

Vocabulary Learning Tips

Learning new vocabulary is an important part of learning to be a good reader. Remember that the letter **C** in **ACTIVE Skills for Reading** reminds us to cultivate vocabulary.

1 Decide if the word is worth learning now

As you read you will find many words you do not know. You will slow your reading fluency if you stop at every new word. For example, you should stop to find out the meaning of a new word if:
  a. you read the same word many times.
  b. the word appears in the heading of a passage, or in the topic sentence of a paragraph—the sentence that gives the main idea of the paragraph.

2 Record information about new words you decide to learn

Keep a vocabulary notebook in which you write words you want to remember. Complete the following information for words that you think are important to learn:

New word	collect
Translation	收集
Part of speech	verb
Sentence where found	Jamie Oliver collected more than 270,000 signatures from people.
My own sentence	My brother collects stamps.

3 Learn words from the same family

For many important words in English that you will want to learn, the word is part of a word family. As you learn new words, learn words in the family from other parts of speech (nouns, verbs, adjectives, adverbs, etc.).

Noun	happiness
Verb	
Adjective	happy
Adverb	happily

4 Learn words that go with the key word you are learning

When we learn new words, it is important to learn what other words are frequently used with them. These are called collocations. Here is an example from a student's notebook.

		long		
take		two-week		next week
go on	a	short	vacation	in Italy
need		summer		with my family
have		school		by myself

5 Create a word web

A word web is a picture that helps you connect words together and helps you increase your vocabulary. Here is a word web for the word "frightened":

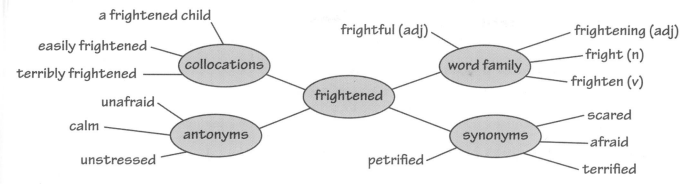

6 Memorize common prefixes, roots, and suffixes

Many English words can be divided into different parts. We call these parts *prefixes*, *roots*, and *suffixes*. A *prefix* comes at the beginning of a word, a *suffix* comes at the end of a word, and the *root* is the main part of the word. In your vocabulary notebook, make a list of prefixes and suffixes as you come across them. On pages 238–239 there is a list of prefixes and suffixes in this book. For example, look at the word "unhappily."

prefix: un- (meaning "not")   suffix: -ly (meaning "an adverb")

unhappily

root: happy

7 Regularly review your vocabulary notebook

You should review the words in your vocabulary notebook very often. The more often you review your list of new words, the sooner you will be able to recognize the words when you see them during reading. Set up a schedule to go over the words you are learning.

8 Make vocabulary flash cards

Flash cards are easy to make, and you can carry them everywhere with you. You can use them to study while you are waiting for the bus, walking to school or work, or eating a meal. You can use the flash cards with your friends to quiz each other. Here is an example of a flash card:

Front   Back

Tips for Fluent Reading

F
L
U
E
N
T

Find time to read every day.

Find the best time of day for you to read. Try to read when you are not tired. By reading every day, even for a short period, you will become a more fluent reader.

Look for a good place to read.

It is easier to read and study if you are comfortable. Make sure that there is good lighting in your reading area and that you are sitting in a comfortable chair. To make it easier to concentrate, try to read in a place where you won't be interrupted.

Use clues in the text to make predictions.

Fluent readers make predictions before and as they read. Use the title, subtitle, pictures, and captions to ask yourself questions about what you are going to read. Find answers to the questions when you read. After reading, think about what you have learned and decide what you need to read next to continue learning.

Establish goals before you read.

Before you read a text, think about the purpose of your reading. For example, do you just want to get a general idea of the passage? Or do you need to find specific information? Thinking about what you want to get from the reading will help you decide what reading skills you need to use.

Notice how your eyes and head are moving.

Good readers use their eyes, and not their heads, when they read. Moving your head back and forth when reading will make you tired. Practice avoiding head movements by placing your elbows on the table and resting your head in your hands. Do you feel movement as you read? If you do, hold your head still as you read. Also, try not to move your eyes back over a text. You should reread part of a text only when you have a specific purpose for rereading, for example, to make a connection between what you read previously and what you are reading now.

Try not to translate.

Translation slows down your reading. Instead of translating new words into your first language, first try to guess the meaning. Use the context (the other words around the new word) and word parts (prefixes, suffixes, and word roots) to help you guess the meaning.

Read in phrases rather than word by word.

Don't point at each word while you read. Practice reading in phrases—groups of words that go together.

Engage your imagination.

Good readers visualize what they are reading. They create a movie in their head of the story they are reading. As you read, try sharing with a partner the kinds of pictures that you create in your mind.

Avoid subvocalization.

Subvocalization means quietly saying the words as you read. You might be whispering the words or just silently saying them in your mind. Your eyes and brain can read much faster than you can speak. If you subvocalize, you can only read as fast as you can say the words. As you read, place your finger on your lips or your throat. Do you feel movement? If so, you are subvocalizing. Practice reading without moving your lips.

Don't worry about understanding every word.

Sometimes, as readers, we think we must understand the meaning of everything that we read. It isn't always necessary to understand every word in a passage in order to understand the meaning of the passage as a whole. Instead of interrupting your reading to find the meaning of a new word, circle the word and come back to it after you have finished reading.

Enjoy your reading.

Your enjoyment of reading will develop over time. Perhaps today you do not like to read in English, but as you read more, you should see a change in your attitude. The more you read in English, the easier it will become. You will find yourself looking forward to reading.

Read as much as you can.

The best tip to follow to become a more fluent reader is to read whenever and wherever you can. Good readers read a lot. They read many different kinds of material: newspapers, magazines, textbooks, websites, and graded readers. To practice this, keep a reading journal. Every day, make a list of the kinds of things you read during the day and how long you read each for. If you want to become a more fluent reader, read more!

Are You an ACTIVE Reader?

Before you use this book to develop your reading skills, think about your reading habits, and your strengths and weaknesses when reading in English. Check the statements that are true for you.

		Start of course	End of course
1	I read something in English every day.	☐	☐
2	I try to read where I'm comfortable and won't be interrupted.	☐	☐
3	I make predictions about what I'm going to read before I start reading.	☐	☐
4	I think about my purpose of reading before I start reading.	☐	☐
5	I keep my head still, and move only my eyes, when I read.	☐	☐
6	I try not to translate words from English to my first language.	☐	☐
7	I read in phrases rather than word by word.	☐	☐
8	I try to picture in my mind what I'm reading.	☐	☐
9	I read silently, without moving my lips.	☐	☐
10	I try to understand the meaning of the passage, and try not to worry about understanding the meaning of every word.	☐	☐
11	I usually enjoy reading in English.	☐	☐
12	I try to read as much as I can, especially outside class.	☐	☐

Follow the tips on pages 8–9. These will help you become a more active reader. At the end of the course, answer this quiz again to see if you have become a more fluent, active reader.

Getting Ready

Check (✔) your answer for each question in the survey below. Then discuss your answers with a partner.

What Kind of Job Is Right for You?

		Agree	Somewhat Agree	Disagree
1	I would like to work at the same company for my whole life.			
2	I can't enjoy a job unless it is quite challenging.			
3	I prefer working with other people to working alone.			
4	I get the most satisfaction out of working with my hands.			
5	For me, a position with power and status is attractive.			
6	If I take on a job, I always have a very strong sense of responsibility about it.			
7	I want to do a job that makes a contribution to society.			
8	My main motivation for working is to make money and, with luck, plenty of it.			
9	If I could, I'd work part time rather than full time.			
10	Balancing work time with my own private time is a challenge for me.			

Chapter 1: The Idol Life: Entrepreneurial Geniuses

Before You Read:
Real-Life Entrepreneurs

A Discuss the following questions with a partner.

1 Look at the photos on the next two pages. Can you name these two entrepreneurs? Can you name the world-famous businesses that each one started?

2 Can you name any other famous entrepreneurs? What line of business are they in? Which country are they from?

3 What do you think it takes to be a successful entrepreneur in today's business climate?

B Match these terms from the reading with their definitions.

1 entrepreneur _____
2 start-up capital _____
3 end-users _____
4 shareholders _____
5 franchising _____
6 going public _____

a. customers; consumers of a product
b. part owners of a public company who own its stock
c. a private company selling stock to the public for the first time
d. money used to create a new company
e. a pioneer in business
f. the practice whereby a company gives another company the right to sell its products in an area

Reading Skill:
Scanning

When we need to read something to find specific information, we move our eyes very quickly across the text. When we "scan" like this, we do not read every word or stop when we see a word we do not understand; we read quickly and pause only to find the particular information we are looking for.

A Read these statements about the reading. Without reading the passage, check (✔) if you think they are true (T) or false (F).

		T	F
1	Michael Dell set up his business with just $1,000.		
2	Michael Dell started IBM.		
3	Michael Dell was 36 years old at the time of the interview.		
4	Michael Dell and Anita Roddick define "entrepreneur" in the same way.		
5	The Body Shop was opened in 1986.		
6	The Body Shop sells more than 1,000 items.		
7	Anita Roddick believes that experimenting seems to kill entrepreneurial spirit.		
8	Anita Roddick hopes to be remembered for contributing to the awareness that business can and must be a force for positive social change.		

B Now scan the reading to find out if the statements above are really true or false.

C Read the passage again; then answer the questions that follow.

The Idol Life: Entrepreneurial Geniuses

When you think of the word "entrepreneur," who comes to mind? Whether you look at historical innovators such as Henry Ford[1] or John D. Rockefeller[2] or at today's headlines, there are just **a handful of** entrepreneurs who stand out in each generation. We recently talked to two of today's entrepreneurial icons—people whose names are synonymous with success, risk-taking, and independent thinking.
5 How have they changed from their early days in business through today's **volatile** market, ever-changing technology, and crowded business landscape? And how has their entrepreneurial spirit endured? Let's find out.

Michael Dell

As a college student, Michael Dell declared that he wanted to
10 beat IBM. In 1983, he began conducting business out of his dorm room at the University of Texas in Austin, selling custom-made PCs and components. A year later, with $1,000 in start-up capital, Dell officially set up his business and left school. "Being an entrepreneur wasn't on my mind," insists
15 Dell. "What was on my mind was the opportunity I saw ahead, which was so **compelling**."

He had no idea how big that opportunity really was. Dell Computer Corporation is now a $31.9 billion company. Though Dell himself had "no idea the Internet would come along," his
20 company now runs one of the world's largest Windows-based e-commerce websites. These days, Dell spends most of his time planning company strategy. "Strategy is the biggest point of impact I can have as the company is much, much larger—it has 40,000 employees," he says. "So my ability to make an impact
25 on anything else is pretty small."

Dell says he feels as entrepreneurial now as when he started. "There are plenty of markets to discover," he says, "and each new **venture** requires **tenacity** and a willingness to take risks." Dell shares his thoughts on what being an entrepreneur is about below.

Q: **How do you define "entrepreneur"?**
30 A: Somebody who has a new idea, or different idea, and takes a risk, and works hard to make it work.

Q: **How do you keep your entrepreneurial spirit alive?**
A: There's always a new challenge, whether it's a new product line, a new customer, a new service, or some new milestone.[3]

Q: **What was your dream when you started out?**
35 A: My plan was to sell built-to-order computer systems directly to end-users. I recognized there was a big opportunity there because of the inefficiencies of the indirect system.[4]

Q: **What would you hope to be your *legacy*?**
A: Well, I don't plan to be remembered any time soon. I'm 36 years old. But I hope they would think, this is a guy who built a company that created tremendous value for its customers, its employees,
40 and its shareholders. And perhaps, this is a guy who helped people realize the power of computing and the Internet. And then the last piece, which is something only a few people would know, that this is a guy who was a great dad and a great husband.

Anita Roddick

This interview was conducted in 2002. Anita Roddick died in 2007. She was 64 years old.

45 As a young girl, starting a business was the last thing on Anita Roddick's mind. "I wanted to be an actress," she says. Even when she began to pursue what would become The Body Shop, her environmentalism-minded skin- and hair-care company with more than 1,800 stores around the world, Roddick's goal
50 was not to be an icon.

Roddick opened her first shop in 1976 with twenty-five hand-mixed products, eventually franchising The Body Shop, and then going public in 1984. The Body Shop now offers more than 1,000 items and reached sales of more than one billion
55 dollars in 2001/2002.

In 1997, Roddick helped launch a master's degree program **in conjunction with** Bath University in England, with the aim of making business education more socially responsible. More recently, she established The Body Shop's Human Rights Award,
60 which recognizes individuals and organizations that focus on social, economic, and cultural rights.

The biggest challenge has been people's **cynicism**. "People feel there has to be an **ulterior motive** to The Body Shop's activism, as though our principles are a marketing **ploy**," Roddick says. Have the challenges affected Roddick's feelings about entrepreneurship? Not even slightly. "I don't think being
65 an entrepreneur is something you question," says Roddick. "It's just something you are."

Q: **How do you define "entrepreneur"?**
A: Entrepreneurs are obsessive visionaries, pathological[5] optimists, passionate storytellers, and outsiders[6] by nature.

Q: **How do you keep your entrepreneurial spirit alive?**
70 A: By being experimental. Success is double-edged:[7] Managing success seems to kill the entrepreneurial spirit. So to maintain it, you must keep on experimenting.

Q: **What was your dream when you started out?**
A: My business was a response to the extravagance and waste of the cosmetics industry. I felt there were plenty of people like me hungry for an alternative.

75 Q: **What would you hope to be your legacy?**
A: The future is being shaped by the forces of global business, so I would hope that I've helped change the vocabulary and practice of business, and contributed to the awareness that it can, and must, be a force for positive social change.

This reading was adapted from *The Idol Life* by Aliza Pilar Sherman.
Reprinted with permission from *Entrepreneur* Magazine © January 2002.

---

[1] **Henry Ford (1863–1947)** developer of the gasoline-powered motor car and founder of the Ford Motor Company
[2] **John D. Rockefeller (1839–1937)** famous early entrepreneur in the oil business and great philanthropist
[3] **milestone** important event or achievement
[4] **indirect system** system where the manufacturer sells to another company or store that the customer buys from
[5] **pathological** a state of disease or illness; used non-literally here to mean "obsessive"
[5] **outsiders** not members of a group; very independent people
[7] **double-edged** having two sides—usually one positive, one negative

A Complete the sentences with the correct answer, then discuss your answers with a partner.

1 Michael Dell and Anita Roddick are the foci of this article because they are both _____.

2 Now that his company is so large, Michael Dell mainly focuses on planning company _____.

3 As a young girl, Anita Roddick wanted to be _____.

4 In 1997, Anita Roddick helped launch a master's degree program with the aim of making business education more _____.

5 Anita Roddick's business was a response to the extravagance and waste of the _____.

B Decide if the following statements about the reading are true (T) or false (F). If you check false, correct the statement to make it true.

	T	F
1 In college, Michael Dell dreamed of beating IBM.		
2 Michael Dell predicted that the Internet would come along years before it actually did.		
3 Michael Dell doesn't plan to retire soon.		
4 The biggest challenge for The Body Shop has been selling their products.		
5 Anita Roddick believes that the future is being shaped by the forces of global business.		

C Critical Thinking

Discuss these questions with your partner.

1 If you were to start your own company, what kind of business would you go into? Why?

2 What difficulties and competition would you face if you were to start the business you talked about in question one?

3 How do you feel about entrepreneurs like Michael Dell and Anita Roddick? Do you admire them? Why or why not?

Vocabulary Comprehension:
Word Definitions

A Look at the list of words and phrases from the reading. Match each one with a definition on the right.

1 a handful of _____
2 volatile _____
3 compelling _____
4 venture _____
5 tenacity _____
6 legacy _____
7 in conjunction with _____
8 cynicism _____
9 ulterior motive _____
10 ploy _____

a. hidden or secret reason for doing something
b. likely to change suddenly or unexpectedly
c. something said or done in order to trick someone or gain advantage over them
d. an attitude of scornful negativity
e. forceful and persuasive
f. something that is passed on from one generation to the next
g. a plan, often in business, that involves uncertainty or risk
h. persistence
i. a small number or quantity
j. together (with)

B Complete the sentences below using the vocabulary from A. Be sure to use the correct form of the word.

1 Most people will tell you that the key to entrepreneurial success is _____.

2 Other people's _____ is something that most entrepreneurs continually have to fight against.

3 Working on new business _____ is what keeps many entrepreneurs enthusiastic about their work.

4 Though many people try to become billionaires through entrepreneurship, only _____ them succeed.

5 Everyone assumed that the businessman who was running for Congress had a(n) _____ when he donated a large percentage of his earnings to charity.

6 Eliza refuses to vote as she thinks most politicians tell lies as a(n) _____ to get people to vote for them.

7 If Derek's new business venture takes off, he will end up working _____ some of the biggest names in the computer industry.

8 My grandfather's _____ to his students was the love for math that he passed on to them.

9 Most business people will tell you that they are driven by some sort of _____ notion that their ideas will work.

10 Many people think it is very risky to invest while the stock markets are so _____.

A The words below can all be completed by adding the root *ten* or *tain*. Decide which form each word uses and write it in the space provided. Then write which part of speech each word is and, using your knowledge of prefixes and suffixes, write a definition.

Vocabulary	Part of Speech	Definition
1 abs_____		
2 un_____able		
3 de_____		
4 at_____		
5 re_____		
6 con_____er		
7 sus_____able		
8 _____ant		
9 _____ure		
10 main_____		
11 ob_____		
12 _____acious		

B Use your dictionary to make sure you have the correct meaning for each word. Then, complete the following sentences using words from A. Be sure to use the correct form of each word.

1 Jan's business grew so fast due to the _____ attitude of her employees.

2 As all the evidence in the murder case supported the defendant's guilt, his lawyer found himself in a(n) _____ position.

3 Julio _____ a nearly perfect grade point average during all his four years in college.

4 Martin wants to sell his house and use the money to buy a property overseas but his _____ refuses to move out.

5 Anna wants to go and work in Thailand but is having trouble _____ a work permit at the moment.

C Now write four more sentences using any of the remaining words from the list in A. Share your ideas with a partner.

1 _____

2 _____

3 _____

4 _____

Vocabulary Skill:

The Root Word *ten/tain*

In this chapter, you read the words "maintain" and "tenacity." Both are formed using the root word "ten" or "tain," which comes from the Latin word "tenere," meaning "hold on" or "persist." "Ten" or "tain" can be combined with prefixes, suffixes, and other root words to form many words in English.

Before You Read:
You're Hired!

A Discuss the following questions with a partner.

1 Have you ever had a job interview? What job was the interview for?
2 Did you feel nervous before the interview? If so, what did you do to calm your nerves?
3 How are job interviews in your country structured? Are there different types of interviews? What are they, and when are they used?

B Match the verbal expressions from the reading with their definitions.

1 have a say in _____
2 jot down _____
3 take something personally _____
4 weed out _____
5 win others over _____

a. write down quickly and simply
b. be part of an action or decision
c. remove what isn't needed or wanted
d. gain the approval of people
e. interpret something said as a personal attack

Reading Skill:
Skimming for Content

Skimming for content is a useful skill that can help you read and comprehend faster. You can get a good idea of the content of a passage without reading every word or sentence. By skimming quickly over the text you can pick up on the main points of the passage as well as the main idea of what the reading is about.

A Do you know anything about the different types of job interviews? Read the following statements and see how many you can complete by circling the correct word or phrase. If you do not know anything about the subject, just read the statements to get an idea of what the reading is about.

1 Unqualified candidates are weeded out early at a (screening / one-on-one) interview.
2 Notes are (unnecessary / a good idea) in a telephone interview.
3 Salary issues are best (dealt with / avoided) in a telephone interview.
4 Rescheduling surprise interviews is probably a (good / bad) idea.
5 If you are given a one-on-one interview, you probably (might get / have already gotten) the job.
6 At a lunch interview, you should order (whatever you like / what the interviewer suggests).
7 Employers see how candidates interact with each other at a (committee / group) interview.
8 An interviewer might purposely fall silent at a (group / stress) interview.

B Now, spend ONE minute skimming over the passage to get a basic grasp of the content. Do NOT try to read every word. Don't stop when you see words you do not know, or read the footnotes; just let your eyes skim quickly back and forth over the text.

C Now go back to the statements above and see how many of them you can confidently complete. Change any answers that you now think are incorrect. Read through the passage to confirm your answers.

Job Interview Types

If you are going to apply for a job in the United States, be prepared in advance for the types of interviews you can expect during the hiring process. Here are the
5 major ones and tips on how to handle them.

Screening[1] Interview

A screening interview is meant to weed out unqualified candidates. Interviewers will work from an outline of points they want to cover,
10 looking for **inconsistencies** in your résumé and challenging your qualifications. Provide answers to their questions, and never volunteer any additional information. That could work against you. One type of screening interview is the telephone interview.

Telephone Interview

15 Telephone interviews are merely screening interviews meant to eliminate poorly qualified candidates so that only a few are left for personal interviews. You might be called out of the blue,[2] or a telephone call to check on your résumé might turn into an interview. Your mission[3] is to be invited for a personal face-to-face interview.

Here are some tips for telephone interviews:

20 *Anticipate the dialogue.* Write a general script with answers to questions you might be asked. Focus on skills, experiences, and accomplishments. Practice until you are comfortable.

Keep your notes handy.[4] Have any key information, including your résumé and notes about the company, next to the phone. You will sound prepared if you don't have to search for information. Make sure you also have a notepad and pen so you can jot down notes and any questions you would
25 like to ask at the end of the interview.

Be prepared to **think on your feet.** If you are asked to participate in a role-playing situation, give short but **concise** answers. Accept any criticism with **tact** and grace.[5]

Avoid salary issues. If you are asked how much money you would expect, try to avoid the issue by using a delaying statement or give a very broad range. At this point, you do not know how much the
30 job is worth.

Push for a face-to-face meeting. Sell yourself by closing with something like: "I am very interested in exploring the possibility of working in your company. I would appreciate an opportunity to meet with you in person. I am free either Tuesday afternoon or Wednesday morning. Which would be better for you?"

35 *Try to reschedule surprise interviews.* If you were called unexpectedly, try to set an appointment to call so you can be better prepared by saying something like: "I have a scheduling conflict right now. Can I call you back tomorrow after work, at 6 P.M.?"

One-on-One Interview

40　In a one-on-one interview, it has already been established that you have the skills and education necessary for the position. The interviewer wants to see if you will fit in with the company, and how your skills will **complement** the rest of the department. Your goal in a one-on-one interview is to establish **rapport** with the interviewer and show him or her that your qualifications will benefit the company.

Lunch Interview

45　The same rules apply in lunch interviews as in those held at the office. The setting may be more casual, but remember, it is a business lunch and you are being watched carefully. Use the lunch interview to develop common ground[6] with your interviewer. Follow his or her lead in both selection of food and in etiquette.

Committee Interview

50　Committee interviews are a common practice. You will face several members of the company who have a say in whether you are hired. When answering questions from several people, speak directly to the person asking the question; it is not necessary to answer to the group. In some committee interviews, you may be asked to demonstrate your problem-solving skills. The committee will outline a situation and ask you to formulate a plan that deals with the problem. You don't have to come up
55　with the ultimate solution. The interviewers are looking for how you apply your knowledge and skills to a real-life situation.

Group Interview

A group interview is usually designed to uncover the leadership potential of prospective managers and employees who will be dealing with the public. The front-runner[7] candidates are gathered
60　together in an informal, discussion-type interview. A subject is introduced and the interviewer will start off the discussion. The goal of the group interview is to see how you interact with others and how you use your knowledge and reasoning powers to win others over. If you do well in the group interview, you can expect to be asked back for a more extensive interview.

Stress Interview

65　Stress interviews are a **deliberate** attempt to see how you handle yourself. The interviewer may be **sarcastic** or argumentative, or may keep you waiting. Expect this to happen and, when it does, don't take it personally. Calmly answer each question as it comes. Ask for **clarification** if you need it and never rush into an answer. The interviewer may also become silent at some point during the questioning. Recognize this as an attempt to unnerve you. Sit silently until the interviewer **resumes**
70　the questions. If a minute goes by, ask if he or she needs clarification of your last comments.

This reading was adapted from *Job Interview Types*.
Reprinted with permission from www.careerbuilder.com © 2001.

¹ **screening** looking carefully at someone/something in order to evaluate them/it
² **out of the blue** without warning; suddenly
³ **mission** object or goal
⁴ **handy** ready to hand; nearby (for reference)
⁵ **grace** goodwill
⁶ **common ground** agreement or understanding between two people
⁷ **front-runner** a leading contender for a job or competition

A How much do you remember from the reading? For each question or statement, choose the best answer. Try not to look back at the reading for the answers.

1 What is the main purpose of the reading?
   a. to prepare employers for interviews
   b. to compare different types of interviews
   c. to explain which type of interview is best
   d. to inform job seekers about different types of interviews
2 What is NOT a type of interview mentioned in the article?
   a. a screening interview
   b. a committee interview
   c. a candidate interview
   d. a stress interview
3 What is the purpose of a screening interview?
   a. to identify unqualified candidates
   b. to invite the candidate to a telephone interview
   c. to make a final decision about the candidate
   d. to find the most qualified candidate
4 Your main goal during a telephone interview is _____.
   a. to get information about the company
   b. to be invited for a personal face-to-face interview
   c. to make friends with the interviewer
   d. to find out who else is applying for the job
5 If the interviewer becomes sarcastic or argumentative, the interview is probably _____.
   a. lasting too long
   b. almost finished
   c. a stress interview
   d. going very well

B The following statements are all about the reading. Complete each one using a word or phrase you have read.

1 One purpose of a one-on-one interview is for the employer to see how your _____ will complement those of the other employees.
2 A _____ interview may appear casual, but remember you are being _____ carefully.
3 During a committee interview, _____ to the person asking the question.
4 One purpose of a group interview is to identify your _____ potential.
5 A _____ interview is an attempt to see how you _____ yourself under pressure.

C Critical Thinking

Discuss these questions with a partner.

1 Which type of interview do you think is the easiest for the candidate? Which is the easiest for the interviewer?

2 What other methods do companies use to find new job candidates and choose the best among them?

Vocabulary Comprehension:
Odd Word Out

A **For each group, circle the word that does not belong. The words in *italics* are vocabulary items from the reading.**

1	similarities	*inconsistencies*	variations	conflicts
2	act spontaneously	react quickly	plan ahead	*think on your feet*
3	*concise*	wordy	succinct	brief
4	diplomacy	insensitivity	*tact*	courtesy
5	*complement*	supplement	enhance	clash
6	harmony	disagreement	*rapport*	understanding
7	*deliberate*	purposeful	hasty	planned
8	jeering	mocking	*sarcastic*	pleasant
9	*clarification*	disorganization	disorder	misunderstanding
10	starts over	*resumes*	begins again	overdoes

B **Complete the sentences using the words in *italics* from A. Be sure to use the correct form of the word.**

1 I thought Carlos was serious when he told me Maria used to be a chef. Once I tasted her soup, I realized he was being _____. It was terrible.

2 Leon was very embarrassed in the board meeting as his report contained a lot of _____.

3 The reason Cynthia got the job was because she had an excellent _____ with the interviewer.

4 If you are asked to criticize anything in an interview, be sure to use _____. You don't want to appear rude or insensitive.

5 Quick decisions are critical in an emergency situation; as a manager you are expected to be able to _____.

6 The terrorist attack brought business to a halt; the earliest that people were able to _____ working was three weeks later.

7 I'm afraid that your report was very confusing, and several points required _____.

8 Parker claimed he spilled coffee on Jun's papers by accident, but we all know that it was _____.

9 Our office staff consists of a small and varied group of people, but we all have skills that _____ each other very well.

10 Martin's presentations are so well organized and _____ that his training sessions are well attended and always end on time.

A Compare the words *complement* and *compliment*. Use each in the sentences below. Be sure to use the correct form of each word.

> **complement** /ˈkɒmpləmənt/ **n.** Something that completes, makes up a whole, or brings to perfection.

> **compliment** /ˈkɒmpləmənt/ **n.** An expression of praise, admiration, or congratulation.

1 The famous painters Diego Rivera and Frida Kahlo were excellent partners because they truly _____ each other.
2 Sometimes just by _____ people, you can make them feel very good about themselves.

B Look at the words below. For each pair of homophones, look up the definitions in a dictionary and write them down. Then, write a sentence that uses each word correctly.

1 **a.** council: _____
   use: _____
   b. counsel: _____
   use: _____
2 **a.** faze: _____
   use: _____
   b. phase: _____
   use: _____
3 **a.** profit: _____
   use: _____
   b. prophet: _____
   use: _____
4 **a.** led: _____
   use: _____
   b. lead: _____
   use: _____

Vocabulary Skill:
Homophones

In this unit, you read the word "complement." There is another word, "compliment," that is pronounced the same as "complement," and is spelled almost the same, but has a different meaning. Words like these are called "homophones," and there are many of these in English.

Real Life Skill:
Reading Job Ads

The most common place to find job ads is in newspapers and magazines. Because advertising is expensive and space is limited, the ads often contain many abbreviations. It is important to understand the meaning of these abbreviations when looking for a job that fits your experience, skills, and educational background.

A Read this job advertisement.

BOOKKEEPER
Imm opening in large medical office. Exp only. Req strong background in payroll, invoices, w/ knowledge of BookkeeperPro or similar software. Flexible PT sched, some wknds req. Excellent salary (neg) plus full benefits. **Call Sara at 555-0011.**

B Match each abbreviation with its definition.

1 neg _____
2 exp only _____
3 imm _____
4 wknds _____
5 w/ _____
6 req _____
7 PT _____
8 sched _____

a. Saturdays and Sundays
b. working hours
c. not full-time
d. this is necessary
e. we will discuss this
f. right now
g. only people who have done this work before
h. having

C With a partner, discuss what the exact meaning of each abbreviation is.

Example: *exp only* stands for "experienced only"

D Read the following ad and try to figure out the meaning of each abbreviation.

INTERNATIONAL SALES: Office Equipment
For Asia/Australia/NZ. Extensive travel.
Base salary (up to $30K neg) + excellent commission. Req four-yr degree, computer literate, excellent spoken/written English (other langs a plus). Imm start. Send res to: phil@globalhireonline.net

NZ _____   K _____   yr _____
langs _____   res _____

E Do you think this would be a good job for you? Tell your partner why or why not.

What Do You Think?

1 What kinds of jobs are most popular for graduates in your country at the moment?
2 When do college and university students in your country start looking for jobs? Are there any special resources to help them?
3 Around the world, attitudes toward work differ. We use the phrase "work ethic" to talk about these attitudes. Phrases such as "live to work" and "work to live" are used to describe different work ethics. What do you understand by these phrases? What is the difference in meaning between them?
4 What is the work ethic in your country? Do you think this is good? Do you know of any countries where the work ethic is very different from that of your country?

Computer Culture

Getting Ready

A Complete the quiz about computer viruses below. Then check your answers at the bottom of the page.

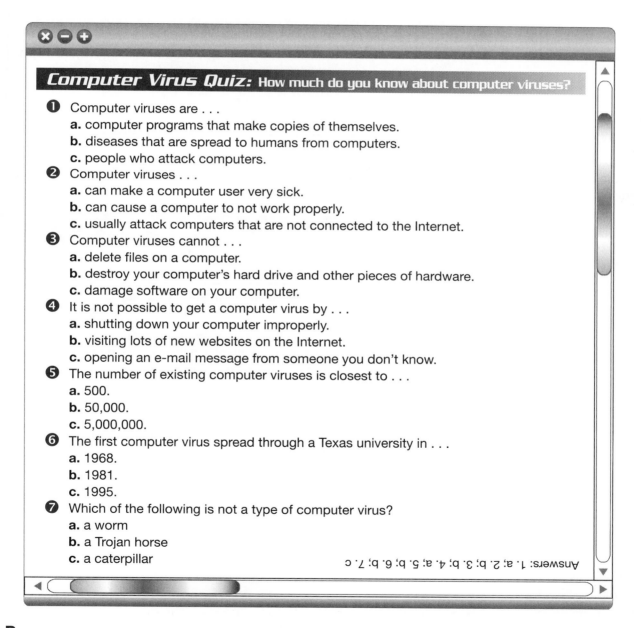

Computer Virus Quiz: How much do you know about computer viruses?

❶ Computer viruses are . . .
   a. computer programs that make copies of themselves.
   b. diseases that are spread to humans from computers.
   c. people who attack computers.

❷ Computer viruses . . .
   a. can make a computer user very sick.
   b. can cause a computer to not work properly.
   c. usually attack computers that are not connected to the Internet.

❸ Computer viruses cannot . . .
   a. delete files on a computer.
   b. destroy your computer's hard drive and other pieces of hardware.
   c. damage software on your computer.

❹ It is not possible to get a computer virus by . . .
   a. shutting down your computer improperly.
   b. visiting lots of new websites on the Internet.
   c. opening an e-mail message from someone you don't know.

❺ The number of existing computer viruses is closest to . . .
   a. 500.
   b. 50,000.
   c. 5,000,000.

❻ The first computer virus spread through a Texas university in . . .
   a. 1968.
   b. 1981.
   c. 1995.

❼ Which of the following is not a type of computer virus?
   a. a worm
   b. a Trojan horse
   c. a caterpillar

Answers: 1. a; 2. b; 3. b; 4. a; 5. b; 6. b; 7. c

B What was your score? Were any answers surprising? Discuss your results with a partner.

Chapter 1: Unmasking Virus Writers and Hackers

Before You Read:

Criminal or Cool?

A Answer the following questions.

1 What do you understand by the word "stereotype"? In your country, is there a stereotypical image of someone who is a computer expert? Describe this image.
2 Why do you think people hack into computers or write computer viruses?
3 What is your personal view of computer hackers and virus writers?
4 Is it a criminal act in your country to hack into a computer or spread any kind of computer virus? If so, do you agree with this law? Why or why not? If it is not law, do you think it should be made law?

B Discuss your answers with a partner.

Reading Skill:

Understanding Inference

Information in a reading passage can be found in two ways: by what is stated directly and written clearly on the page, or by what we can infer. When we infer, we use the information that is stated directly to draw conclusions about events, or the writer's opinion or purpose. Knowing how to infer can help you to better understand the writer's purpose and ideas. It is a useful skill to know when reading for pleasure, and can help you better understand reading passages in exams.

A Read through each of the following statements carefully. Scan through the reading passage and decide if each statement is stated (S) or inferred (I). Check (✔) the correct column.

	S	I
1 Most people think that the majority of virus writers and hackers are male.		
2 One stereotypical image of virus writers is that they are introverted loners.		
3 Although hackers and virus writers tend to be grouped together as similar, they differ greatly in their knowledge of computers and motivation for what they do.		
4 Hacking into a computer tends to require a higher level of skill than virus writing.		
5 Hackers tend to be people who like to have control over what they do in life.		
6 Young virus writers like to think they can bring about social change.		
7 Computers act as a barrier that can cause us to become desensitized to others' feelings.		
8 Virus writing was once considered an exciting and trendy pursuit.		

B Check your answers with a partner. Discuss the reasons for your answers by making reference to the relevant parts of the reading.

C Now read the passage again and answer the questions that follow.

Unmasking Virus Writers and Hackers

When we think of the people who make our lives miserable by hacking into computers or spreading **malicious** viruses, most of us imagine an unpopular teenage boy, brilliant but geeky, venting his frustrations[1] from the safety of a suburban bedroom.

Actually, these stereotypes are just that—stereotypes—according to Sarah Gordon, an expert in computer viruses and security technology, and a Senior Research Fellow with Symantec Security Response. Since 1992, Gordon has studied the psychology of virus writers. "A hacker or a virus writer is just as likely to be the guy next door to you," she says, "or the kid at the checkout line bagging[2] your groceries. Your average hacker is not necessarily some Goth[3] type dressed entirely in black and sporting a nose ring: she may very well be a 50-year-old female."

The virus writers Gordon has come to know have varied backgrounds; while **predominantly** male, some are female. Some are solidly[4] academic, while others are athletic. Many have friendships with members of the opposite sex, good relationships with their parents and families; most are popular with their peers. They don't spend all their time in the basement. One virus writer volunteers in his local library, working with elderly people. One of them is a poet and a musician, another is an electrical engineer, and others work for a university quantum physics[5] department. You wouldn't pick them out of a lineup as being the **perpetrator**.

Hackers and virus writers are actually very different, distinct populations. "Hackers tend to have a more thorough knowledge of systems and a more highly developed skill set," Gordon says, "whereas virus writers generally take a shallower approach to what they're doing." Hackers tend to have a much deeper knowledge of individual applications and are still regarded as being somewhat "sexy" in today's counterculture,[6] while virus writing is looked down upon, mostly for its random damage and lack of required skill.

Their motivations[7] may also differ. While both hackers and virus writers are initially attracted by the technical challenge, hacking is more about power and control. When you're hacking and you get into a system, you remain involved with that system—you take it over and **dominate** it. On the other hand, once a virus writer releases a program into the wild, the virus goes off and keeps on making copies of itself independently of the author. It's not as **intimate** or connected a relationship as between a hacker and the computer—the virus writer **relinquishes** control and becomes disassociated from the actual activity he or she has set in motion.

Gordon explains that people write viruses for a number of reasons. Some may perceive it as a technical challenge, even though writing a virus is actually very easy. It can take two minutes or less, depending on

the application you're using. And the part of the program that makes it viral, i.e., that makes it **replicate** itself, is generally very simple—just one or two lines of **code**. It's much more complicated to write a useful
40 application than it is to write a virus.

Younger virus writers like to be part of a group. They look for peer identity, which is important to them. Or it may be a way to make a social statement. If you're a young person who doesn't have a lot of power and you can **assert** yourself with a political statement in a virus that travels all around the world, you might think you're making a difference, imagining yourself a modern-day social activist.[8] Gordon says, "It's a big
45 deal to them when they see it on CNN. They feel like they've reached the world."

"Furthermore," Gordon says, "most virus writers don't understand the damage they do. Most of them just don't make the connection between actions and their consequences." This is understandable to a degree because the computer has introduced a shift in the way we communicate. Desensitization[9] occurs; you miss all the visual cues, the contextual clues, and you don't see the impact you're having on another
50 person. We've all gotten e-mail from people who are actually abusive in writing when they'd never speak to us that way in person.

People who make mischief with their computers seem to distance themselves from their actions. They justify their behavior with the **rationale** that "It's not really wrong, it's not illegal." Or they may tell themselves, "Well, everybody has antivirus software, so if I send this out, it won't really hurt anybody."

55 Fortunately, social pressure is changing the impressions people have of hackers and virus writers. Their own peers are beginning to say to them, "This is not cool." And, while it is still widely legal to make viruses publicly available, Gordon's research has shown a decrease in acceptance of online publication of virus source code. Gordon says the media used to promote virus-writers as being geniuses and heroes. But now the press has changed its tune.[10] They no longer portray virus writers as brilliant and misunderstood.
60 "We're seeing the media start to turn around," she says. "We're getting the message out to young people that writing viruses really isn't cool."

This reading was adapted from *Unmasking Virus Writers and Hackers* by Sarah Gordon. First published by Symantec Corporation, April 24, 2002. Copyright © 2002 Symantec Corporation. Reprinted with permission.

[1] **venting (his) frustrations** getting rid of feelings of anger or resentment
[2] **bagging** putting something in a bag
[3] **Goth** abbreviation of Gothic—of or relating to the Middle Ages; in modern terms, of or relating to a style emphasizing mystery and darkness, characterized by dark or black clothing and dark make-up
[4] **solidly** definitely; firmly
[5] **quantum physics** science of measuring energy
[6] **counterculture** a culture, usually prevalent among young people, with values that oppose those of the establishment
[7] **motivations** the reasons why a person does certain things
[8] **social activist** person who campaigns or takes action to bring about changes in society
[9] **desensitization** process of becoming less sensitive toward something
[10] **changed (its) tune** changed the view or opinion of something usually in a spoken or written form

A Choose the best answer for each question or statement. Compare your answers with a partner.

1 What is the article mainly about?
a. why hacking and virus writing are bad and why people shouldn't do them
b. how people become hackers and virus writers and what we can do about them
c. who hackers and virus writers are, what they do, and what people think about them
d. the history of hackers and virus writers

2 The average hacker tends to be _____.
a. a stereotypical geek
b. more often male
c. socially frustrated
d. scientifically inclined

3 What does the reading tell us about the social backgrounds of virus writers?
a. They come from many different backgrounds.
b. Most of them work in grocery stores.
c. Female virus writers like to dress in black.
d. They are very antisocial.

4 Which of the following statements is NOT true about the differences between hackers and virus writers?
a. Hackers tend to possess more technical knowledge.
b. Virus writers take a shallower approach to what they do.
c. Hackers have more knowledge of program applications.
d. Hackers are initially more attracted by the technical challenge of what they do.

5 One main motivation that drives a hacker is _____.
a. power and control
b. fame
c. it is easier than writing a virus
d. friendship

B Decide if the following statements about the reading are true (T) or false (F). If you check (✔) false, correct the statement to make it true.

	T	F
1 Virus writers and hackers are male or female and almost any age, although most are male.		
2 Writing a virus is a difficult technical task.		
3 Young virus writers like to feel part of a group.		
4 Most virus writers believe that what they do is wrong.		
5 There is social pressure to increase the acceptance of virus writers and hackers.		

C Critical Thinking

Discuss these questions with a partner.
1 Why do you think society has had a tendency to be lenient and even understanding of virus writers and hackers?
2 What are some of the ways in which hackers can be dangerous to society?
3 The article claims that computer communication desensitizes us. Do you feel this is true for you? Explain your reasons.

Vocabulary Comprehension:
Word Definitions

A Look at the list of words from the reading. Match each one with a definition on the right.

1 malicious _____
2 predominately _____
3 perpetrator _____
4 dominate _____
5 intimate _____
6 relinquishes _____
7 replicate _____
8 code _____
9 assert _____
10 rationale _____

a. very closely associated or familiar
b. most noticeably or largest in number
c. to influence or control something or someone
d. someone who commits a crime or harmful act
e. to copy or repeat something
f. gives up or surrenders something
g. wanting to cause harm to others
h. reasoning or justification for something
i. to express oneself in a bold or forceful way
j. language used to tell computers what to do

B Complete the sentences using the vocabulary from A. Be sure to use the correct form of each word.

1 One of the main reasons that people seek therapy is because they have a fear of _____ relationships.
2 For years the workforce in this company was _____ by men; now there are roughly equal numbers of men and women.
3 Though top executives in many international corporations are still _____ male, an increasing number of women are attaining high level positions.
4 In most ball games, one player or team wins when their opponent _____ control of the ball.
5 That is a completely unique piece of art, and nobody knows the technique for making it anymore: it is quite impossible to _____ it.
6 After spending years being shy and introverted, Ling decided to _____ herself and asked Michael out on a date!
7 That video game is simple to play, but it required 5,000 lines of _____ to create the software for it.
8 Some people thought Carly's attempts to get promoted over Sunil were purely _____. Others viewed her actions as healthy competition.
9 As a teenager, I never understood my parents' _____ when they prohibited me from staying out after midnight.
10 Some psychologists say that if you stare into the eyes of the _____ of any crime for long enough, you will see if he or she is guilty or not.

A For each word, study its different parts. Use your knowledge of prefixes, suffixes, and word roots to write the part of speech and a simple definition. Use your dictionary to check your answers. Share your ideas with a partner.

Vocabulary	Part of Speech	Definition
1 implicate		
2 inexplicable		
3 explicit		
4 pleat*		
5 pliable		
6 multiply		
7 multiplex		
8 implicit		

*Some words can have more than one part of speech.

B Now complete the following sentences using the words from A. Be sure to use the correct form of each word.
1 Carl is quite particular about how his pants are pressed; the _____ have to be starched and ironed as straight as possible.
2 Does anyone want to see a movie at the new _____ tonight?
3 Joanne gave me very _____ directions to her house, but I still managed to get lost.
4 This new type of molding clay feels much more _____. It can be molded into shape more easily; the children love it.
5 The number of people outside the theater quickly _____ when word spread that free concert tickets were being given away.
6 As Jason had been seen hanging out with known thieves, the police _____ him in the robbery of the convenience store.
7 Even though Sara and Jin Soo do not believe in the supernatural, they had to admit to some _____ occurrences in their house.
8 Juliana and Keith had a(n) _____ agreement not to discuss family issues around the dinner table.

Vocabulary Skill:
The Root Word *plic*

In this chapter, you read the words "replicate," which means "to repeat" or "to copy," and "complicate," which means "to make more difficult." The root word "plic," also written as "ply," "plex," or "pli," comes from the Latin word "plicare," meaning "fold," "bend," "layer," or "entwine." This root is combined with other prefixes and suffixes to form many words in English.

Chapter 2: Female Virus Writer Packs a Punch

Reading Skill:
Arguing For and
Against a Topic

Many reading passages present two sides of an argument—one argues for, or in favor of, the topic; the other argues against it. Phrases such as "advocates of," "proponents of," and "in favor of" signal that information that supports one side of the argument will be introduced. Phrases like "advocates against," "critics of," "skeptics of," or "concerns about" signal that information against the topic is coming. Also, words and phrases like "argues that," "questions," "however," "though," "in contrast," and "in spite of" signal that an opposite or different opinion is about to be introduced.

A Discuss the following questions with a partner.

1 Based on your knowledge of computer virus writers, how common is it for them to be female?
2 At what age do you think most virus writers would become interested in computers?
3 What damage can computer viruses cause?

B Match the computer terms on the left with their definitions.

1 Commodore 64 _____
2 C# _____
3 .Net _____
4 Microsoft Outlook _____

a. a computer programming language
b. an e-mail program
c. an early desktop computer from the 1980s
d. a software platform that integrates various technologies

C Scan the reading for the terms and check your answers.

A Scan the reading passage and complete the chart with information from the passage.

Computer Virus Writing

Arguments For	Arguments Against
1 _____	1 _____
2 _____	2 _____
3 _____	3 _____
4 _____	4 _____

B Compare your answers with a partner. Are there any other reasons you can add to your list?

C Now read the passage again and complete the comprehension exercises that follow.

Female Virus Writer Packs a Punch

She can kick you in the pants *and* wipe your hard drive cleaner than a dog's dinner plate. So when the young kickboxer and virus writer known as "Gigabyte" tells you she doesn't want her face on TV, well, you **play along**.

"I'll just shoot[1] you from behind," I say, carrying my
5 TV camera across the large mat that covers the health club's gymnasium floor. It's almost time for the 6 P.M. kickboxing class, and Gigabyte is the only woman there. Of course, she's used to that. In the male-dominated world of virus writers, she stands out. And
10 not only because of her gender. She is also something of a virus-writing **prodigy**, having started programming at age six. "I figured out how to write a few lines of code on my uncle's Commodore 64," says Gigabyte. "Later, I wanted to learn more about programming, so I went to
15 the store and asked for books. The salespeople were surprised. It was like, 'Why do you want a book? Why don't you just buy a game and go play?' But games are not very interesting to me. I wanted to learn how to write real executable[2] programs."

20 So she did.

At age fourteen, she wrote her first computer worm,[3] which took over the shutdown screens of infected users. Two years later, she wrote a powerful virus that **mangles** MP3 files. More recently she became only the second person to write a virus in C#, the language of Microsoft's .Net platform. Her so-called "Sharpei" worm, which comes in an e-mail attachment, spreads via Microsoft's Outlook e-mail program
25 and infects certain files in computers where the .Net framework is present.

The morning after kickboxing class, I arrive at Gigabyte's house at 6:30. She's having tea with her grandmother in the kitchen of a tiny, **immaculate** cottage. She has lived with her grandparents most of her life, for reasons she **declines** to discuss. We catch the public bus downtown to her school. Although the bus is packed with other teenagers, she speaks to no one.

30 We walk a few blocks to her school, where I meet her computer teacher. "She is a good young programmer," she says. "But I do not approve of her virus writing. I know she says she is not causing any harm, and it is true that she does not intentionally spread these viruses, but I do not think it is appropriate, and viruses can cause a lot of damage." Nevertheless, teacher and student are **cordial** to each other throughout the long morning class. Later that afternoon, Gigabyte walks around the computer
35 room her grandparents have set aside for her, flicking on[4] no fewer than four Windows machines. She's comfortable here, and full of opinions.

On being some sort of feminist icon, she says, ". . . I'm a virus writer. If I wanted to make a [feminist] statement, don't you think it would be part of the viruses I've written? I mean, yeah, I do want to admit I'm female because there is nothing to hide about it. The world should know there are female virus writers out there. But it's certainly not my motivation for virus writing. I do this for myself, not for the whole world. Other females don't need me to **stand up for** them; they can do it for themselves."

On the ethics of writing viruses: "I'm not responsible for stupid people who open e-mail attachments that erase their files."

"Hey," she says, "let's go outside. I want to show you something."

I'm led out into the backyard garden, which is beautifully **groomed**. There are painted gnomes, and a small pond, and then, suddenly, there is a ferret,[5] Gigabyte's pet ferret, out for a little afternoon walk. How right they are for each other, I think, looking at the ferret and the virus writer. Both are **cunning** and quick, and you wouldn't want either of them to bite you.

"Virus writing is so aggressive, and most reasonable people consider it an act of vandalism,[6] or at least potential vandalism," I say. "Would you spray paint **graffiti** on somebody's wall?"

"We are not coming inside anyone's walls," she said. "The users are running the virus. They are the ones clicking on it."

"So you think the people who execute these programs are responsible for the damage that your viruses do?" I ask.

"Actually," she says, "I think stupid people should have to have some sort of license to get on the Internet."

There's a pause in the conversation. The ferret is turning somersaults[7] in the grass at our feet. "Do you think of what you do as art?" I ask.

"I want to do something original, that not everyone does," she says. "If you write something that's new or funny or special in a way, then I think it is a form of art, yes."

I ask her if she wants to work with computers for a living. When she grows up, I mean.

"Yes. But not with an antivirus company," she says. "I will never do antivirus." That would run counter to her code.

This reading was adapted from *Female Hacker Packs Punch* by Rick Lockridge, reprinted with permission of *TechTV* © 2002.

[1] **shoot** film; colloquial term used to mean "take a photo" or "record on film"
[2] **executable** effective; able to perform and do the job for which it was designed
[3] **worm** a type of computer virus that replicates itself and destroys information or interferes with software
[4] **flicking on** switching on
[5] **ferret** small, brown, furry animal kept as a pet and often trained to hunt rats and rabbits
[6] **vandalism** the act of destroying property for fun
[7] **somersaults** rolling the body over headfirst to land on the feet

A

The following questions are all about the reading. Answer each one using the information you have read. Try not to look back at the reading for the answer.

1 How would you describe the author's attitude toward Gigabyte?
_____

2 In the first paragraph, why did the author decide to "play along" with Gigabyte? _____

3 Did Gigabyte like to play computer games at a young age?
_____

4 How does Gigabyte's "Sharpei" worm spread from one computer to another? _____

5 What can we infer from the reading about Gigabyte's relationship with her parents? _____

B

Complete the sentences with information from the reading. Write no more than three words for each answer.

1 Gigabyte started computer programming at the age of _____.
2 Gigabyte wrote her first computer virus when she was _____.
3 Gigabyte lives with her _____.
4 The author thinks Gigabyte and her ferret are both _____.
5 Gigabyte thinks stupid people should be required to have a license to get on _____.

C Critical Thinking

Discuss these questions with a partner.
1 Would you like to meet Gigabyte? Why or why not?
2 Why doesn't Gigabyte use her real name in the interview? Do you think she wishes she could?
3 Gigabyte says she would never work for an antivirus company. What do you think her reasons are?

A

The words in *italics* are vocabulary items from the reading. Read each question or statement and choose the correct answer. Compare your answers with a partner.

1 If someone is playing a joke on someone, and he or she asks you to *play along*, that person wants you to _____.
   a. say what the joke is   **b.** act as if the joke is real
2 A *prodigy* shows his or her talent at an unusually _____ age.
   a. young   **b.** old
3 If someone *mangles* the engine in their car, it will _____.
   a. work better   **b.** not work at all
4 If your desk is *immaculate*, it is _____.
   a. disorganized and messy   **b.** very neat and tidy

5 If somebody *declines* to comment on a topic, it means they _____.
   a. want to speak about it   **b.** don't want to speak about it
6 A *cordial* letter is one that is _____.
   a. pleasant and friendly   **b.** malicious
7 You should *stand up for* your rights means that you should _____.
   a. stand up when you speak   **b.** assert yourself
8 Well-*groomed* is an adjective used to describe someone who is _____.
   a. well-traveled   **b.** neat in appearance
9 A *cunning* person would be _____ toward others.
   a. deceptive   **b.** sincere
10 Where would you most likely find *graffiti*?
   a. on a dinner menu   **b.** on the walls of public bathrooms

B **Answer these questions. Share your answers with a partner.**

1 Talk about a time that you *played along* with a joke.
2 Give an example of a child *prodigy* whom you know, or have heard of. What is he/she good at?
3 Give an example of something that can be *mangled*. How would this object most likely end up in this state?
4 If somebody were to look around your bedroom or house right now, would they say it is *immaculate*? If not, what adjectives would they use?
5 When was the last time you *declined* an invitation to go out? What circumstances usually cause you to do this?
6 What is an example of a *cordial* greeting? Give an example of a greeting that is not so cordial.
7 Talk about someone you know, or someone in history, who is known for *standing up for* his or her rights, or the rights of others. What did they achieve by doing this?
8 On what occasions in your culture is it especially important to be well-*groomed*?
9 Do you know anyone who you could describe as *cunning*? Explain why you would describe this person as *cunning* using examples.
10 Do you see a lot of *graffiti* in your country or in your neighborhood? Do you consider *graffiti* to be a form of vandalism, or a form of art? Explain your answer.

Vocabulary Skill:

The Root Word
graph/graphy

In this chapter, you read the word "graffiti," a variation of the Greek word "graphein," meaning "to write" or "record" something. The root "graphy" also refers to "the study of something." The root words "graph" and "graphy" are combined with prefixes and suffixes to form many words in English.

A **Look at the word stems in the box below, then read the list of definitions that follow. Add the root *graph* or *graphy* to each word stem to make words that match the definitions. Use your dictionary to check your answers.**

biblio   photo   para   bio   carto   mono
autobio   demo   seismo   choreo

1 the life memoirs of a person, written by that person _____
2 a short section of a text, made up of two or more sentences, that deals with the same idea throughout _____
3 a written account, such as a book or scholarly pamphlet, on a particular and usually limited subject _____

4 the study of the characteristics of human populations, for example: size, growth, density, distribution, and vital statistics _____

5 the art and science of making maps or navigational charts _____

6 an image of an object, person, or landscape recorded digitally or on special film or paper _____

7 an instrument for automatically detecting and recording the duration, intensity, and direction of an earthquake _____

8 a list of writings related to a given subject, or referenced within a particular written work _____

9 the art of creating and arranging dance sequences _____

10 a written account of a person's life _____

B Now go back to the word stems in A, and decide which form of the root *graph* or *graphy* each one uses, and which can use both. Complete the chart below. Use your dictionary to check your answers.

graph	both	graphy
_____	_____	_____
_____	_____	_____
_____	_____	_____
_____	_____	_____

C Now complete the sentences below using words from the chart; not all the words are used. Be sure to use each word in its correct form.

1 The standard academic essay in English is made up of at least five _____.

2 Many pop stars work with _____, who create original dances and develop new dance moves for them.

3 It's important to include a(n) _____, citing all referenced works, as part of your research project.

4 In order to write someone's _____, you have to conduct an extensive amount of research on them.

5 As Della was a well-known chef, her _____ contained numerous recipes along with her memoirs.

6 Jun believes that living in Tokyo and experiencing numerous earthquakes as a young child inspired him to become a(n) _____.

7 Though Annelise originally studied color _____, she recently learned more about using black and white film and now works primarily in that medium.

8 Sebastian has been unable to find much published material on his chosen field of study except for an old _____ in the reference library.

9 Anybody who studies _____ trends will know that the continual dramatic increase in global population is creating a huge strain on the environment.

10 Hyun Suk hopes that by getting a bachelor's degree in geography, he will eventually be able to enter the field of _____.

Real Life Skill:
Reading Computer Advertising

If you want to buy a computer system, it's important to compare the specifications (technical details) of different computers, as well as their prices. Advertising for computers often contains a lot of abbreviations for technical terms, as well as computer jargon. Being familiar with these terms can help you better understand exactly what it is you are buying.

A Read the following advertisements for computers.

The Techron MZ4000 Desktop System features:	The Techie AZ2000Laptop features:
• 2 GB RAM at 3 GHz	• 1,024 MB RAM
• Big 360 GB HD	• 120 GB HD
• DVD-ROM Drive	• DVD-ROM Drive
• 52X max CD-RW drive	• 3 USB ports
• 6 USB ports	• Doorways Unlimited OS
• Doorways Forever OS	• Free word processing & spreadsheet software
• One year free ISP service	
New low prices!	**New low prices!**

B Write the abbreviations in the ads that stand for the following:

1 operating system—the basic software in the computer _____
2 hard drive—the part of the computer that stores information _____
3 Internet service provider—the company that gives you access to the Internet _____
4 digital video disk read-only memory—use this to watch movies on your computer _____
5 universal serial bus—a type of plug that allows you to connect devices such as a printer or mouse to your computer _____
6 random access memory—the part of the computer that enables the programs to work _____
7 a unit of computer memory capacity that measures one million bytes _____
8 compact disk rewritable—use this to listen to recordings and save information _____
9 gigahertz—controls the speed at which the computer can carry out instructions _____
10 a unit of computer memory capacity that measures one billion bytes _____

C Imagine you want to buy a computer. What do you need it for? What specifications do you need? Talk to a partner and discuss which features you would want or need to have in your computer. Which of the computers featured in the advertisements above would you buy?

What Do You Think?

1 Can you think of any incidents in the news that involved hackers or virus writers?
2 Crimes on the Internet cross international borders. Should an international Internet police organization be set up to fight them? Explain your answer.
3 Virus writing has been compared to vandalism, taking pleasure in destroying things. Why do some people seem to enjoy such destruction simply for the sake of destruction?

Getting Ready

Complete the survey below. Then discuss your answers with a partner.

What Kind of Traveler Are You?
Choose the best answer for each question below.

1 How often do you go on trips abroad?
  a. once a year
  b. a few times a year
  c. when you can afford it

2 How often do you travel around your home country?
  a. once a year
  b. a few times a year
  c. when you can afford it

3 Who do you like to travel with?
  a. alone or with a friend or partner
  b. family
  c. a big group of friends

4 How do you like to travel?
  a. in comfort
  b. you like to figure it out yourself
  c. on an organized package tour

5 Which of the following is the primary reason you go on vacation?
  a. rest and relaxation
  b. education and cultural learning
  c. adventure
  d. to spend time with family or friends

6 Which of the following holidays appeals to you most?
  a. island hopping in the South Pacific
  b. city tours of Australia
  c. backpacking across Europe
  d. resort holiday with plenty of amenities

7 How do you usually pay for your vacation?
  a. max out your credit card
  b. find the cheapest way to get there and budget carefully
  c. spend no more than a couple of weeks' salary
  d. save all year for your big trip

Chapter 1: Into the Heart of a Family in Casablanca

A **Discuss the following questions with a partner.**

1 When was the last time you went on a trip? Where did you go? Why?
2 What did you do while you were on the trip?
3 Did any unusual or interesting events happen on this trip? If so, what?
4 Did you meet, or talk to, anyone interesting on this trip? If so, who? Have you kept in touch with this person?

B **Complete the sentences with a word from the box.**

> winding   broken   split

1 She tried to speak with us, but it was difficult to understand her _____ English.
2 On a _____ road, a driver should expect to make lots of turns.
3 I'll be there "in a _____ second" means that I'll be there very, very soon.

C **Scan the reading for the words and check your answers with a partner.**

Dates and times, as well as words such as "then," "next," "later," "soon," and "eventually" are often used in text to indicate the order in which certain events happened. Being aware of how a reading is organized can help you to understand it better, and enable you to find specific information in a passage more easily.

A **Read through the sequence of events below and think about the correct order in which they probably happened.**

A Traveler's Timeline

_____ Abdelatif wrote down his address.
_____ Miguel and the writer found their friend.
_____ The family members took turns sitting with Miguel and the writer.
_____ Miguel, Abdelatif, and the writer worked as volunteers in Kenitra.
_____ The taxi driver asked for directions.
_____ Miguel and the writer decided to visit their friend in Casablanca.
_____ Miguel and the writer realized they had made a mistake.
_____ The family gave Miguel and the writer some couscous and chicken to eat.
_____ A policeman and a young boy helped Miguel and the writer.
_____ They took photos and exchanged addresses.

B **Now scan through the reading passage and put the events above into the correct order.**

C **Which words or expressions helped you to put these events in the correct order? Go back over the reading and circle any words or information that helped you.**

Into the Heart of a Family in Casablanca

Here's what I love about travel: strangers can often amaze you. Sometimes a single day can bring a beautiful surprise, a simple kindness that opens your heart and makes you a different person by the time you go to sleep—more tender, less **jaded** than you were when you woke up.

This particular day began at seven in the morning in Casablanca. My friend Miguel[1] and I were going to visit Abdelatif, a young man we'd worked with on a volunteer project in Kenitra, an industrial city on the Moroccan coast. He'd been expecting us to arrive in Casablanca for a few days now, and since he had no telephone, he'd written down his address and told us to just show up—his mother and sisters were always at home. As my plane was leaving from Casablanca the following morning, we wanted to get an early start so we could spend the whole day with him.

Apparently[2] the address Abdelatif had written down for us was hard to understand, and when we got into the neighborhood, our taxi driver started asking directions. Eventually, with the help of a policeman and then a little boy, we were led to a house down a winding road. Our driver went to the door and **inquired**. He came back to the cab saying Abdelatif's sister was in this house visiting friends and would come along to show us where they lived.

Soon a girl of about sixteen **emerged** from the house. Surprisingly, she didn't resemble Abdelatif at all. Still, I'd seen other families where children didn't look alike, so I didn't give it too much thought. We waited in the yard while the sister went in and returned accompanied by her mother, sisters, and brother-in-law, all of whom greeted us with cautious warmth. We were shown into a **pristine** home with multicolored tiles lining the walls. The mother told us in broken French that Abdelatif was out, but would be home soon. We sat on low, cushioned seats in the living room, drinking sweet mint tea and eating sugar cookies, while the family members took turns sitting with us and making shy, polite conversation that frequently **lapsed** into uncomfortable silence. As anything was said, Miguel would say, "What?" and I would translate the simple phrase for him: "Nice weather today. Tomorrow perhaps rain."

An hour passed, and as the guard kept changing, more family members emerged from inner rooms. I was again struck[3] by the fact that none of them looked a thing like our friend. How did Abdelatif fit into this picture? Was he adopted? I was very curious to find out.

After two hours had passed with no sign of Abdelatif, the family insisted on serving us a meal of couscous[4] and chicken. "Soon," was the only response I got when I inquired as to what time he might arrive. But at last, we heard the words we had been waiting for. "Please," said the mother, "Abdelatif is here."

"Oh, good," I said, and for a moment, before I walked into the living room, his face danced in my mind—the brown eyes, the smile filled with **radiant** life. We entered the lovely tiled room we'd sat in before and a young man came forward to shake our hands with an uncertain expression on his face.

40 "Hello, my friends," he said cautiously. "Hello," I smiled, slightly confused. "Is Abdelatif here?" "I am Abdelatif."

"But . . . but . . ." I looked from him to the family and then began to **giggle** nervously. "I - I'm sorry. I'm afraid we've made a bit of a mistake. I - I'm so embarrassed."

"What? What?" Miguel asked urgently. "I don't understand. Where is he?" "We've got the wrong
45 Abdelatif," I told him, and then looked around at the entire family who'd spent most of the day entertaining us. "I'm afraid we don't actually know your son."

For a split second no one said anything, and I wished I could disappear right there on the spot. Then the uncle **exclaimed heartily**, "It's no problem!" "Yes," the mother joined in. "It doesn't matter at all. Won't you stay for dinner, please?"

50 I was so overwhelmed by their kindness that tears rushed to my eyes. "Thank you so much," I said fervently. "It's been a beautiful, beautiful day, but please . . . could you help me find this address?"

I took out the piece of paper Abdelatif had given me back in Kenitra, and the new Abdelatif, his uncle, and his brother-in-law came forward to **decipher** it. "This is Baalal Abdelatif!" said the second Abdelatif, recognizing the address. "We went to school together! He lives less than a kilometer from here. I will bring
55 you to his house."

And that is how it happened. After taking photos and exchanging addresses and hugs and promises to write, Miguel and I left our newfound family and arrived at the home of our friend Abdelatif as the last orange streak of the sunset was fading into the dark night. There, I reached out and hugged him with relief, exclaiming, "I thought we'd never find you!"

This reading was adapted from *Looking for Abdelatif, an Unexpected Journey into the Heart of a Family in Casablanca* by Tanya Shaffer. Reprinted with permission from Salon.com © 1999.

¹ **Miguel** /mɪgel/ Spanish man's name; equivalent of English "Michael"
² **apparently** clearly; obviously; according to what is easy to see
³ **struck** hit by an idea or awareness
⁴ **couscous** /kʊskʊs/ a North African pasta

A **The statements below are about the reading. Choose the correct answer to complete each one.**

1 What the writer loves about travel is being _____.
   a. amazed   **b.** comfortable   **c.** free   **d.** shocked
2 The writer and the family communicated in broken _____.
   a. English   **b.** Spanish   **c.** French   **d.** Arabic
3 When the mother found out about the writer's mistake, she immediately _____.
   a. brought the writer to Baalal Abdelatif
   b. invited the writer to dinner
   c. started to cry
   d. asked them to leave
4 The writer's friend named Abdelatif and the new Abdelatif she met were _____.
   a. father and son   **b.** enemies   **c.** brothers-in-law   **d.** schoolmates

B **Decide if the following statements about the reading are true (T) or false (F). If you check (✔) false, correct the statement to make it true.**

		T	F
1	Abdelatif gave friends his address and phone number.		
2	The writer and Miguel planned to stay with Abdelatif for a few days.		
3	The taxi driver had a difficult time finding the address.		
4	The taxi driver found Abdelatif's sister who showed them to the house.		
5	The writer was surprised as Abdelatif's sister looked so little like him.		

C Critical Thinking

Discuss these questions with a partner.
1 Why do you think the writer felt that this experience was a valuable one?
2 What do you think the writer, Miguel, and their friend Abdelatif said to each other after they finally met?

Vocabulary Comprehension:
Word Definitions

A Look at the list of words from the reading. Match each one with a definition on the right.

1 jaded _____
2 inquired _____
3 emerged _____
4 pristine _____
5 lapsed _____
6 radiant _____
7 giggle _____
8 exclaimed _____
9 heartily _____
10 decipher _____

a. warmly and sincerely
b. very clean; pure
c. to read or interpret; to decode
d. slipped gradually into a less favorable condition; passed by
e. appeared by coming out of something
f. tired or worn out, usually after overexposure to something
g. asked for information
h. filled with emotions of love or happiness; glowing or beaming
i. to laugh in a silly, uncontrolled way
j. cried out or spoke suddenly

B Complete the sentences using the vocabulary from A. Be sure to use the correct form of each word.

1 If you are planning to take a trip overseas, you should _____ about the accommodations, climate, and culture of the country you are going to visit.
2 Even though I cannot _____ the language, I think it's fun to look at hieroglyphics and imagine what they might say.
3 Martin was shocked to see his girlfriend _____ from a restaurant with another man.
4 It is said that most New Yorkers are _____ with celebrities. They don't react to them like most tourists do.
5 The woman stood in the middle of the supermarket and _____ that her son was missing.
6 At her wedding, you couldn't help noticing how _____ Sheena looked.
7 When Tina and Lisa are together, they never stop _____, even when there is no reason to laugh.
8 The crowd cheered _____ when their team scored the first goal of the match.
9 After seeing how much his exam scores had _____ since last term, Eric's father grounded him for the rest of the year.
10 I have no idea how Marianne keeps her home so _____ with five children running around.

Vocabulary Skill:

Adverbs of Emotion

In this chapter you read the adverbs "fervently," "heartily," "urgently," and "cautiously." They all describe the way in which the speakers in the reading passage expressed their feelings. Adverbs are often used in written texts to convey the emotions of a speaker. Knowing how these adverbs work, and what they mean, can help you to better understand readings that contain them.

A Look at the list of adverbs below. For each one, write the feeling you think a person would be expressing if they spoke in this way; the first one has been done for you. Use your dictionary to help you.

Adverb	Feeling
1 furiously	*very angry about something*
2 cautiously	
3 urgently	
4 pensively	
5 firmly	
6 tactfully	
7 flatly	
8 humbly	
9 confidently	
10 joyously	

B Now complete each sentence below using adverbs from A. More than one answer may be possible. Share your answers with a partner.

1 The waiter _____ apologized for the delay in showing us to our table. We had, after all, made reservations weeks ago.

2 Mario _____ never mentioned and pretended not to notice the large pimple on Maria's nose.

3 The writer stared _____ at the girl, trying to find some resemblance between her and her brother Abdelatif.

4 Although the suspect was interrogated by the police for three hours, he still _____ denied having anything to do with the incident.

5 Kumiko's grandmother looked both ways and then _____ began to cross the street.

6 Sam screamed _____ at the man who crashed into her car; her baby was in the car with her.

7 When news of the stock market crash reached the office, Ed immediately got on the phone and _____ requested an update on his financial portfolio.

8 Alicia phoned and _____ told us about the birth of her first grandchild yesterday.

C Now write your own sentences using two of the adverbs from A. Share your ideas with a partner.

1 _____

2 _____

Unit 3   Chapter 2: Canaima—Eco-tours with Angels and Devils

Before You Read:
Tourism with a Difference

A Discuss the following questions with a partner.

1 What do you understand by the term "eco-tourism"?
2 Would you like to go on an eco-tour? Why or why not?
3 Do many tourists visit your country each year? Which places do they usually go to?
4 Are eco-tours offered to any of the main tourist areas in your country? If so, what do they involve?

B What do you think the following words and phrase mean? Match each word or phrase with a definition on the right.

1 mesa _____
2 vantage point _____
3 overcast _____
4 carnivorous_____
5 hammock_____

a. a hanging bed made of netting
b. cloudy
c. a good spot to view something from
d. a flat-topped mountain
e. meat-eating

Reading Skill:
Previewing

Previewing is something good readers do when they first encounter new reading material. They ask themselves questions like these: *What is this about? What kind of text is this? What do I already know about it?* Previewing can involve skimming, scanning, and predicting to help us get acquainted with the reading passage.

A Take one minute to preview the reading passage. Think about the title, scan the passage for interesting information, and skim the beginning and ending paragraphs.

B Discuss these questions about the reading passage with a partner.

1 What do you think the passage is about?
2 Where could you find this kind of an article?
3 What do you already know about this subject?
4 What interesting points did you notice?
5 Do you think you'll enjoy reading the passage?

C Try to predict which of the following the writer will encounter on an eco-tour to Venezuela. Check (✔) your answers.

☐ a comfortable hotel   ☐ a new kind of drink

☐ a Jacuzzi   ☐ UFOs

☐ many other tourists   ☐ interesting new foods

D Now read through the passage; then answer the questions that follow.

Canaima—
Eco-tours with Angels and Devils

I threw my bags into the back, went around to the passenger side, and slid into the front seat. Moments later the wheels started turning and our journey to Canaima National Park began. We
5 climbed to a cruising altitude[1] of around 5,000 feet.[2] At this height, the jungle looked like a gigantic green carpet, except for the red rivers snaking through it. Our pilot followed the path of the Churún River, and as it approached the edge of the mesa, the
10 plane took a dramatic dive along the trajectory[3] of the mighty Angel Falls—the longest waterfall in the world—as it **plummeted** down into Devil's Canyon.

A half hour later, we landed on a dirt strip alongside six mud huts that constitute the Pemón Indian village of Uruyen. As the trip continued, I became increasingly amazed at the lack of
15 tourists. Nowhere was it more surprising than in Devil's Canyon, the principal vantage point at the base of the 3,200-foot (975-meter) Angel Falls. It was one of the most **awe-inspiring** sights I have ever **beheld**, but almost equally incredulous was the fact that we were the only ones there!

How could this be? After all, you can barely move for crowds even on overcast days at Niagara. Canaima's remoteness is one reason; there is no road access so you must charter a flight from
20 Puerto Ordaz, a one-hour journey from the Venezuelan capital of Caracas. Flights are limited and the trip is expensive. Another major factor is that until recently, the Venezuelan government did not promote tourism to Canaima and Angel Falls. Of the few tourists who come here, most fly directly into Canaima village, which gives easiest access to the Falls via a three-hour boat ride, and a moderately challenging two-hour hike.

25 The tour operators at Angel Eco-Tours take an interesting approach in that they emphasize the park and its people more than Angel Falls. In doing so, they create an experience that I found to be truly unique. This is in large part due to the close interaction we had with the Pemón Indians, to whom Angel Eco-Tours donates five percent of its earnings. In previous stays at indigenous villages, I had often gotten the sense that tourists were well received primarily because they
30 contribute significantly to the village's income. But the Pemón are extremely **gracious** hosts. From the moment we arrived in their village, it was clear that they were genuinely excited to share their culture and learn about us.

We slept in their huts, played soccer with them, tried traditional dishes such as cassava bread dipped in a beetle-based hot sauce, and even learned a few phrases in the Pemón language
35 (although most speak at least some Spanish). My fondest memory is of spending an evening watching three generations of Pemón, **decked out** in their traditional garb,[4] perform a ceremonial dance. The show became increasingly amusing as Pemón and tourists alike drank more and

more of their homemade cassava beer. Our inhibitions[5] quickly disappeared and before we knew it, we were dancing alongside the Pemón.

40 Through our interactions with the Pemón, we gained a very special understanding of the land they inhabit. They were our guides on hiking excursions, bringing us to some of their most sacred spots. These included caves with **eerie** rock formations resembling human faces, towering waterfalls where we swam underneath the powerful spray, a spot in the river that formed a natural Jacuzzi, and a riverbank with pink sandstone that can be used for natural
45 facials. As we walked through the forest, they pointed out the many trees and plants that they use for medicinal or ceremonial purposes. Given the other-worldliness of the park, I was not surprised to hear that a large number of the flora, including several carnivorous plant varieties, are **endemic** to the region.

The Pemón also introduced us to their system of beliefs and spirituality. I had heard that the
50 planet's major energy meridians,[6] which connect spiritual centers such as Machu Picchu and Stonehenge, all run through Canaima. After a few days, I didn't doubt it. Nearly everyone in our group reported having extremely **lucid** dreams. Mysteries seemed commonplace; the sky at night constantly flickered with lightning, although there was never any thunder or rain. Supposedly, there are more UFO sightings here than anywhere in the world. Sightings or not, by
55 the end of the trip, everyone in the group felt that their batteries had been totally recharged.

As much as I found the trip **exhilarating**, I would not say it is for everyone. Eco-tourism means responsible, low-impact travel, and generally involves some degree of "roughing-it." This trip is no exception. Three of the five nights were spent in hammocks, which did not suit everyone's natural contours. You must not be **averse** to sun, sweat, mosquitoes, or bathing in rivers with
60 little or no privacy. At $1,500 per person for the week-long trip, it's an excellent deal, but still prohibitively[7] expensive for some people. If you can afford it, and don't mind a few ants in your pants, this trip will provide you with an incredibly unique experience that I guarantee you will never forget.

This reading was adapted from *Canaima: Where Angels and Devils Collide* by Brad Weiss © 2001.
Reprinted from IgoUgo with permission of the author; http://www.igougo.com/experience/archive43.html.

[1] **cruising altitude** height at which airplanes travel
[2] **5,000 feet** equal to 1,524 meters
[3] **trajectory** the path of something moving through space
[4] **garb** distinctive clothing
[5] **inhibition** restraint or reservation; feeling unable to express what one really thinks
[6] **meridian** invisible line or circle on the earth's surface that passes through certain points
[7] **prohibitively** causing something to be impossible

A Decide if the following statements about the reading are true (T), false (F), or if the information is not given (NG). If you check (✔) false, correct the statement to make it true.

	T	F	NG
1 The passage is mainly about the author's experiences on an eco-tour in Venezuela.			
2 To the author, the Canaima National Park looked like a big red snake from 5,000 feet.			
3 The easiest way to get to Angel Falls from Canaima village is by airplane.			
4 Some of the plants in Canaima National Park eat meat.			
5 A travel magazine paid for the author to go to Venezuela.			

B How much do you remember from the reading? Choose the best answer for each question or statement.

1 Devil's Canyon is situated _____.
   a. at the bottom of Angel Falls
   b. in a popular tourist spot
   c. near Niagara Falls
   d. near Caracas
2 Angel Falls is _____.
   a. too far from Caracas to visit
   b. a spiritual mecca for eco-tourists
   c. the longest waterfall in the world
   d. as popular as Niagara Falls
3 The writer considers the trip to Canaima National Park to be _____.
   a. very easy for most eco-tourists
   b. challenging, but well worth the effort
   c. inexpensive considering what you receive
   d. too difficult for most people
4 The writer describes _____ as evidence of Canaima's spiritual energy.
   a. ceremonial dances and carnivorous plants
   b. strange rock formations and pink sandstone
   c. medicinal plants and herbs
   d. energy lines and UFO sightings
5 The writer thinks that this eco-tour is not for everyone as it involves _____.
   a. living in natural settings without many amenities
   b. hiking for long periods through rough terrain
   c. a considerable expense
   d. all of the above

C Critical Thinking

Discuss these questions with a partner.

1 Would you like to go on the eco-tour described in the passage? Why or why not?

2 Do you think involvement with the tourist industry is of benefit to the Pemón people or not? In what ways?

Vocabulary Comprehension:
Odd Word Out

A **For each group, circle the word that does not belong. The words in *italics* are vocabulary items from the reading.**

1	plunged	ascended	descended	*plummeted*
2	*awe-inspiring*	magnificent	astounding	unimpressive
3	held on	*beheld*	saw	observed
4	considerate	surly	courteous	*gracious*
5	*decked out*	dressed up	costumed	unadorned
6	wonderful	*eerie*	weird	strange
7	native	indigenous	*endemic*	foreign
8	*lucid*	incoherent	clear	explicit
9	invigorating	depressing	stimulating	*exhilarating*
10	dislike	*averse*	willing	opposed

B **Complete the sentences using the words in *italics* from A. Be sure to use the correct form of each word.**

1 I'm sure I have never _____ as beautiful a sunset as the one I saw in Acapulco.

2 Nigel has a(n) _____ to cats and will not visit any house that keeps one as a pet.

3 When traveling to certain tropical countries, find out what diseases are _____ to the region and take the necessary medications.

4 When Olivia, whose grandparents are from Spain, visited the country for the first time, she had a(n) _____ feeling that she had been there before.

5 Although traveling can be exhausting, I always feel _____ when I arrive in a new country.

6 After spending several days hiking across the mountains with little food and water, Chen's speech was slurred and he did not appear _____.

7 Every New Year's Eve, James loves to get _____ in his party hat and clothes.

8 There are many amazing places to see in Egypt, but the Temple of Karnac, in Luxor, is certainly one of the most _____ sights I have ever seen.

9 We planned to have a barbecue last night, but the temperature _____ in the afternoon so we ended up eating indoors with the heat turned on.

10 I've found that in most countries the local people are quite _____; they want visitors to leave with wonderful impressions of their country.

A For each word, study the different parts. Using your knowledge of prefixes and suffixes, write the part of speech and a simple definition for each word. Working with a partner, use your dictionary to check your answers.

Vocabulary Skill:
The Root Word *ject*

In this chapter, you read the noun "trajectory," meaning "the path of something moving through space." The root word "ject" comes from the Latin word "jacere," which means "to throw." It is combined with prefixes and suffixes to form many words in English.

Vocabulary	Part of Speech	Definition
1 eject	_____	_____
2 projector	_____	_____
3 injection	_____	_____
4 reject	*verb / noun*	_____
5 dejected	_____	_____
6 interject	_____	_____
7 project	*verb / noun*	_____
8 objection	_____	_____

B Complete each sentence using the words from A. Be sure to use the correct form of each word.

1 Every time Jae-Woo suggests a new idea, his boss _____ it. As a result, his motivation has plummeted.
2 Carla closed her eyes and braced herself for the painful _____ the doctor was about to give her.
3 The CEO reported today that total earnings are expected to exceed _____ figures in the coming months.
4 The journalist who shouted at the president as he made his speech was _____ from the press conference by security guards.
5 It's customary for students in the United States to _____ while other classmates, or even the lecturers, are speaking.
6 After his girlfriend told him she didn't want to date him anymore, Carl felt totally _____.
7 Stefan's computer crashed the night before his 9 A.M. presentation. Luckily, the _____ was set up so he copied his notes onto transparencies.
8 Mrs. Fahid made her _____ to the nuclear power station quite clear at the meeting.

C Can you think of any other words in English that include the root *ject*?

Real Life Skill:
Choosing a Travel Guidebook

When you travel, the more information you have before you set out on your trip, the more you'll get from it. That's why there are dozens of different series of travel guidebooks, covering thousands of destinations worldwide. Each series caters to a different type of traveler, so it's important to know what kind of approach you take to travel in order to choose the guidebook that's right for you, and your trip.

A Match these types of travelers with the definitions below.

1 Budget travelers _____
2 Luxury travelers _____
3 Armchair travelers _____
4 Business travelers _____
5 Adventure travelers _____
6 Family travelers _____

a. make frequent short trips, and may have little free time to see the sights. They require efficiency and comfort.
b. travel together with their spouse and children, and look for safe destinations and activities that all ages can enjoy together.
c. want "only the best"—the most elegant hotels, the most succulent meals, the most exclusive shops. Expense is not a concern.
d. enjoy reading about travel as a hobby. Many never actually use the guidebook to take a trip.
e. are looking for unusual experiences and undiscovered destinations, and do not mind discomfort or even some degree of danger.
f. want to travel as much as possible for the lowest price possible. The cost of everything is very important.

B Read the following descriptions from the back covers of travel guidebooks. Which type of traveler are they intended for?

1 The world's most beautiful guidebooks—full-color photography on every page, plus poetry and art from the indigenous people.
2 Double rooms for only $20, three-course meals for just $5—who says travel has to be pricey? We'll help you get top value for your vacation dollar, every time!
3 Outdoor fun, kid-friendly museums, lots of rainy-day sights to see—even hotels that offer baby-sitting. You'll find it all here!
4 All the essential facts you need for a productive stay, with suggestions to help you make the most of your leisure hours.
5 Don't follow the crowd—follow us, to pristine rainforests, wild rivers, and remote mountain villages where life hasn't changed in centuries.
6 For those who appreciate the finer things in life. We share inside tips, hot new discoveries, and the very best localities for everything you're looking for.

C Work with a partner. Go back to the travel survey in Getting Ready on page 39. Look at your partner's answers to the survey and decide what type of traveler he/she is. Which of these guidebooks would you recommend for him/her? Explain your answer.

What Do You Think?

1 Are there any monuments or natural sites in your country that are being damaged by mass tourism? What kind of damage is being inflicted on these places? What is being done to protect them? Do you think this action is enough?
2 Do you think it is possible for mass tourism to coexist with environmental conservation? If so, how is it possible? If not, what can be done to change this situation?

Fluency Strategy: *Muscle Reading*

When you build your physical muscles, you focus on a specific muscle at a time and work it over and over again. Likewise, Muscle Reading involves engaging with a passage in multiple ways in order to build your knowledge and comprehension. There are a total of nine steps to follow in Muscle Reading.

Preview

Preview "The Internet Entrepreneur" by reading the first paragraph, the first sentence in paragraphs 2–4, and the final paragraph.

Outline

Making an **outline** requires a slow, careful reading, which will help you build your fluency when you read again later on.

Complete the outline of "The Internet Entrepreneur."

The Internet Entrepreneur

1 Most Internet businesses, known as _____, have _____.

2 A review of the dot-com era
 • Some entrepreneurs deliberately _____.
 • Dot-coms were called _____ because so many failed.
 • A huge amount of _____ was lost.

3 Some Internet businesses have done well.
 • Most successful ones were started by _____ people.

4 Characteristics of successful Internet entrepreneurs
 • They are able to _____.
 • They do constant _____ to keep track of _____.
 • They must be _____ and _____.
 • They need to _____ and be _____.

5 High-tech economy
 • What it is not: a place where anyone with _____ can _____.
 • What it is: a business environment where people can _____ to produce successful _____.

Question

Good readers ask themselves questions as they read. Sometimes the **questions** are answered in what they are reading; other times you have to go to additional readings to find the answers.
What questions come to your mind as you read "The Internet Entrepreneur"? Where do you think you would find answers to these questions? Share your questions and ideas with a classmate.

1 _____

2 _____

3 _____

Read

Now, following your pre-reading preparation, read as fluently as possible.

The Internet Entrepreneur

The late 1990s was a volatile time for the Internet entrepreneur. There were a large number of new high-tech and Internet-based businesses being started up, some
5 based on little more than dreams. And, nearly any entrepreneur with a high-tech or Internet-based business plan could receive a large amount of money from investors to develop the business. These businesses
10 were called "dot-coms" after the last part of their Internet addresses, and that time in business history has become known as the dot-com era. Most dot-com ventures failed as the inconsistencies between
15 high-tech dreams and realities clarified, but a handful of entrepreneurs from that time remain successful today.

Larry Page and Sergey Brin, founders of Google

Many people look back at the dot-com era with a certain amount of cynicism. Some charge that there were entrepreneurs who deliberately misled investors about the potential of their business plans; that they had the ulterior motive of getting their hands
20 on large amounts of cash before anything else—a ploy that some say was common in the dot-com era. By 2001, most of the dot-coms had disappeared and were sarcastically referred to as "dot-bombs." By the time the hype died down, incredible amounts of money had been lost. This is an unfortunate legacy of the dot-com era.

Why did companies like Microsoft, Apple, and Google find success, while so many others disappeared? There is no concise answer, but one interesting coincidence is that many of them were started by two or more entrepreneurs working in conjunction with each other. At Microsoft, Bill Gates and Paul Allen complemented each other; Apple had Steve Jobs and Steve Wozniak; and we owe Google to the rapport between founders Larry Page and Sergey Brin.

Besides collaborating with others, today's entrepreneurs need to be able to think on their feet because the business situation changes so quickly. Entrepreneurs need to do constant research to keep track of changing trends. Today's entrepreneurs need to be hardworking and tenacious—the easy money of the dot-com era is history. Experimentation and innovation are critical in a rapidly changing and highly competitive marketplace.

It seems that the mistakes of the dot-com era have shown the world what the high-tech economy truly is—and what it isn't. It isn't a place where anyone with a dream can get rich. It is, however, a powerful and flexible business environment where people with sound business ideas and effective business models can work together to produce successful business innovations—sometimes very successful ones indeed. But, as has always been true in the business world, there is no substitute for thorough planning and hard work.

Underline

Go back through the reading and <u>underline</u> the main ideas and important information from the reading. Compare what you have underlined with the outline that you made. How is the information in your outline similar to the ideas you underlined? How is it different? Share what you have underlined with a classmate.

Answer

Without looking back at the passage, answer the following questions.

1 What is the author's main purpose in writing this passage?
   a. to expose the negative side of the dot-com era
   b. to explain the history and qualities of a type of entrepreneur
   c. to convince the reader to become an entrepreneur
   d. to show how being an entrepreneur is easier today than ever before

2 What is most likely the reason that it was easy to get money from investors in the dot-com era?
   a. Investors were mainly Internet entrepreneurs.
   b. Investors didn't expect to get their money back in those days.
   c. Investors were confused about the potential of high-tech business ideas.
   d. Investors knew that any idea would succeed.

3 Why do many people look back on the dot-com era with cynicism?
   a. because many companies misled their investors
   b. because they are jealous of the success of dot-coms
   c. because the level of technology was so much lower then
   d. because there were no true entrepreneurs in that era

4 Why did some people probably refer to dot-coms as "dot-bombs" by 2001?
   a. because most dot-com companies were short-lived failures
   b. because dot-com companies started up extremely quickly
   c. because some dot-coms became extremely successful
   d. because many people wished to eliminate dot-com businesses

5 According to the passage, what do Microsoft, Apple, and Google all have in common?
   a. They all produce high-quality computers.
   b. They are all cynical about dot-coms.
   c. They all have a good rapport with each other.
   d. They were all developed by more than one person.

6 Which quality of today's entrepreneurs is NOT mentioned in the passage?
   a. They need to be able to think on their feet.
   b. They need to work in more than one company at a time.
   c. They need to collaborate with others.
   d. They need to do constant research.

7 According to the passage, what have we learned from the dot-com era?
   a. that most high-tech and Internet-based businesses will succeed
   b. that anyone with a dream can get rich in today's environment
   c. that sound business ideas and effective plans are needed for success
   d. that investors should give money freely to new companies

Recite

You can increase your comprehension by talking with someone about what you have read.
Turn to a partner and recite the main ideas from "The Internet Entrepreneur."

Review

Review each of the comprehension questions above. Did you get any questions incorrect? If so, why?

Review Again

Review your outline and the comprehension questions. What have you learned from the reading? Write the main ideas you learned and why they are important.

Self Check

Write a short answer to each of the following questions.

1. Have you ever used the Muscle Reading strategy before?

   Yes   No   *I'm not sure*

2. Will you practice Muscle Reading in your reading outside of English class?

   Yes   No   *I'm not sure*

3. Do you think Muscle Reading is helpful? Why or why not?

   _____

   _____

4. Which of the six reading passages in units 1–3 did you enjoy most? Why?

   _____

   _____

5. Which of the six reading passages in units 1–3 was easiest? Which was most difficult? Why?

   _____

   _____

6. What have you read in English outside of class recently?

   _____

   _____

7. What do you think you can do to become a better reader?

   _____

   _____

   _____

Review Reading 1: White Hat and Black Hat Hackers

Time yourself as you read through the passage. Try to read as fluently as you can. Record your time in the Reading Rate Chart on page 240. Then answer the questions on page 61.

White Hat and Black Hat Hackers

All hackers seem to have one thing in common: they enjoy figuring out how things work. They are often, but not necessarily, computer prodigies. They apply their natural curiosity to understanding
5 computer applications and systems. They gain an intimate knowledge of these applications and systems: a level of knowledge sometimes equal or superior to the creators' themselves. This knowledge is not in itself a bad thing nor a good
10 thing; it is what the hacker does with the knowledge that makes the hacker an ethical or an unethical one. While it is difficult to fit hackers neatly into distinct categories, one popular way of dividing them up is into these three groups:
15 *white hat* hackers, *black hat* hackers (also known as *crackers*), and *gray hat* hackers.

Ideally, the white hat hacker has immaculate computer ethics. For example, if a white hat hacker discovers a security weakness in a computer network, the hacker would naturally inform the network administrator of the problem and perhaps cordially offer some advice on how to address
20 the problem. While white hat hackers do gain access to private networks and information, they do so with the permission of the owner, and they can be counted on to "do the right thing." White hat hackers often work for organizations and businesses to enhance the businesses' level of computer security.

Linus Torvalds is an example of a white hat hacker. He studied computer science at the University
25 of Helsinki, where in 1991 he wrote the first version of a computer operating system called Linux. Unlike so many other software authors who have enriched themselves, Torvalds gave his operating system away for free, relinquishing profits he might have made from it.

The black hat hacker, on the other hand, can be cunning and even malicious. In some circles, the

term *cracker* is used instead. It is predominantly black hat hackers that perpetrate computer
crimes. Black hat crackers have broken into computer networks and used that access to steal
money. They have damaged or threatened to damage computers and computer networks.

Kevin Poulson, who went by the name of Dark Dante, was an early black hat hacker. In a famous
incident, Poulson used his understanding of computers and telephones to unethically win a
Porsche automobile. A radio station had promised the automobile to the 102nd caller. Poulson
simply kept control of all the phone lines and made sure that he was the one to win the car. Like
many black hat hackers, Poulson spent time in prison and then took a job as a white hat hacker
for a computer security company.

Another example of a black hat hacker is Vladimir Levin of Russia. He was arrested in 1995 for
planning a theft from a large American bank, Citibank. He was accused of being the leader of
a group of criminals who fooled the Citibank computers into giving them $10 million. He was
convicted, spent three years in jail, and had to give back the money he took. Thanks to this crime,
Citibank has since greatly upgraded its security systems.

In between the white hat and the black hat there is the gray hat hacker. Gray hat hackers find
their way into computer systems and networks, but they are not quick to inform the owner of the
security problem. At the same time, they are not usually intent on mangling the system software
or memory, either. There have been cases of gray hats leaving behind messages or defacing
websites with electronic graffiti in order to let others know that they were capable of getting
in, but not doing any real damage. So, while gray hats wouldn't likely stand up for the rights of
network owners or managers, they are also likely to do little or no damage.

Because gray hats are rarely arrested, their names usually remain unknown. The Apache Software
Foundation's website was broken into in 2004 by hackers. They did not, as might be feared,
release viruses to replicate in Apache's computers or damage them in any way. Instead, they left
a message explaining the security problem that had allowed them to gain access. The hackers
asserted: "This is a general warning. Learn from it. Fix your systems, so we won't have to." In
their own strange way, the gray hat hackers had assisted Apache in making their networks more
secure.

In conclusion, it seems the future of white hat hackers is secure as their skills are in demand to
secure the vast number of computer networks around the world. There is certainly more pressure
than ever on gray hat hackers to stop their activities. More people are questioning their rationale,
because today's corporations and governments simply have too much at stake to allow them to
casually enter their networks. In recent years, gray hats have been arrested and prosecuted for
crimes that might have been ignored in the past. And finally, while the early black hat hackers
were never severely punished, their activities are today taken more seriously than ever before.
However, the problem of the black hat hacker is sure to continue.

845 words   Time taken _____

Reading Comprehension

1 What is the author's purpose in writing this passage?
- **a.** to inform the reader about various types of hackers
- **b.** to convince the reader that gray hats are mostly ethical
- **c.** to warn the reader to avoid hackers while on the Internet
- **d.** to show that black hats aren't as bad as people think

2 Which of the following actions would a white hat probably NOT do?
- **a.** ask permission before entering a computer network
- **b.** take a job in a company to enhance computer security
- **c.** tell his friends how to break into a computer network
- **d.** report the activities of black hat hackers

3 What is another term for a black hat hacker?
- **a.** Linux
- **b.** cracker
- **c.** breaker
- **d.** blacker

4 How did Kevin Poulson win a Porsche automobile?
- **a.** He controlled the telephone calls going to the radio station.
- **b.** He changed the winning numbers in the radio station computer.
- **c.** He asked 101 friends to call the radio station before him.
- **d.** He knew a black hat hacker at the radio station.

5 What has Citibank done since it lost $10 million to hackers?
- **a.** It has offered $10 million for information about the thieves.
- **b.** It has greatly enhanced its security.
- **c.** It hasn't changed very much.
- **d.** It has stopped doing business in Russia.

6 Which action would be typical of a gray hat hacker?
- **a.** entering and taking control of a computer network
- **b.** asking permission before entering a computer network
- **c.** breaking into a computer network but doing little or no damage
- **d.** e-mailing computer viruses to unethical companies

7 Why are the names of gray hat hackers usually unknown?
- **a.** because they never do anything wrong
- **b.** because they are too clever for the police
- **c.** because they don't like publicity
- **d.** because they are rarely arrested

8 Which type of hacker might the author say is most likely to disappear in the future?
- **a.** the white hat hacker
- **b.** the gray hat hacker
- **c.** the black hat hacker
- **d.** They are all likely to disappear.

Review Reading 2: A Kenyan Safari

Fluency Practice

Time yourself as you read through the passage. Try to read as fluently as you can. Record your time in the Reading Rate Chart on page 240. Then answer the questions on page 64.

A Kenyan Safari

By Richard Mantle

In September of last year, I joined a tour group and visited several of the national parks of Kenya on a tour that lasted about two weeks. It was an absolutely exhilarating experience. Although the group of veteran
5   tourists seemed a bit jaded to me at the beginning of the trip, the awe-inspiring wildlife, the pristine natural settings, and some fascinating encounters with native people seemed to change everyone. We all emerged from the safari radiant with joy and inspiration.

10   The park where we encountered the most impressive array of endemic wildlife was the Maasai Mara. We saw lions, zebras, wildebeest, gazelles, giraffes, elephants, and more. It was an eerie feeling when a large lion came up to our minibus and started to lick the window. The terrified woman sitting next to the
15   window exclaimed, "Driver! Get us out of here now!" The driver giggled and said we had nothing to worry about; the lion could never break the reinforced windows of the minibus. The frightened woman turned red, and we all laughed heartily.

At Amboseli National Park, we had our first encounter with the Maasai people. This famous warrior tribe lives by herding cattle, but they also make extra money by selling jewelry to and
20   performing for tourists like us. We found them to be exceptionally gracious people, decked out in their traditional red and blue clothes. After laying out their jewelry on cloths near our camp, they timidly entered the camp and inquired if we would like to buy something. This gentle approach was very effective—our group always bought jewelry from the Maasai, but rarely from the other sellers.

25   On our last day in Amboseli, our tour guide had a surprise in store for us. The Maasai put on a music and dance show. Without any musical instruments, just using their voices, they created wonderfully intricate music that was very soothing and almost magical. The Maasai danced

back and forth, sometimes leaping high in the air. Some people in our group even lost their inhibitions and joined in, dancing and leaping with the Maasai! When the Maasai finished, we roused ourselves from our dreamy state and thanked them heartily. Long after, the memory of the music stayed with us, giving everyone a warm and special feeling.

The next morning we left for our next destination: Lake Bogoria, famous for its thousands of pink flamingos. The lake is in a valley between two very high cliffs. As we drove along one of the cliffs, most of us were incredulous that we could ever get down to the lake without plummeting to our deaths. Our trusty driver made it down the steep road safely, of course. We spent an hour watching the flamingos take off from and land on the shimmering surface of the lake. Soon the sun was directly overhead, and it was time for lunch. Our guide led us over to one area of the lakeshore that had hot springs and geysers. We cooked boiled eggs for lunch in the natural boiling water. (No, not flamingo eggs—chicken eggs, of course!)

After lunch, the guide surprised us by saying we were going to go looking for hippopotamuses. I was a little nervous about this, as I had heard that hippos were actually more dangerous even than lions. As we were all getting into several large canoes on the shore of the lake, I asked the guide if this was indeed true. He said that in fact, hippos could be very dangerous, and that I was right to respect their power. After about fifteen minutes of paddling across the lake, the guide told us to look to our left and we would see a large male hippopotamus. Well, he didn't seem to mind being looked at, until everyone in the group started taking photos of him. I guess he was averse to the sound of the cameras, and he started to make some unmistakably aggressive sounds. With that, our guide turned our canoes around, and we headed away from the hippo and back to the safety of the shore.

That evening, we all ate dinner together in a little restaurant called Mamalina. It was an interesting mixture of modern Kenya and traditional Kenya. Our guide helped us to decipher our menus, which, while written in English, contained lots of dishes we had never heard of before. Many of the dishes were prepared from the fish of Lake Bogoria, and there were various chicken and goat dishes as well. They were prepared with a variety of interesting vegetables endemic to the area that I had never seen before. When the food was brought, it smelled wonderful, and everyone dug in heartily.

While we were eating, we were amazed to see three men from the Samburu tribe enter the restaurant. They were decked out in the traditional clothes of their people, which included beautiful bird feathers and hair dyed bright red. It was really a surprise for us when these mighty African warriors all sat down at the bar and ordered a cola to drink! It was an unforgettable final scene from what was for me an unforgettable trip.

858 words   Time taken _____

Reading Comprehension

1 What was the author's main purpose in writing this account?
  a. to convince the reader to go on an African safari
  b. to entertain the reader with a description of his African safari
  c. to warn the reader about the dangers of an African safari
  d. to encourage the reader to learn more about African people

2 According to the author, how did the safari seem to change the tourists?
  a. It made them more jaded.
  b. It made them less afraid of Africa.
  c. It made them more joyful and inspired.
  d. It made them braver.

3 Why did the group laugh at the woman in the minibus at the Maasai Mara?
  a. because she panicked when a lion licked the window
  b. because she was afraid of zebras and wildebeest
  c. because she wanted to go home
  d. because she wanted to drive the minibus herself

4 Why did the tourists prefer to buy jewelry from the Maasai people?
  a. because they had the best jewelry
  b. because they wore red and blue clothes
  c. because they also lived from herding cattle
  d. because they were gracious and polite

5 Which phrase best describes the music performed by the Maasai?
  a. modern and annoying
  b. primitive and simple
  c. soothing and magical
  d. loud and overwhelming

6 Why did the guide decide to turn the boats around and head back to the shore of Lake Borogia?
  a. Everyone had taken all the photos they needed.
  b. Some tourists were getting very hungry.
  c. The hippopotamus was becoming aggressive.
  d. There were too many flamingos.

7 The meat of which type of animal was NOT on the menu at Mamalina?
  a. fish
  b. sheep
  c. goat
  d. chicken

8 Why was the final scene with the Samburu men so amazing to the author?
  a. because he thought they were going to be aggressive
  b. because the feathers they wore were very beautiful
  c. because they looked very traditional but drank cola
  d. because they were clearly part of a tourist show

Haunted by the Past

Getting Ready

Discuss the following questions with a partner.

1 Do you know of any well-known ghost stories or tales of hauntings? What happened?
2 Do you believe in ghosts? If not, how do you think these stories come to exist?
3 Do you ever read books or watch movies about ghosts or hauntings? Can you name some famous book or movie titles?
4 What feelings do you experience when you read ghost stories or watch scary movies?

Chapter 1: The Bell Witch

Before You Read:
Ghosts and Ghouls

A Answer the following questions.

1 Have you seen the movie entitled (in English) *The Blair Witch Project*? If so, what did you think of it? If not, what do you know about the story that inspired this movie?
2 What is one thing that many ghost stories have in common?
3 Some people claim that ghost stories are simply tricks or practical jokes, played on others, to scare people. What do you think? Are there logical explanations for what some people claim to be ghost stories?
4 Why do you think this story is called "The Bell Witch"? Scan the reading quickly to find the answer.

B Discuss your answers with a partner.

Reading Skill:
Identifying Meaning from Context

You can guess the meaning of important but unfamiliar words in a reading passage by using the following strategy: 1. Think about how the new word is related to the topic of what you are reading about. 2. Identify which part of speech the new word is by looking at how it fits with the other words in its sentence. 3. Look at how the word relates to the rest of the information in the paragraph surrounding it. 4. Use your knowledge of prefixes, suffixes, and word roots to identify the basic meaning of the word.

A The following is an extract from the reading passage. As you read through it, think about the topic of the reading, and what you already know about this topic. Pay attention to the words in bold.

Her voice, according to one person who heard it, "spoke at a **(1) nerve-racking** pitch when displeased, while at other times it sang and spoke in low musical tones." The spirit of Old Kate led John and Betsy Bell on a **(2) merry chase**. She threw furniture and dishes at them. She pulled their noses, **(3) yanked** their hair, **(4) poked** needles into them. She yelled all night to keep them from sleeping, and snatched food from their mouths at mealtimes.

B Decide which part of speech each bold expression is, and write them below.

(1) _____   (3) _____
(2) _____   (4) _____

C Circle the words in the sentence that work with or affect the items in bold, and tell you the part of speech. Look at how the word relates to the rest of the paragraph. Are there any other words or phrases that give you clues to the meaning of each item? If so, circle them. Now try to identify the meaning of each word. Replace each one with a word or phrase, or write a definition.

(1) _____   (3) _____
(2) _____   (4) _____

D Use your dictionary to check whether you have interpreted the meaning of the words correctly. Share your answers with a partner.

The Bell Witch

In 1817, one of the most well-known hauntings in American history took place in the small town of Adams, Tennessee.[1] In fact it was so well known that the story caught the attention of a future president of the United States.

Known as the Bell Witch, the strange activity that caused fear in the small farming community has remained unexplained for nearly 200 years. It is the **inspiration** for many fictional ghost stories, including the film *The Blair Witch Project*. Although they both attracted a great deal of public interest, the facts of the Bell Witch story share little in common with those created for *The Blair Witch Project*. Because it really happened, the Bell Witch story is perhaps much more frightening.

Like many stories, certain details of who or what the Bell Witch was vary from version to version. The **prevailing** account is that it was the ghost of a woman named Kate Batts, a mean old neighbor of John Bell. Batts believed Bell cheated her in a land purchase and on her deathbed,[2] she **swore** that she would haunt John Bell and his family. This version appears in a Tennessee guidebook published in 1933:

"Sure enough, tradition says, the Bells were **tormented** for years by the malicious spirit of Old Kate Batts. John Bell and his favorite daughter Betsy were the principal targets. Toward the other members of the family the witch was either **indifferent** or, as in the case of Mrs. Bell, friendly. No one ever saw her, but every visitor to the Bell home heard her all too well. Her voice, according to one person who heard it, 'spoke at a **nerve-racking** pitch when displeased, while at other times it sang and spoke in low musical tones.' The spirit of Old Kate led John and Betsy Bell on a merry chase. She threw furniture and dishes at them. She pulled their noses, yanked their hair, poked needles into them. She yelled all night to keep them from sleeping, and snatched food from their mouths at mealtimes."

News of the Bell Witch spread quickly. When word of the haunting reached Nashville,[3] one of its most famous citizens, General Andrew Jackson, decided to gather a group of friends and go to Adams to investigate. The future president wanted to come face to face with the phenomenon and either expose it as a hoax or send the spirit away. According to one account, Jackson and his men were traveling over a smooth section of road when suddenly the wagon stopped. The men pushed and pushed, but the wagon could not be moved. The wheels were even removed and inspected. Then came the sound of a voice from the bushes saying, "All right general, let the wagon move on. I will see you tonight." The astonished men could not find the source of the voice. The horses then unexpectedly started walking on their own and the wagon moved along again. Jackson indeed encountered the witch that night and left early the next morning, claiming he would rather fight the British than the Bell Witch!

The haunting of the Bell house continued for several years, ending with the ghost's ultimate act of **vengeance**. In October 1820, John Bell suffered a stroke.[4] In and out of bed for several weeks, his health never improved. The Tennessee State

University in Nashville recounts this part of the story:

"On the morning of December 19, he failed to awake at his regular time. When the family noticed he was sleeping unnaturally, they attempted to **rouse** him. They discovered Bell was in a stupor[5] and couldn't be completely awakened. John Jr.[6] went to the medicine cupboard to get his father's medicine and noticed it was gone but a strange vial[7] was in its place. No one claimed to have replaced the medicine with the vial. A doctor was **summoned** to the house. The witch began **taunting** that she had placed the vial in the medicine cabinet and given Bell a dose of its contents while he slept. The substance was tested on a cat and discovered to be highly poisonous. John Bell died on December 20. 'Kate' was quiet until after the funeral. However, after the grave was filled, the witch began singing loudly and joyously until all of John Bell's friends and family left his graveside."

A few explanations of the Bell Witch phenomena have been offered over the years. One is that the haunting was a hoax created by Richard Powell, the schoolteacher of Betsy Bell and Joshua Gardner, the boy with whom Betsy was in love. It seems Powell was deeply in love with Betsy and would do anything to destroy her relationship with Gardner. Through a variety of tricks, and with the help of several friends, it is believed that Powell created all of the ghostly effects to scare Gardner away. In fact, Gardner eventually did break up with Betsy and left the area. It has never been satisfactorily explained, however, how Powell achieved all the effects. But Powell did come out the winner. In the end, he married Betsy Bell.

This reading was adapted from *The Bell Witch* by Stephen Wagner, About.com Guide to Paranormal Phenomena. Reprinted with permission of the author © 1999.

[1] **Tennessee** a state in the southeast of the United States
[2] **on her deathbed** in the bed she died in; just before her death
[3] **Nashville** the capital city of Tennessee
[4] **stroke** a blocked or broken blood vessel in the brain that causes a lack of muscle control, difficulty speaking, and sometimes death
[5] **in a stupor** in a state of mental and/or physical inactivity
[6] **Jr.** junior; sons with the same name as their fathers often have "junior" put after the first name
[7] **vial** a small glass container, often holding medicinal liquid

A The following questions are all about the reading. Answer each one using the information you have read. Try not to look back at the reading for the answers.

1 Where did the Bell Witch story take place? _____

2 What was the name of the ghost in the Bell Witch story? _____

3 Who did the ghost haunt? _____

4 Why did the ghost haunt these people? _____

5 Did the ghost make any noises? Describe the kind of noises it made.

_____

B Decide if the following statements about the reading are true (T), false (F), or if the information is not given (NG). If you check (✔) false, correct the statement to make it true.

	T	F	NG
1 Andrew Jackson thought that the Bell Witch was a hoax.			
2 The haunting ended soon after the death of John Bell.			
3 The poison that killed John Bell also killed a cat.			
4 The Bell Witch may have been a hoax created by Richard Powell.			
5 Powell died before he could marry Betsy Bell.			

C Critical Thinking

Discuss these questions with a partner.

1 Do you think people were more or less likely to believe in ghosts in the 1800s compared with today?

2 How would you have reacted to the ghost if you had been a part of the Bell family?

3 Does it seem possible to you that Richard Powell could have created such a hoax? Why or why not?

Vocabulary Comprehension:
Word Definitions

A The words in *italics* are vocabulary items from the reading. Read each question or statement and choose the correct answer. Compare your answers with a partner.

1 Something that is an *inspiration* gives a person _____.
   a. new ideas   **b.** a boring feeling

2 A *prevailing* view is one that is _____.
   a. unaccepted   **b.** generally accepted

3 You might ask someone to *swear* to return some borrowed money if you _____.
   a. didn't trust them completely   **b.** knew for sure they would give it back.

4 If you are *tormented* by something, it causes you to feel _____.
   a. pain and anguish   **b.** confused

5 Which person is *indifferent*?
   a. someone who doesn't care about anything
   b. someone who worries about most things

6 Something *nerve-racking* is _____.
   a. stressful and frightening   **b.** extremely relaxing

7 An act of *vengeance* is _____.
   a. forgiving someone who hurt you   **b.** hurting someone who hurt you

8 If you were trying to *rouse* someone, you would be _____.
   a. trying to get him/her to sleep   **b.** trying to awaken him/her

9 If a crime is committed, who is *summoned* to the crime scene?
   a. the police   **b.** criminals

10 If someone is *taunting* you, it means he or she is _____.
   a. teasing you   **b.** encouraging you

B Answer these questions. Share your answers with a partner.

1 When was the last time you had a feeling of *inspiration*? What were you inspired to do?

2 Have you ever been *tormented* by something?

3 What is the *prevailing* view of politicians in your country?

4 What is something you feel *indifferent* about?

5 What kinds of situations do you find *nerve-racking*?

6 In what situations do people *swear* to tell the truth, to be loyal, or to carry out another person's wishes?

7 Why would someone want to perform an act of *vengeance*?

8 Are you easy or difficult to *rouse* in the morning?

9 Have you ever *summoned* the police or firefighters to your home?

10 When you were at elementary school, was *taunting* common on the playground?

A For each word, study the different parts. Then, write the part of speech and a simple definition. Use the list of prefixes and suffixes below, as well as your dictionary, to help you. Share your ideas with a partner.

Vocabulary Skill:
The Root Word
pos/pon

In this chapter, you read the word "expose," which contains the root "pos," meaning "put," "place," or "stand," and the prefix "ex-" which means "to show." Thus, "expose" means "to put on show" or "to reveal." The root "pos," or "pon," is used with a variety of prefixes and suffixes to form many different words in English.

Prefixes		Suffixes	
com-	with, together	**-tion**	the state of something
dis-	not, apart	**-able**	able to
de-	remove, down, away		
post-	after		
op-	against		
pro-	for		
trans-	across, change		

Vocabulary	Part of Speech	Definition
1 deposition	noun	a sworn statement used in court
2 compose	_____	_____
3 component	_____	_____
4 disposable	_____	_____
5 postpone	_____	_____
6 oppose	_____	_____
7 propose	_____	_____
8 position	_____	_____
9 transpose	_____	_____
10 deposit	_____	_____

B Now complete the sentences using words from A. Be sure to use the correct form of each word.

1 Albert was saving his money, so he _____ his entire paycheck in the bank.
2 Even two months after her car crash, Sheena was too ill to attend the court trial of the other driver. Instead her lawyer took a _____ from her in the hospital.
3 I'm trying this alternative cold remedy. It's _____ of different plant roots and herbs, and tastes very strange.
4 Because of the pouring rain, we decided to _____ the picnic.
5 Mary lost the spelling contest, because she _____ the last two letters of the word *theater*.
6 After years of working in a junior _____, Trina was promoted to management.

Chapter 2: *Vanishing Hitchhikers*

Before You Read:
Spooky Strangers

A Discuss the following questions with a partner.

1 What do you think the differences are between a *ghost*, a *phantom*, and a *poltergeist*? Use your dictionary to help you understand the meaning of each word.
2 Do you know of anyone, or of any stories, where living people have come into close contact with ghosts? What happened?
3 Do you believe ghostly tales of people seeing vanishing figures? Why or why not?
4 Where do you think such stories come from?

B Match the words and phrase from the reading on the left with their definitions.

1 resurrection _____
2 cemetery _____
3 vanish into thin air _____
4 imprints _____

a. idiomatic expression meaning disappear
b. marks made on a surface in the shape of something
c. the act of coming back to life from the dead
d. a place where the dead are buried

C Scan the reading for the words and phrase and check your answers.

Reading Skill:
Recognizing Sequence Markers

Sequence markers are words and phrases that signal the reader about the order of events. Expressions such as "then," "soon after that," "subsequently," as well as days, dates, and times can act as sequence markers. The past perfect can also signal the order of events.

A Scan the reading to find the sequence marker that connects each pair of events from the stories in the text. Write the sequence marker in the blank.

1 _____ she can pull over to the side of the road, the youth simply vanishes.
2 _____ he arrives at the address, he turns to speak to her . . .
3 _____ driving a short distance, she suddenly tells him to stop . . .
4 The driver sees the flash of the lighter, _____, on turning his head . . .

B In each sentence in A above, circle the event that occurred first. If the events happened at the same time, circle both events.

C Read the passage again; then answer the questions that follow.

Vanishing Hitchhikers

One of the most entertaining types of ghost stories is that of the phantom, or **vanishing**, hitchhiker.[1] It's also one of the most **chilling** because, if true, they bring ghosts in very
5   close contact with **mortals**. Perhaps more **disconcerting** still, the stories describe the ghosts as looking, acting, and sounding like living people—even physically interacting with the unsuspecting drivers who pick them up.

10   The basic story usually goes something like this: a tired driver traveling at night picks up a strange hitchhiker, drops him or her off at some destination, and then somehow later finds out that the hitchhiker had in fact died
15   months or years earlier—often on that very same date. Like most ghost stories, tales of phantom hitchhikers are impossible to **verify**, and are most often considered to be urban legends.[2] There are many such stories, and
20   it's up to you to determine whether or not you believe any of them. Here are just a few:

The Basketball Player

A woman, driving to her sister's house on a winter evening, sees a boy of about eleven or twelve years of age hitchhiking on the side of the road. She stops for him; he gets into the
25   front seat next to her, and they chat as they drive down the highway. The boy says he's a basketball player for a local school, and she sees that, indeed, he has the height and build of an athlete. She also notices that he is not wearing a jacket of any kind, **despite the fact** that it's winter. The boy seems to have no particular destination in mind as he points to the side of the road and asks to be let out there. The woman is **puzzled** because she can see
30   no houses or lights anywhere. Before she can pull over to the side of the road, however, the youth simply vanishes. She immediately stops the car, gets out, and looks around, but the boy is nowhere to be seen. She later learns that the same vanishing hitchhiker was first picked up at the same spot twenty-nine years earlier!

The Girl on the Side of the Road

35   A doctor, while driving home from a country club dance, picks up a young girl in a white dress. She climbs into the back seat of his car because the front seat is crowded with golf clubs, and tells him an address to take her to. As he arrives at the address, he turns to speak to her but she is gone. The curious doctor rings the doorbell of the address given to him by the mysterious girl. A gray-haired man answers the door and reveals that the girl was
40   his daughter. She had died in a car accident exactly two years earlier.

Resurrection Mary

The story of Resurrection Mary begins on a winter night when a young girl named Mary is killed in a car accident while on her way home from a dance. Five years later, a taxi driver picks up a young girl in a white dress on the same street. She sits in the front seat and
45 instructs him to drive north. After driving a short distance, she suddenly tells him to stop, and then simply vanishes from the taxi. The taxi is stopped in front of Resurrection Cemetery, where the girl is buried. According to an **account** many years later, a woman witnessed Mary locked inside the iron fence of the cemetery. Reportedly, the metal bars of the fence bore the imprints of her hands.

50 ## The Smoking Ghost

On a dark winter night, a man stops for a stranger hitchhiking on the side of the road. The stranger is dressed in a military uniform and, after he gets into the car, asks if he can have a cigarette. The man gives him one, and a lighter with which to light it. With his peripheral vision,[3] the driver sees the flash of the lighter, but then, on turning his head, is astonished to
55 see that his passenger has vanished into thin air. Only the cigarette lighter remains on the seat.

The Grandmother

Two businessmen stop for a little old lady in a lavender[4] dress walking along the side of the road in the middle of the night. She tells them she is going to see her daughter and
60 granddaughter, and they offer to drive her to the next town. On the way, she proudly tells them all about her children and grandchildren, such as their names and where they live. After a while, the men become **engrossed** in their own business conversation, and when they reach their destination, the old woman is no longer in the back seat. **Fearing the worst**, the men retrace their route, but do not find the woman anywhere. Finally, recalling the daughter's
65 name, they go to her house to report what they fear might have been a horrible accident. The men identify her from photos in the daughter's house. It turns out that the old woman was buried exactly three years ago that day.

This reading was adapted from *Phantom Hitchhikers* by Stephen Wagner, About.com Guide to Paranormal Phenomena. Reprinted with permission of the author © 1999.

---

[1] **hitchhiker** a person who travels free by getting vehicles to stop at the roadside and pick him/her up
[2] **urban legend** an invented story that is believed to be true
[3] **peripheral vision** the outermost edge of the entire area that a person can see; out of the corner of the eye
[4] **lavender** pale or light purple color

A Decide if the following statements about the reading are true (T) or false (F). If you check (✔) false, correct the statement to make it true.

		T	F
1	All of the stories in the text feature a hitchhiker that is a ghost which suddenly disappears.		
2	The writer believes that the stories in the text could be proven true.		
3	A common phantom in many ghost stories is a vanishing taxi driver.		
4	Many ghost stories are considered to be urban legends.		

B The statements below are about the reading. Complete each one using the correct word or phrase.

1 The woman who picked up the boy in *The Basketball Player* noticed that he _____.
   a. didn't look like an athlete
   b. wasn't wearing a jacket
   c. was riding a bicycle
   d. spoke a foreign language

2 In *The Girl on the Side of the Road*, the doctor discovered that his phantom passenger had _____.
   a. directed him to her father's house
   b. played golf earlier
   c. been dancing
   d. quickly run away

3 In the story of *Resurrection Mary*, Mary died because she _____.
   a. was locked inside the cemetery
   b. got lost in the woods
   c. forgot to take her medicine
   d. was in a car accident

4 In the story of *The Smoking Ghost*, the ghost vanishes with _____.
   a. the man's car
   b. the man's lighter
   c. the man's cigarette
   d. the man's uniform

5 In the story of *The Grandmother*, the old lady died _____.
   a. in a lavender dress
   b. in a horrible accident
   c. three years before
   d. with her family

C Critical Thinking

Discuss these questions with a partner.
1 Which of the five stories in the reading did you find the scariest? Why?
2 Do you think this type of story is found in all cultures of the world or only some? Explain your answer.
3 Would you pick up a hitchhiker on a lonely road late at night? Why or why not?

Vocabulary Comprehension:
Word Definitions

A **Look at the list of words and phrases from the reading. Match each one with a definition on the right.**

1 vanishing _____
2 chilling _____
3 mortals _____
4 disconcerting _____
5 verify _____
6 despite the fact _____
7 puzzled _____
8 account _____
9 engrossed _____
10 fearing the worst _____

a. having one's attention completely occupied
b. to prove; make certain of the accuracy of something
c. confused or baffled
d. in spite of something; even though
e. feeling that the worst possible thing has happened
f. a spoken or written description of an event
g. upsetting; making one feel worried or uncertain
h. beings who will eventually die
i. disappearing
j. frightening

B **Complete the sentences using the vocabulary from A. Be sure to use the correct form of each word.**

1 The way Seow Lin gives a(n) _____ of her flying lessons is hilarious.
2 This crossword has had me _____ for hours.
3 In the ancient Greek myths, the gods, who lived forever, often involved themselves in the lives of _____.
4 Don't try calling Rachel on Monday evenings; she gets so _____ in TV soap operas that she doesn't respond to anything.
5 _____ that Alan cut back on his spending, he still didn't have enough money to pay all his bills.
6 So-ra wanted to _____ that her interviewee was a good worker, so she called his former boss for a reference.
7 The most _____ story I heard wasn't a ghost story; it was a true story about a burglar who murdered all six people who lived in the house.
8 When I met Melissa's boyfriend, he kept telling me he'd met me somewhere before and asked me lots of really personal questions. It was quite _____.
9 As quickly as she made the cookies, they _____ from the plate.
10 When Fred didn't come home from his fishing trip, his wife immediately _____. She called the coastguard to ask for help.

A

Study the words in the chart. What do you think they mean? Use your knowledge of prefixes, suffixes, and the root *mort* to match each word with a definition.

Vocabulary Skill:
The Root Word *mort*

Noun	Verb	Adjective
mortuary mortgage* murder* morgue mortality post-mortem**	amortize mortify	immortal moribund morbid

* can also be a verb   ** can also be an adjective

In this chapter, you read the word "mortal." This word is formed from the root "mort," also written "mor" or "mur," which means "to die" or "death." There are many words in English that use this root and they are used in a variety of contexts.

1   lasting or living forever _____
2   obsessed with disturbing subjects like death _____
3   a place where bodies of people found dead are kept for examination or identification _____
4   to cause one to feel extreme shame or embarrassment _____
5   the crime of intentionally killing a person _____
6   an agreement that allows one to borrow money to finance a purchase, usually of property _____
7   medical examination of a dead body to determine the cause of death _____
8   to reduce a debt or expenditure by making installment payments over time _____
9   a place, especially a funeral home, where dead bodies are kept before a funeral _____
10 the quality or state of not living forever _____
11 at, or near, the point of death; on the verge of becoming obsolete _____

B

Use the words from A to complete the paragraphs below. Which words are left over? Check your answers with a partner.

News in Brief   *Six Feet Under* **Reaches Six Million Viewers**

All of us, at one point or another, face death and our own **(1)**_____. Perhaps this is what the creator of the television show *Six Feet Under* was thinking when he conceived of the program to which six million people—the highest viewing figures so far—tuned in last night. Despite the fact that some consider the theme quite **(2)**_____, it's obviously a popular topic. The show takes place in a funeral home. The characters frequently have to go to the **(3)**_____ to retrieve bodies of the deceased, many of whom were **(4)**_____ or accident victims. The bodies are then placed in the **(5)**_____ until the funeral takes place. The show examines many issues related to death, and reminds us that though our loved ones may pass away, our thoughts will keep them **(6)**_____.

Real Life Skill:
Types of Stories

The same story, or set of events, can be narrated in many different ways, for different purposes. They might be told in a humorous way for entertainment, in a factual way as a news report, or in a certain order using specific phrases and language for educational purposes. Knowing how and why events are being told in a certain way can help you to understand the purpose of the information being provided.

A Read these different types of stories and their definitions. Where would you most likely read each one? Match each story type to a type of reading material. Some of them can be used more than once. Can you add any other examples?

> children's book   joke book   newspaper   corporate document   magazine
> police report   self-help book   advice column   historical information

1 **tale**—an old story that has been told many times _____
2 **report**—a detailed and objective presentation of facts _____
3 **anecdote**—a short story about a real event, used to illustrate an idea _____
4 **account**—an explanation from one person's point of view _____
5 **chronicle**—a long narrative of events over time _____
6 **yarn**—an entertaining story that is loosely based on truth _____
7 **proverb**—a short sentence that expresses a moral lesson, e.g., "When the cat's away, the mice will play." _____
8 **statement**—a short summary of facts _____
9 **fable**—a short piece of fiction (often about animals) that teaches a moral lesson _____
10 **gossip**—a rumor about someone that is possibly untrue _____

B Now complete the sentences below using one of the story types from A. Be prepared to give reasons for your choice.

1 My grandfather loves to tell _____ about when he was a boy.
2 The Ministry of Environmental Protection recently published its _____ on changes in air quality over the past ten years.
3 I don't believe that Carl is getting married. I think it's just _____.
4 That article has some interesting _____ about women who have started their own businesses.
5 "Look before you leap" is my favorite _____.
6 At the meeting, Dr. Kim gave a(n) _____ of his research trip to the Arctic.
7 In my country, we have a lot of _____ about giants and monsters.
8 The government decided to release a(n) _____ about crimes committed by congressmen.

What Do You Think?

1 Do you believe that any of the ghost stories recounted in Unit 4 are true?
2 What other logical explanations are there for these stories?
3 Do you think some people are more likely to see ghosts than other people? What type of person is more likely to see a ghost?
4 How many of your class members believe in ghosts? How many are skeptics? What reasons do they give to support their beliefs? Take a class poll to find out.

Getting Ready

Complete the survey below. Then, discuss your choices with a partner.

What Do You Like to Read?

A What genres of reading material do you enjoy?
Check (✔) all the genres you have read in the past year.

☐ adventure

☐ science-fiction

☐ popular science

☐ hobbies or collecting

☐ fantasy

☐ horror

☐ romance

☐ biography/autobiography

☐ sports

☐ how-to

☐ other: _____

B What characters or people do you like to read about?
Check (✔) all those that you have read about in the past year.

☐ people who are like myself in some way

☐ celebrities

☐ people who have had interesting adventures or experiences

☐ characters from television and from movies

☐ people who are challenged and overcome problems

☐ super heroes

☐ non-human characters such as animals or aliens

☐ famous athletes

☐ historical figures

☐ other: _____

Chapter 1: What Exactly IS a Short Story?

Reading Skill:
Recognizing Simile and Metaphor

Good writers choose their words very carefully. Often, the words that an author chooses describe an image that expresses their ideas, and can help the reader understand them better. These images can be expressed as "similes" or "metaphors." Similes are figures of speech in which direct comparisons are made between two things, illustrated by the use of "like," or "as," for example, "love is like a bed of roses." Metaphors are figures of speech that suggest a comparison is being made between two things by describing how one thing resembles another, for example, "love is a battlefield."

A Answer the following questions.

1 Do you usually read one book at a time, or do you read several different books at a time?
2 What was the last book you finished? Who wrote it? What was it about? Briefly retell the story.
3 How often do you read short stories? What do you understand to be the main differences between a short story and a novel?
4 What do you think are the main differences between a short story and a poem?

B Discuss your answers with a partner.

A Read through the following paragraph taken from the reading passage. Look at the bold sections. Which is an example of a simile, and which is an example of a metaphor? Write your answer below. Which words tell you this?

> In a recent class I was asked "What is a short story?" My first answer was that it was something that could be read in one sitting and brought **(1) an illumination** to the reader, sudden and golden **(2) like sunlight cracking through** heavy cloud. I went on to say that in my opinion a "real" short story was closer to poetry than to the novel.

(1) _____ (2) _____

1 Which example compares reading a short story to experiencing the light of understanding? 1 / 2
2 Which example compares the light of understanding to sunlight appearing through the clouds? 1 / 2

B Now go to paragraph three and find an example of simile OR metaphor. Circle the correct choice below, then write the words that tell you which it is.

Simile / Metaphor: _____
What two things does the writer compare in this example?

C Now read through the passage again and answer the comprehension questions that follow.

What Exactly Is a Short Story?

In a recent class I was asked "What is a short story?" My first answer was that it was something that could be read in one sitting and brought an illumination to the reader, sudden and golden
5 like sunlight cracking through heavy cloud. I went on to say that in my opinion a "real" short story was closer to poetry than to the novel.

Not all my students were convinced. Let's discuss word count: when is a short story too long to still
10 be a short story? Is there an official point where a short becomes a novella,[1] another where a novella becomes a novel? Is Hemingway's *The Old Man & the Sea* truly a novel? Let's set an **arbitrary** limit of words. For now let's agree that stories up to 10,000
15 words in length are short stories.

I'm not trying to be definitive here, so let's look at some definitions of the short story. My favorite is Benét's,[2] "something that can be read in an hour and remembered for a lifetime." One writer said, "The theme of a novel will not fit into the framework of a short story; it's like trying to squeeze a mural[3] into the frame of a **miniature**. And as in a miniature painting, the details need
20 to be sharp."

The short story is an example of one **facet** of human nature. Often a character undergoes some event and experiences something that offers him or her change. This is why it's said that short stories usually "say something," often a small something, but sometimes delivered with such precision that the effect is **exquisite**, even a life-moment for some readers, something similar to
25 a religious experience or to witnessing a never-to-be-repeated scene in nature.

The perfect short story is written with a poet's sensitivity for language, with a poet's precision. The shape and sounds and rhythms of the words are more commonly part of the effect than they usually are in the novel. Just as in a poem, the bare words themselves are never the complete meaning. They interact with each other. Their sounds do things. How they are placed
30 on the page matters. The poem tries to create a piece of truth, an insight into being human, and the form is so tight, so **sparse** that we can argue over exact meanings long into the night.

One reason for the confusion students often have over the definition of short stories is that other word forms, **anecdotes**, sketches, vignettes,[4] or slices of life often find their ways into them. These are often pretty and faintly moving, but somehow they leave us with a slightly
35 unsatisfied feeling. The fewer words we use, below a certain point—let's imagine this point is 1,500 words—the harder it is to have something clearly happen to a character, and have that occurrence change him or her.

So, for now, under 10,000 words is at the long end of short stories, but how short? Are we saying under 1,500 words is not a short story? Great writers can do in 600 words what a
40 solid writer might manage in 1,100. Maybe at 500 words, the **confinement** begins to create a new form, often very interesting, but more of an intellectual exercise; literary showing off rather than a natural giving of truth.

In the United Kingdom, there's an annual competition for "stories," complete in exactly fifty words. Here is one: *Frank believed in his luck. Frank smoked too much but he knew he'd*
45 *never die of a heart attack or lung cancer. Frank smoked all the time. One day there was a gas leak in Frank's kitchen. Frank went to fix it. He didn't die of a heart attack or lung cancer.*

It's fun and sort of complete, but it isn't likely to find a place in our hearts and change our outlook on life. Technically it's a story, and short it definitely is, but "short story," I argue, it is not.

50 There is a degree of **unity** in a well thought out short story, one I tend to call its theme. This kind of intensity in a novel would indeed tire the reader. But in the one-sitting contract with the reader of a short story, it is presumed that he or she will cope. Hence, when the story has quality, often the experience seems **profound**.

Okay, so let's form a definition here: A short story is a narrative,[5] rarely over 10,000 words
55 or below 500 words—more commonly 1,500 to 5,000 words, a single-sitting read, but with enough time and weight to move the reader. It is narrow and focused to produce a singular effect through the story, most commonly through events affecting some change, or denial of change, in an individual. All aspects of a short story are closely integrated and cross-**reinforcing**—language, point of view, tone and mood, the sounds as well as the meanings
60 of the words, and their rhythm.

Writer Isabelle Allende once wrote: "Novels are, for me, adding up details, just work, work, work, then you're done. Short stories are more difficult—they have to be perfect, complete in themselves."

This reading was adapted from *What IS a Short Story?* by Alex Keegan.
Reprinted with permission of the author © 1999.

---

[1] **novella** a story that is longer than a short story but shorter than a novel
[2] **Benét** Stephen Vincent Benét (1898–1943), American author
[3] **mural** /mjuːrəl/ a large work of art usually applied directly onto a wall
[4] **vignettes** /vɪnˈjets/ short, descriptive scenes from a story
[5] **narrative** the telling of a story

A Use the information you have read to select the correct answer to each statement. Try not to look back at the reading for the answers.

1 We can infer from the opening paragraph that the author is a _____.
   a. teacher   b. poet   c. student   d. painter
2 According to the author, the ideal short story should be _____.
   a. at least 10,000 words in length   b. below 500 words
   c. under 1,500 words   d. around 1,500 to 5,000 words
3 The author suggests that in a short story, the main character _____.
   a. experiences a change   b. falls in love
   c. is confident and strong   d. is intense
4 Well-written short stories are written with a poet's sensitivity for _____.
   a. poetry   b. unity   c. language   d. life
5 Included in a short story may be all the following *except* _____.
   a. anecdotes   b. vignettes   c. novellas   d. sketches

B Complete the sentences with the correct answer, then discuss your answers with a partner.

1 The title of the text suggests that many people do not know _____.
2 The author considers the unifying concept of a short story to be its
   _____.
3 To the author, writing a _____ is an example of literary showing off.
4 Benét defined a short story as something that can be read in an hour and remembered _____.
5 Isabelle Allende felt that short stories were _____ to write than novels.

C Critical Thinking

Discuss these questions with a partner.
1 Which of the definitions of a short story from the text do you most agree with? Explain your choice.
2 Does this text inspire you to read more short stories? Why or why not?

Vocabulary Comprehension:
Odd Word Out

A For each group circle the word that does not belong. The words in *italics* are vocabulary items from the reading.

1	*arbitrary*	subjective	discretionary	objective
2	reduced	scaled down	*miniature*	deliberate
3	perspective	*facet*	aspect	falsehood
4	horrific	elegant	*exquisite*	beautiful
5	dense	thin	scant	*sparse*
6	rationales	tales	stories	*anecdotes*
7	limitation	freedom	*confinement*	restriction
8	association	separation	connection	*unity*
9	*profound*	deep	superficial	intense
10	*reinforcing*	strengthening	supporting	weakening

B Complete the sentences using the words in *italics* from A. Be sure to use the correct form of the word.

1 The soldiers put hundreds of bags of sand behind the seawall in order to _____ it before the storm arrives.

2 During his interview, Chris told a(n) _____ about something that happened in his last job that made his interviewer smile.

3 This book is so true to my own life that reading it was a(n) _____ emotional experience.

4 I really don't think Jun thought about these sales figures at all. I'm sure he must have picked some _____ numbers out of thin air.

5 Some people find it easy to work in this small office; others feel too restricted by the _____.

6 If we lived in the country we'd get a full-sized dog, but because we live in a small city apartment, we chose to get a _____ poodle.

7 Just one _____ of our business is to provide online training for employees.

8 _____ of ideas is important, not only in stories, but for any written work to make sense.

9 Natasha has created a minimalist home. She's decorated as _____ as she can and, I must admit, the house has a certain elegance about it.

10 Everybody has different taste in home furnishings. What one person considers to be _____, another might think is horrendous.

A Study each word in the chart below. Using your knowledge of prefixes and suffixes, write the part of speech and a simple definition for each one. Use your dictionary to help you. Share your answers with a partner.

Vocabulary	Part of Speech	Definition
1 subscribe	_____	_____
2 manuscript	_____	_____
3 postscript	_____	_____
4 scribble	_____	_____
5 prescription	_____	_____
6 describe	_____	_____
7 superscript	_____	_____
8 inscription	_____	_____
9 transcribe	_____	_____
10 conscript	_____	_____

The root word "scribe," also written as "scrip" or "script," comes from the Latin word "scribere," meaning "to write." Many words in English that are related to writing contain this root so it is a useful one to know.

B Now use some of the words from A to complete the sentences below. Be sure to use the correct form of the appropriate word.

1 Who _____ on my folder? It's covered in ink now!
2 Read the _____ on this stone. This building is over 500 years old!
3 In every letter or e-mail she sends, Emily adds a _____ and writes a joke.
4 Do you _____ to this magazine or do you buy it at the newsstand?
5 Most actors like to receive their _____ to read over before rehearsals begin.
6 From the way Steven _____ his girlfriend, you'd think she were a model.
7 I don't believe it. I only have a sore throat but this _____ is for three different medications!

C Now ask and answer the following questions with a partner.

1 Do you *subscribe* to any newspapers, magazines, or websites? Which ones?
2 Do you ever add *postscripts* to letters or e-mails?
3 *Describe* a member of your family—his or her appearance and character.
4 When was the last time you had to get a *prescription* from the doctor?

Chapter 2: An Interview with J.K. Rowling

Before You Read:
A Writer's Story

A How much do you know about J.K. Rowling and Harry Potter? Read each statement below and decide if it is true (T) or false (F).

		T	F
1	J.K. Rowling was born into a rich family.		
2	Rowling wrote *Harry Potter and the Philosopher's Stone* in a library.		
3	Rowling wrote a book about a rabbit called Rabbit.		
4	Rowling writes primarily for children.		
5	Rowling names her characters after members of her family.		
6	Some of the characters in Rowling's books are based on real people.		
7	Snitch, Bludgers, and Quaffle are characters in Rowling's books.		
8	Rowling doesn't use a computer to write her novels.		

B Compare and discuss your answers with a partner. Share any other interesting facts you know about J.K. Rowling and Harry Potter.

Reading Skill:
Scanning

When we need to read something to find specific information, we move our eyes very quickly across the text. When we "scan" like this, we do not read every word or stop when we see a word we do not understand; we read quickly and pause only to find the particular information we are looking for.

A Scan the article to find out if the statements above are really true or false.

B Scan the article to find these words. Read the sentence containing each word and the sentences before and after. Then match each word with a definition.

1 Quidditch _____   a. a wizards' school in the Harry Potter books
2 Hermione _____   b. a non-wizard human in the Harry Potter books
3 Muggle _____   c. an imaginary sport played in the Harry Potter books
4 Hogwarts _____   d. a female character in the Harry Potter books

C Read the article again; then answer the questions that follow.

An Interview with J.K. Rowling

Divorced, living on public assistance[1] in an Edinburgh apartment with her **infant** daughter, J.K. Rowling wrote *Harry Potter and the Philosopher's Stone* at a café table. Fortunately, Harry Potter rescued her! In this Amazon.co.uk

5 interview, Rowling discusses the birth of our hero, the Manchester hotel where Quidditch was born, and how she might have been a bit like Hermione when she was 11 years old.

How old were you when you started to write, and
10 **what was your first book?**
Rowling: I wrote my first finished story when I was about six. It was about a rabbit called Rabbit. Very imaginative. I've been writing ever since.

Why did you choose to be an author?
15 **Rowling:** If someone asked for my recipe for happiness, step one would be finding out what you love doing most in the world and step two would be finding someone to pay you to do it. I consider myself very lucky indeed to be able to support myself by writing.

Do you have any plans to write books for adults?
Rowling: My first two novels—which I never tried to get published—were for adults. I suppose I
20 might write another one, but I never really imagine a target audience when I'm writing. The ideas come first, so it really depends on the idea that **grabs me** next.

Where did the ideas for the Harry Potter books come from?
Rowling: I've no idea where ideas come from and I hope I never find out; it would spoil the excitement for me if it turned out I just have a funny little **wrinkle** on the surface of my brain
25 which makes me think about invisible train platforms.

How do you come up with the names of your characters?
Rowling: I invented some of the names in the Harry books, but I also collect strange names. I've gotten them from medieval[2] saints, maps, dictionaries, plants, war memorials, and people I've met!

30 **Are your characters based on people you know?**
Rowling: Some of them are, but I have to be extremely careful what I say about this. Mostly, real people inspire a character, but once they are inside your head they start turning into something quite different. Professor Snape and Gilderoy Lockhart both started as **exaggerated** versions of people I've met, but became rather different once I got them on the page. Hermione is a bit like
35 me when I was 11, though much cleverer.

Are any of the stories based on your life, or on people you know?
Rowling: I haven't **consciously** based anything in the Harry books on my life, but of course that doesn't mean your own feelings don't **creep in**. When I re-read chapter 12 of the first book, *The Mirror of Erised*, I saw that I had given Harry lots of my own feelings about my own mother's
40 death, though I hadn't been aware of that as I had been writing.

Where did the idea for Quidditch come from?
Rowling: I invented Quidditch while spending the night in a very small room in the Bournville Hotel in Didsbury, Manchester. I wanted a sport for wizards, and I'd always wanted to see a game where there was more than one ball in play at the same time. The idea just amused me.
45 The Muggle sport it most resembles is basketball, which is probably the sport I enjoy watching most. I had a lot of fun making up the rules and I've still got the notebook I did it in, complete with **diagrams**, and all the names for the balls I tried before I **settled on** Snitch, Bludgers, and Quaffle.

Where did the ideas for the wizard classes and magic spells come from?
50 **Rowling:** I decided on the school subjects very early on. Most of the spells are invented, but some of them have a basis in what people used to believe worked. We owe a lot of our scientific knowledge to the alchemists![3]

What ingredients do you think all the Harry Potter books need?
Rowling: I never really think in terms of ingredients, but I suppose if I had to name some I'd
55 say humor, strong characters, and a **watertight** plot.[4] These things would add up to the kind of book I enjoy reading myself. Oh, I forgot scariness—well, I never set out to make people scared, but it does seem to creep in along the way.

Do you write longhand[5] or type onto a computer?
Rowling: I still like writing by hand. Normally I do a first **draft** using pen and paper, and then
60 do my first edit when I type it onto my computer. For some reason, I much prefer writing with a black pen than a blue one, and in a perfect world I'd always use narrow feint[6] writing paper. But I have been known to write on all sorts of weird things when I didn't have a notepad with me. The names of the Hogwarts houses were created on the back of an airplane sick bag. Yes, it was empty.

[1] **public assistance** government money to provide food, shelter, or medical care to unemployed people
[2] **medieval** related to the Middle Ages, a period of European history from about A.D. 476 to 1450
[3] **alchemists** scientists from the Middle Ages who tried to change ordinary metals into gold
[4] **plot** the main storyline in a novel, story, play, or film
[5] **longhand** writing by hand onto notepaper rather than typing onto a computer
[6] **narrow feint** a particular type of lined writing paper

A Decide if the following statements about the reading are true (T) or false (F). If you check (✔) false, correct the statement to make it true.

	T	F
1 J.K. Rowling was married when she wrote the first Harry Potter novel.		
2 J.K. Rowling wrote her first story when she was six years old.		
3 Rowling has already published two books for adults.		
4 Rowling does not know exactly where the ideas for the Harry Potter books came from.		
5 All the characters in the Harry Potter books are based on people Rowling knows well.		

B The statements below are about the reading. Complete each one using the correct word or phrase.

1 Rowling subconsciously gave Harry Potter many of the feelings that she experienced _____.

2 Quidditch most resembles _____, but with multiple balls in play at the same time.

3 Rowling thinks four things are necessary to make any book successful: humor, strong characters, a plot, and _____.

4 Rowling writes first _____; then edits as she types the story into her computer.

C Critical Thinking

Discuss these questions with a partner.

1 Have you ever read a Harry Potter novel or seen a Harry Potter movie? Which ones did you see? What did you think of them?

2 Have you ever considered writing some fiction yourself? What kind of story might you like to write?

Vocabulary Comprehension:

Word Definitions

A Look at the list of words and phrases from the reading. Match each one with a definition on the right.

1 infant _____
2 grabs me _____
3 wrinkle _____
4 exaggerated _____
5 consciously _____
6 creep in _____
7 diagrams _____
8 settled on _____
9 watertight _____
10 draft _____

a. perfectly designed; without flaws or loopholes
b. with awareness; deliberately
c. sketches or drawings to show how something works
d. overstated; presented as greater than in actuality
e. a line or crease in something
f. sneak in; enter surreptitiously
g. finally decided
h. a preliminary outline or version of a plan, document, or picture
i. a very young child
j. captures my attention

B Complete the sentences using the vocabulary from A. Be sure to use the correct form of each word.

1 Even though Mei Ling is usually a very optimistic person, she sometimes lets negative thoughts about her future _____.
2 It wasn't until our daughter was born that we finally _____ a name for her.
3 Bill was half asleep, so he really wasn't _____ of what he was saying.
4 Even famous writers will go through multiple _____ of a work before coming up with the final manuscript.
5 Leonardo da Vinci produced some amazing _____ for inventions that were only made real hundreds of years after he died.
6 Some people may think that _____ are a sign of aging, but others believe they are a sign of living.
7 Much to everyone's disbelief, Christina's mother claims that she started singing and dancing as a(n) _____.
8 The best storytellers know how to _____ just enough to make their tales more fascinating, but still believable.
9 This book really isn't that interesting. Unless something on the next page _____, I'm not going to finish it.
10 Police were stunned by the skills the bank robbers had. Their plan was completely _____ and they escaped with a fortune without leaving any clues.

A Each of the sentences below contains an idiom in *italics*. Read the idioms and look at how each one is used in the context of the sentence. Try to determine what they mean, and write a short definition for each one. Compare your ideas with a partner.

1 Juan thought about his study problem all night, but he just couldn't *come up with* a solution.

  _____

2 Alex could not *make up his mind* which shirt to wear to the party. In the end, his girlfriend had to decide for him.

  _____

3 Sue hates doing housework and, rather than getting it done quickly, she always tries to *think up* some way of delaying it.

  _____

4 Although Satoshi's boss has made him an incredible offer of promotion, it will mean moving overseas. Rather than make an immediate decision, he has decided to *think it over* for a day or two.

  _____

5 With unemployment as bad as it is, you really ought to *think twice* before you quit your job.

  _____

6 When Alan's position was made redundant, he assumed he would get another job. The thought of going back to school never *crossed his mind* until his wife suggested it to him.

  _____

7 This course is way too difficult. That lecture went right *over my head*; I couldn't understand any of it.

  _____

8 Oh no! I meant to call that client back but it completely *slipped my mind*. I'll have to call tomorrow.

  _____

9 Look at the price of this! Nobody *in their right mind* would pay that much money.

  _____

Vocabulary Skill:
Idioms of Thinking

In this chapter you read the idiom "come up with." An idiom is a fixed group of words that has a special meaning. There are many idioms that relate to the subject of thinking. Sometimes it's possible to know what the idiom means by looking at the individual words, but it can also be helpful to look at the idiom in context in order to understand its meaning.

B Ask and answer the questions below with a partner. Share your answers with other students in the class.

1 Can you *come up with* a way to make learning English vocabulary easier?
2 Have you *made up your mind* about what kind of job you would like to do when you graduate?
3 *Think up* two ways you can get more practice reading in English.
4 What would you advise somebody to *think twice* about? Why?
5 Has it ever *crossed your mind* to quit school and go traveling for a year? Where would you like to go?
6 Do you have a good memory or do things tend to *slip your mind*?
7 If you had to write a story now, would you have to *rack your brain* to think of an idea, or would one come easily? Share your story idea if you have one.

Real Life Skill:
Understanding
Literary Terms

The analysis of literature uses a special set of terms and vocabulary. Knowing these terms will help you to talk about literature you read in your classes, and to understand book reviews and other writings about aspects of literature.

A Read these common literary terms and their definitions below. Do you have any similar terms in your native language?

> **simile:** a direct comparison between two things
> Your smile is *like sunlight*.
> **metaphor:** an indirect comparison between two things
> *The journey of life* takes us down many strange roads.
> **alliteration:** a series of words with the same consonant sound repeated
> They *stopped* and *stood still*.
> **assonance:** a series of words with the same vowel sound repeated
> We *reached* the shore of the *deep sleeping sea*.
> **onomatopoeia:** a word that imitates a sound
> Behind the door, Ellen could hear the *murmur* of voices.

B Read the following sentences and write the literary term that applies to each.

1 Lee's expression was as cold as ice. _____
2 In front of us, we saw a sad sight. _____
3 Thunder boomed, and the rain poured down. _____
4 Going back home was like waking up from a dream. _____
5 The black cloud of his anger hung over us all day. _____
6 The dog growled, but the cat purred happily. _____
7 When I was a child, I liked to ride my bike. _____
8 My love for you is a fire that will burn forever. _____

C Read the following poem and identify the literary terms which are incorporated into it.

> Inhale clean, crisp, country morning air,
> Watch sun rise and puffs of cloud
> Drift across a clear blue sky;
> Underfoot, a soft, thick carpet of snow,
> Freshly laid the night before,
> For special guests expected;
> Birds twitter in the trees,
> Robins singing seasonal song,
> And the joyful twenty-fifth begins.

D What do you think this poem is about? Which words tell you this? Share your thoughts and ideas about the poem with a partner.

What Do You Think?

1 Do you have a favorite author? Who is this author and why do you like his/her work?
2 Do you ever read this author's works in any other languages besides the original language in which it was written? Do you think any meaning or originality is lost in translation?
3 Do you tend to read books more than once? What would make you read a book again?
4 List three books you would encourage other people to read. Why would you recommend these books to others?

A New Generation of Thinking

Getting Ready

Discuss the following questions with a partner.

1 What do you understand by the word "intelligence"?
2 Look at the people in the pictures above. Which of these activities do you think require the most "intelligence"?
3 Do you think there are certain qualities or characteristics that all intelligent people display? If so, what are they?
4 Why do you think some people can excel in certain areas of study where others fail, and vice versa?

Chapter 1: Emotional Intelligence

Before You Read:

What's Your EQ?

A **Answer the following questions.**

1 Do you know what an IQ test is? What does it measure? How does it do this?
2 Have you ever taken an IQ test? If so, do you remember your score?
3 Are there other ways we can measure intelligence?
4 Do you know what emotional quotient, or EQ, is? What do you think it measures?

B **Discuss your answers with a partner.**

Reading Skill:

Skimming for Content

Skimming for content is a useful skill that can help you read, and comprehend, faster. You can get a good idea of the content of a passage without reading every word or sentence. By skimming quickly over the text, you can pick up on the main points of the passage, as well as the main idea of what the reading is about.

A **How much do you know about the subject of emotional intelligence? Read the following statements and see how many you can complete by circling the correct word or statement. If you do not know anything about the subject, just read the statements to get an idea of what the reading is about.**

1 *Emotional Intelligence* is a popular (TV show / book).
2 The writer of *Emotional Intelligence*, Daniel Goleman, states that emotional stability is (more / less) important than IQ in achieving success in life.
3 Goleman's findings are based on experiments conducted on (children / teenagers), who were tested again as (teenagers / adults).
4 The experiment highlights differences in (academic / social) competence between individuals.
5 Those individuals who did (better / worse) on the test as children were more organized, confident, and dependable later in life.
6 If more (positive / negative) emotions are stored in our brains as we grow up, we end up possessing a higher level of emotional intelligence.
7 More recent scientific studies have shown (an increase / a decline) in the overall emotional aptitude of children.
8 Goleman feels that his book may make people (more / less) aware of the role our emotions play in everyday life.

B **Now, spend ONE minute skimming over the passage to get a basic grasp of the content. Do NOT try to read every word. Do not hesitate or stop when you see words you do not know, or read the footnotes; just let your eyes skim quickly back and forth over the text.**

C **Now go back to the statements in A and see how many of them you can confidently complete. Change any answers that you now think are incorrect. Read through the passage to confirm your answers.**

Emotional Intelligence

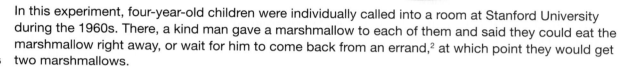

Daniel Goleman is discussing his famous "impulse[1] control" test at a San Francisco lecture and has the entire audience's attention. Goleman, a psychologist and science writer, is the author of the best-seller *Emotional Intelligence*, a fascinating book about recent discoveries in brain research that prove emotional **stability** is more important than IQ in determining an individual's success in life. One of the highlights of the book, Goleman explains to his audience of foundation leaders, educators, and grants donors, is a test administered thirty years ago that Goleman calls "The Marshmallow Challenge."

In this experiment, four-year-old children were individually called into a room at Stanford University during the 1960s. There, a kind man gave a marshmallow to each of them and said they could eat the marshmallow right away, or wait for him to come back from an errand,[2] at which point they would get two marshmallows.

Goleman gets everyone laughing as he describes watching a film of the preschoolers while they waited for the nice man to come back. Some of them covered their eyes or rested their heads on their arms so they wouldn't have to look at the marshmallow, or played games or sang to keep their thoughts off the single marshmallow and waited for the promised double prize. Others—about a third of the group— simply watched the man leave and ate the marshmallow within seconds.

What is surprising about this test, claims Goleman, is its diagnostic power: A dozen years later the same children were **tracked down** as adolescents and tested again. "The emotional and social difference between the grab-the-marshmallow preschoolers and their gratification[3]-delaying peers was dramatic," Goleman says.

The ones who had resisted eating the marshmallow were clearly more socially competent than the others. "They were less likely to go to pieces, freeze or regress under stress, or become rattled and disorganized when pressured; they embraced challenges and pursued them instead of giving up, even in the face of difficulties; they were self-reliant[4] and confident, trustworthy and dependable."

The third or so who grabbed the marshmallow were "more likely to be seen as shying away from social contacts, to be stubborn and indecisive, to be easily upset by frustrations, to think of themselves as unworthy, to become immobilized[5] by stress, to be mistrustful or **prone to** jealousy, or to overreact to certain situations with a sharp temper."

And all because of a single marshmallow? In fact, Goleman explains, it's all because of a lone neuron[6] in the brain, only recently discovered, that **bypasses** the neocortex—the area of the brain where rational decisions are made—and goes straight to the amygdala, or emotional center of the brain. It is here that quicker, more primitive "fight or flight"[7] responses occur, and are stored for future use. The more that emotional memories involving temper, frustration, anxiety, depression, impulse, and fear pile up in early adolescence, the more the amygdala can "hijack[8] the rest of the brain," Goleman says, "by flooding it with strong and inappropriate emotions, causing us to wonder later, 'Why did I overreact?'"

40 But if the emotions stored in the brain are those of **restraint**, self-awareness, self-regulation,[9] self-motivation, **empathy**, hope, and optimism, then we become **endowed** with an "emotional intelligence" that serves rather than enslaves us for the rest of our lives.

The bad news, says Goleman, is that a widely praised but disturbing study from the University of Vermont has shown a "decline in emotional aptitude among children **across the board**." Rich or poor,
45 East Coast or West Coast, inner city or suburb, children today are more vulnerable than ever to anger, depression, anxiety—what he calls a massive "emotional **malaise**." The good news, however, involves another recent discovery—that the amygdala takes a long time to mature, around fifteen or sixteen years, which means to Goleman that "emotional intelligence can be taught, not only in the home but perhaps, more importantly, in school."

50 Goleman's own story is as intriguing as his book. The author or co-author of nearly a dozen other books involving brain research and behavior, he experienced steady but modest sales until *Emotional Intelligence* hit the stores. Later came the cover of *Time* magazine and appearances on television, such as the Oprah Winfrey Show.[10]

"But I think the book also points out the real strength in what has become a feminine preserve in this
55 culture," claims Goleman. "Girls are raised to be emotionally **astute** and perceptive, but sons learn little about emotions except how to control anger. Women are absolutely more empathetic than men on average, but they've felt powerless to bring up the idea of emotions as a serious topic."

The irony, Goleman feels, is that if he had written a book about women and emotions, school reform, emotion-based leadership in business, or child psychology, "the book wouldn't have gotten much
60 attention. As it happens this is a book about all those things, but women and children and school reform are marginalized[11] in this society. So I come along with a lot of scientific data that says, 'Hey, this stuff is consequential'; and maybe some doors are opening in our society."

This reading was adapted from *The Author Talks About Emotions—Success Depends on Self-Control, He Says* by Patricia Holt. Reprinted with permission from the *San Francisco Chronicle* © 1995.

---

[1] **impulse** a sudden urge to do something
[2] **errand** a short trip taken to do a specific task, e.g. mailing letters
[3] **gratification** sense of pleasure and satisfaction
[4] **self-reliant** able to rely on one's own ability to do things
[5] **immobilized** unable to progress; impeded
[6] **neuron** a nerve cell
[7] **fight or flight** psychological and physiological reaction to stress causing one either to be aggressive or to run away
[8] **hijack** take or seize control
[9] **self-regulation** self-control
[10] **Oprah Winfrey Show** U.S. TV talk show hosted by female celebrity Oprah Winfrey
[11] **marginalized** pushed to the outside of something as a result of being considered unimportant

A The following questions are all about the reading. Answer each one using the information you have read. Try not to look back at the reading for the answers.

1 As well as being the author of *Emotional Intelligence*, what else does Daniel Goleman do for a living?
2 What is the "marshmallow challenge"?
3 List two differences that Goleman found between the children who ate the marshmallow and those who resisted it.
4 Where is the neocortex? What happens there?
5 What is the emotional center of the brain called?

B Decide if the following statements about the reading are true (T), false (F), or if the information is not given (NG). If you check (✔) false, correct the statement to make it true.

	T	F	NG
1 Goleman thinks that emotional intelligence cannot be taught.			
2 *Emotional Intelligence* is Goleman's only published book.			
3 Emotional intelligence is declining mainly among poor children.			
4 Children today are less vulnerable to anger, depression, and anxiety.			
5 Women are more empathic than men, on average.			

C Critical Thinking

Discuss these questions with a partner.
1 If you had been involved in the Stanford University experiment, do you think you would have resisted the marshmallow or eaten it? Give reasons for your answer.
2 The reading states that emotional intelligence is more important than IQ in determining an individual's success in life. How much do you agree with this? Give reasons for your answer.
3 The reading describes one way that emotional intelligence was tested and measured in children. How do you think emotional intelligence could be tested and measured in adults?

Vocabulary Comprehension:
Words in Context

A The words in *italics* are vocabulary items from the reading. Read each question or statement and choose the correct answer. Compare your answers with a partner.

1 If you are worried about someone's *stability*, you are afraid that _____.
   a. they may suddenly get sick   **b.** they may become upset easily
2 If you to try to *track down* a book you are looking for, you _____.
   a. order it from a bookstore   **b.** look for it in a bookstore
3 Someone who is described as *prone to* fits of anger is someone who _____.
   a. gets angry easily   **b.** has a calm, stable personality
4 A hungry girl might *bypass* a fast food restaurant because she _____.
   a. wants to eat there   **b.** is trying to avoid eating there
5 Someone who shows *restraint* at an all-you-can-eat lunch would _____.
   a. eat as much as possible   **b.** eat until they are comfortably full
6 Having *empathy* means _____.
   a. you get frequent headaches   **b.** you can understand others' feelings
7 If someone is *endowed with* something, it means he/she has _____.
   a. a natural talent or ability   **b.** a tendency to please other people
8 If your employer announces wage cuts that will "affect staff *across the board*," then _____ will have their salary cut.
   a. everyone in the company   **b.** only senior members of staff
9 A *malaise* is something that makes people _____.
   a. behave positively   **b.** behave negatively
10 Being *astute* is an important quality for _____.
   a. dog walkers   **b.** politicians

B Answer these questions. Share your answers with a partner.

1 Give an example of one way a person could demonstrate that they have a high level of emotional *stability*.
2 How will you go about *tracking down* a good job when you graduate from university?
3 Are you *prone to* catching colds in winter? What do you usually do to prevent them?
4 Give an example of a time when you had to show *restraint*.
5 Can you name someone you know who is always *empathetic* toward others?
6 Do you know anyone who is *endowed with* a special talent? What can they do?
7 What are some things that students *across the board* on your campus would like to change or improve?
8 If one of your friends complained to you that he/she was suffering from general *malaise* and couldn't study, what advice would you give?
9 Do you ever travel by a different route to *bypass* a traffic jam or crowded public transportation?
10 Do you agree with the statement in the reading that girls are raised to be more emotionally *astute* than boys? Give reasons and examples from your own upbringing.

A Following the example below, divide the following list of words into their different parts. Using your knowledge of prefixes, suffixes, and the root *tend*, write a short definition for each word. You can also refer to the chart in Unit 4's Vocabulary Skill. Check your definitions using your dictionary and share your ideas with a partner.

Vocabulary Skill:
The Root Word *tend*

In this chapter you read the word "attention," which contains the root "tent." This root word can also be written as "tend" or "tens," and comes from the Latin word "tendere," meaning to "stretch," "move," or "be pulled." This root is combined with prefixes and suffixes to form many words in English.

---

intensify = in / tens / ify

prefix = in   meaning: into
root = tens   meaning: stretch
ending = ify   meaning: to become

Part of speech: verb   **Meaning:** to become more involved or extreme

---

1 distend = dis / tend

prefix = _____   meaning: _____
root = _____   meaning: _____

Part of speech: _____   **Meaning:** _____

2 tension

root = _____   meaning: _____
ending = _____   meaning: _____

Part of speech: _____   **Meaning:** _____

3 extended

prefix = _____   meaning: _____
root = _____   meaning: _____
ending = _____   meaning: _____

Part of speech: _____   **Meaning:** _____

4 extensive

prefix = _____   meaning: _____
root = _____   meaning: _____
ending = _____   meaning: _____

Part of speech: _____   **Meaning:** _____

5 contend

prefix = _____   meaning: _____
root = _____   meaning: _____

Part of speech: _____   **Meaning:** _____

6 tendency

root = _____   meaning: _____
ending = _____   meaning: _____

Part of speech: _____   **Meaning:** _____

B Now complete the sentences below using the words from A. Be sure to use the correct form of each word.

1 One major reason why many people don't like traveling in the winter is because they have to _____ with bad weather conditions.

2 Even though Laura has a(n) _____ to put things off until the last minute, she always gets things done in the end.

3 After a(n) _____ search for the lost girl that covered five neighborhoods, police finally found her at her school playground.

4 Due to the huge popularity of the band, their tour was _____ by an extra five dates.

5 As the two sides of the leading political party still cannot agree on the issue of welfare, _____ has increased within the government.

6 Children who are victims of famine usually have very _____ stomachs.

Chapter 2: Left Brains, Right Brains, and Board Games

Before You Read:
Brain Games

A Discuss the following questions with a partner.

1 How often do you play board games? Which board games do you play the most?

2 What is the most challenging board game you've played? What made it challenging?

3 What is the most fun board game you've played? What made it fun?

B Write the name of a different board game for each skill.

Skill	Board game
a good vocabulary	
a good memory	
the ability to think ahead	
lots of patience	

Reading Skill:
Identifying Main and Supporting Ideas

Paragraphs often use supporting ideas to give more information about the main idea of a paragraph. Supporting ideas usually follow the main idea. Different types of supporting ideas include examples, illustrations, facts, reasons, etc.

A Read the statements and put **M** next to the statement that is the main idea. Put **S** next to the statement that is a supporting idea.

Paragraph 4

_____ So Tait approached Alexander to help him examine the possibilities of producing a new board game.

_____ When Tait and his good friend Whit Alexander left their jobs at Microsoft, they vowed to jump at any future opportunities to work together.

Paragraph 5

_____ They began conducting research to further develop the concept of their "whole brain" game.

_____ They gathered as much knowledge as they could about the history of social games

Paragraph 6

_____ They discovered a Harvard University researcher named Howard Gardner.

_____ They began researching the field of intellectual psychology.

Paragraph 7

_____ The two inventors identified a number of occupations that people might pursue if they are gifted in one of Gardner's intelligences.

_____ They then broke down the findings into subject matters or areas of interest that those same people would be exceptionally strong in.

B Skim the paragraphs and check your answers.

C Now read the entire article and answer the questions that follow.

Left Brains, Right Brains, and Board Games

It's not an easy task to do: You need to whistle[1] the song *Stayin' Alive* with enough skill for your teammate to identify the 1970s disco hit. On your next turn, your partner draws a clue with his eyes closed, and you have to guess what it is. You might also find yourself spelling words backward in order to win a round. These odd challenges are part of the "whole brain" board game that tries to satisfy the world's intellectual hunger, appropriately called Cranium.

In November 1997, personal experience led Richard Tait to consider this new type of board game that, unlike popular uni-skill games, incorporates a variety of talents. On vacation with his wife and another couple, they found themselves stuck indoors one rainy afternoon and decided to pass the time with a board game. They first played Pictionary[2] and Tait and his wife badly beat the other team. His competitors then sought revenge and quickly challenged Tait and his wife to a game of Scrabble.[3] Tait admits his friends were the overwhelming victors in the popular word game.

"I felt terrible and wondered why there wasn't a game where everyone that plays can have a chance to shine—still a competitive, fun board game, but one where everyone can show what they are good at," explains Tait.

When Tait and his good friend Whit Alexander left their jobs at Microsoft, they vowed to jump at any future opportunities to work together. So Tait approached Alexander to help him examine the possibilities of producing a new board game. In only nine short months, the two former Microsoft employees **conceived** a unique game that is designed to include something for everyone, and took it to a market that's been **craving** something different.

Once they decided to **take the** proverbial[4] **plunge**, they began conducting research to further develop the concept of their "whole brain" game. The two gathered as much knowledge as they could about the history of social games, comparing their findings against the **criteria** for Cranium.

Their conclusion was to develop a left brain/right brain game, but neither knew much about the **hypothesis**, so they began researching the field of intellectual psychology.[5] Tait and Alexander would soon discover a Harvard University researcher named Howard Gardner whose "Theory of Multiple Intelligences" **postulates** that there are eight core competencies where people show intelligence, such as linguistic, mathematical, interpersonal, or spatial.[6] "We thought it was a really rich framework to try to base the game design on, so we built up from Gardner's work," explains Alexander.

The two inventors identified a number of occupations that people might pursue if they are **gifted** in one of Gardner's intelligences. They then broke down the findings into subject matters or areas of interest that those same people would be exceptionally strong in, ensuring each player their moment to shine.

After about three months of research, Alexander and Tait realized the **novelty** of their approach to the board-game market. In total, they had come up with fourteen different activities, each one innovative in its own right. One such example is "sculpterades." As the name suggests, this activity requires players to sculpt clues from clay while their teammates guess what they are sculpting, bringing out the child in the most mature adults. The duo's commitment to research and quality design took them through ten different Cranium Clay recipes and multiple scents before settling on a purple, citrus-smelling clay that boasts a long shelf life. Tait says that customers often e-mail them for more of the stuff because they like it so much.

Next, they decided upon four unique groups of question cards, including "Creative Cat," which features sculpting and drawing activities; "Data Head," which focuses on trivia; "Word Worm," which includes vocabulary-based questions; and "Star Performer" featuring performance-based activities. It is the team with the best combination of these skills that eventually wins the game.

Cranium avoids play **dynamics** that allow one group to overwhelm another by limiting each team to one task before passing the turn to the next player. Tait says this is just one example of hundreds of game dynamics they fine-tuned throughout the play tests. But, he adds, there was one constant throughout the testing period: People were having a good time.

"We originally started with a much broader vision than just a board game," explains Tait. He says they looked at the 1980s and how the heart was so heavily emphasized in conjunction with good health. He thinks that the brain is going to be the organ of focus for the new millennium. "And we would like to be the company that's at the forefront of providing fun things to do with your brain to keep it happy and healthy." This strategy has made Cranium a standout among its competitors in the board-game industry, as there simply is no other game that offers such a large variety of activities.

Today, the pair's main challenge is building the Cranium brand name, and Tait **alludes to** a potential TV show as well as new Cranium products in the distant future.

This reading was adapted from *Left Brains, Right Brains, and Board Games: Cranium Turns the Board Game Industry on Its Head* by Jennifer LeClaire © 1999. Reprinted with permission of the author.

[1] **whistle** a high-pitched noise made by blowing air through the teeth or through pursed lips
[2] **Pictionary** board game whereby one person draws pictures to enable their teammates to guess a word or phrase
[3] **Scrabble** board game played by forming words from sets of randomly chosen letters
[4] **proverbial** well known; widely referred to
[5] **intellectual psychology** branch of psychology that deals with the intellect and mental capacity
[6] **spatial** related to space and relationships with objects in it

A How much do you remember about the reading? For each question, choose the best answer.

1 Why did Tait and Alexander create Cranium?
  a. They hoped to become very rich.
  b. They didn't want to work at Microsoft anymore.
  c. They wanted to create a game in which everyone could do well.
  d. They wanted to compete with Pictionary and Scrabble.

2 How did Tait feel after playing Pictionary and Scrabble?
  a. elated   **b.** furious   **c.** tired   **d.** terrible

3 Which activity type involves using purple, scented clay to shape objects?
  a. Sculpterades   **b.** Word Worm   **c.** Creative Cat   **d.** Star Performer

4 How does Cranium avoid one group overwhelming another?
  a. It allows groups to choose their favorite tasks.
  b. It makes sure people are having a good time.
  c. It limits each team to one task before passing the turn to the next player.
  d. It avoids dynamic play.

5 What idea does Tait have to build the Cranium brand name?
  a. a website   **b.** more advertising   **c.** a TV show   **d.** a newspaper article

B Decide if the following statements about the reading are true (T), false (F), or not given (NG). If you check (✔) false, correct the statement to make it true.

	T	F	NG
1 Cranium is a very popular board game.			
2 The game was developed by two former software company employees.			
3 Cranium is a uni-skill game.			
4 Howard Gardner has played the game and enjoyed it.			
5 No future Cranium products will be developed.			

C Critical Thinking

Discuss these questions with a partner.
1 Do you think you would enjoy playing Cranium? Why or why not?
2 Do you agree with Tait that "the brain is going to be the organ of focus of the new millennium"? Explain your answer.

A Look at the list of words and phrases from the reading. Match each one with a definition on the right.

1 conceived _____
2 craving _____
3 take the plunge _____
4 criteria _____
5 hypothesis _____
6 postulate _____
7 gifted _____
8 novelty _____
9 dynamics _____
10 alludes to _____

a. refers to something or someone in an indirect way
b. interactions; relating to interpersonal relationships
c. being new and unusual or different
d. naturally, and exceptionally, talented
e. a strong or uncontrollable desire
f. a theory or idea based on facts but not yet proven
g. conditions or standard by which something can be measured or judged
h. to immerse oneself in a potentially risky situation
i. to claim something is true without proof
j. thought up

B Complete the sentences using the vocabulary from A. Be sure to use the correct form of each word. Then, answer the questions using your own information, and share your answers with a partner.

1 When buying a new house, what _____ should buyers consider?
2 Have you ever _____ of a new game? If so, explain it. If not, what is your favorite game and how do you play it?
3 Scientists once _____ that Mars and Earth were very much alike.
4 Have you ever _____ and done something daring or unusual? What did you do?
5 Can you think of a trend or fashion in your country for which the _____ has worn off recently?
6 Which of your personal qualities contributes the most to the key _____ in your friendships with others?
7 Do you ever have _____ for certain foods? What foods are they?
8 Do you think it is just a _____ that UFOs exist, or do you think that stories of sightings can be taken as fact?
9 Do you know anyone who is _____ at anything? What is it they can do well?
10 How could someone _____ you without using your name? For example, "the person who wears flashy clothes" or "the tall one," etc.

A For each word, study its different parts. Using your knowledge of prefixes, suffixes, and the root *cap*, write the part of speech and a simple definition. Use your dictionary to check your answers. Share your ideas with a partner.

Vocabulary Skill:
The Root Word *cap*

Vocabulary	Part of Speech	Definition
1 accept	_____	_____
2 intercept	_____	_____
3 recipient	_____	_____
4 anticipate	_____	_____
5 captivate	_____	_____
6 receive	_____	_____
7 capacity	_____	_____
8 captor	_____	_____

In this unit, you read the words "conceive" and "concept," which are formed using the root word "cap," also written as "cep," "cip," or "ceive." This root comes from the Latin word "capere," meaning to "take," "receive," or "seize." It is combined with prefixes and suffixes to form many words in English.

B Now complete each sentence below using the words from the chart. Be sure to use the correct form of each word.

1 I think the maximum seating _____ in a taxi in this country is four people. As there are six of us, we'll have to take two.

2 Due to the global economic downturn, I don't _____ that we will make our original sales goal.

3 Shelly is a great designer, but sometimes her ideas are so avant-garde that they are not always _____ by her colleagues or clients.

4 Customs officials managed to _____ the goods being smuggled into the country at the airport.

5 Anthony's debut stage performance _____ the audience.

6 Did we _____ any mail this morning? I'm waiting on a letter from the bank.

7 The president's daughter has been kidnapped! Her _____ are demanding a six-million-dollar ransom.

8 Those employees who were not _____ of prize money in the annual charity draw will receive restaurant vouchers from the CEO.

Real Life Skill:
Understanding Academic Titles

Teachers and researchers at universities have many different academic titles. These differ from one country to another, and even among universities within the same country, but every university has a ranking system for its faculty members. If you ever apply to, or attend, a university in the United States, it will be helpful to you to know some of these titles.

A Read the following paragraph and note the academic titles in bold.

An American university is organized into many departments, such as English and Chemistry. Among the professors in each department, one is chosen to be **department chair**. The head of the entire university is called the **president**. Many people who want to have a university career begin teaching even before they have earned their Ph.D. As **teaching assistants**, they may teach low-level courses while completing their own studies.

Their goal, of course, is to become a full **professor**, but this may take many years. After completing their Ph.D., many faculty members begin as **instructors**, teaching on a yearly contract, while some are fortunate enough to obtain a position as an **assistant professor**. This puts them on the "tenure track"—the academic ladder that leads to a lifelong position. The next step, reached after several years, is **associate professor**. In order to receive tenure, and a permanent appointment as a professor, candidates must carry out significant research and publish scholarly papers.

B List the titles from the paragraph in order from the highest rank to the lowest.

1 _____   5 _____
2 _____   6 _____
3 _____   7 _____
4 _____

C What academic titles do each of these people probably hold?

1 Janet is the head of twelve professors of mathematics.
_____

2 Jack is extremely busy teaching and studying at the same time.
_____

3 Harold has held his position for thirty-two years, and will retire next year.
_____

4 Sharon really enjoys teaching, and she hopes she will have this job again next year.
_____

5 Elaine hopes to become a full professor next year.
_____

What Do You Think?

1 What activities do you find mentally stimulating? How often do you do these activities?
2 Do you notice differences in the ways your friends or family members approach certain learning tasks? Explain some of these differences. After studying this chapter, do you understand better why these differences exist?
3 Which of the eight "intelligences" that Gardner identified (for example, verbal, musical, logical/mathematical, visual/spatial, interpersonal) do you think best demonstrates your own intelligence? Give examples to explain your answer.

Fluency Strategy: *SQ5R*

> SQ5R stands for **S**urvey, **Q**uestion, **R**ead, **R**espond, **R**ecord, **R**ecite, **R**eview. The SQ5R approach will help you be a better, more fluent reader and increase your reading comprehension.

Survey

Survey is similar to the **A** in the ACTIVE approach to reading: *Activate prior knowledge*. When you survey, you prepare yourself by skimming quickly through the text you will read. You read the title. You read headings. You read the first sentence in each section of the passage. You look for and read words that are written in **bold** or *italics*. Look at any pictures and captions. Through the survey you prepare yourself to read.

Look at "Ghost Hunter's Bookstore" on the next page. Read the title and the first sentence in each of the six paragraphs.

Question

After the survey, but before you read, you ask yourself **questions**: "What do I want to learn as I read?"
Based on your survey of "Ghost Hunter's Bookstore," write two to three questions that you hope to answer as you read.

1 _____

2 _____

3 _____

Read

Following the survey and question stage of SQ5R, you **read**. You focus on comprehending the material. You move your eyes fluently through the material.
Read "Ghost Hunter's Bookstore." As you read, keep in mind the 12 tips on pages 8 and 9. By combining those tips and SQ5R, you will improve your reading fluency.

Ghost Hunter's Bookstore

Welcome to Ghost Hunter's Bookstore, the online bookstore with over five hundred titles related to ghosts and ghost hunting. We want to be your online source for ghost
5 hunting inspiration. This month we highly recommend the following five engrossing books:

Georgia Spirits' Revenge is a chilling collection of ten ghost stories from the state of Georgia
10 in the United States. These ghosts all seem to want one thing—vengeance for wrongs suffered in life. These terrible tales of tormented ghosts are reportedly all based on encounters verifiable by eyewitnesses. It's the perfect bedtime read for ghost lovers!

If you believe in ghosts and want to see more of them, the *Ghost Chaser's Manual* is
15 definitely for you. It reveals the secrets of summoning and detecting those hard-to-find ghosts. You'll learn the right way and the wrong way to investigate old houses and buildings. This book can help you avoid those accidents that so often happen to beginners. As long as you chase ghosts by the book, you'll never need to fear the worst!

Ghostly Technology covers all the prevailing technologies used by serious ghost hunters.
20 If you've ever been puzzled by temperature detection devices, or if you've ever been disconcerted by an electromagnetic field meter, this book has the answers you need. If the ghosts you find keep vanishing before you can photograph them, this book can help. You'll also learn about methods for recording ghostly voices. Buy it soon before another ghost gets away!

25 *Ghost Fever* is the rousing journal of a successful ghost hunter. No reader can remain indifferent to these exciting accounts of chasing and being chased by ghosts. Despite the fact that she is taunted by ghosts wherever she goes, this ghost hunter keeps right on investigating. The pages of her journal reveal many secrets of ghosts trapped in our world. You won't want to miss this authentic ghost hunter's journal. It's full of ideas to help you
30 improve your own ghost hunting technique.

A Ghost in the Graveyard is an excellent resource for those brave ghost hunters who know that graveyards are one of the best places to look for ghosts. In addition to step-by-step instructions on how to find graveyard ghosts, this book also explores burial traditions and customs around the world. There is also a new list of 100 graveyards that are known to have
35 the most ghostly activity. You'll definitely want to have that list before starting out on your next successful ghost hunt!

Respond

Think about what you have read. Respond to the reading comprehension questions. Try to answer the questions without looking back at the passage.

1 Which phrase describes the writer's tone in reviewing these titles?
   a. fair and balanced
   b. somewhat negative
   c. enthusiastically positive
   d. rather critical

2 Where do these book reviews appear?
   a. on a website
   b. in a magazine
   c. in a bookstore
   d. in a library

3 In *Georgia Spirits' Revenge*, why do the ghosts want vengeance?
   a. because they were seen by eyewitnesses
   b. because they didn't want to die
   c. because they were unfairly treated during their lives
   d. because ghosts usually want vengeance

4 Which book tells about the adventures of a successful ghost hunter?
   a. *Ghostly Technology*
   b. *Georgia Spirits' Revenge*
   c. *A Ghost in the Graveyard*
   d. *Ghost Fever*

5 Which book contains advice on methods for recording the voices of ghosts?
   a. *Ghostly Technology*
   b. *Ghost Chaser's Manual*
   c. *Ghost Fever*
   d. *A Ghost in the Graveyard*

6 Which book claims to help ghost hunters avoid accidents?
   a. *Ghostly Technology*
   b. *Ghost Chaser's Manual*
   c. *Ghost Fever*
   d. *A Ghost in the Graveyard*

7 Which information is NOT found in *A Ghost in the Graveyard*?
   a. instructions on how to find ghosts
   b. graveyards where ghosts are likely to be found
   c. information about burial traditions
   d. how to escape from angry ghosts

Record

Record the most important ideas from the reading. Return to the reading and take notes.
This gives you the opportunity to check the answers to the comprehension questions by looking at the reading again. There are many different ways you can do this. You can write down the key words from the passage. You can create a mind map. You can make an outline of what you have read. You can write the main ideas of each paragraph.

Complete the missing information in the word web below. Then, in your notebook, complete the word web for the other books mentioned in the reading.

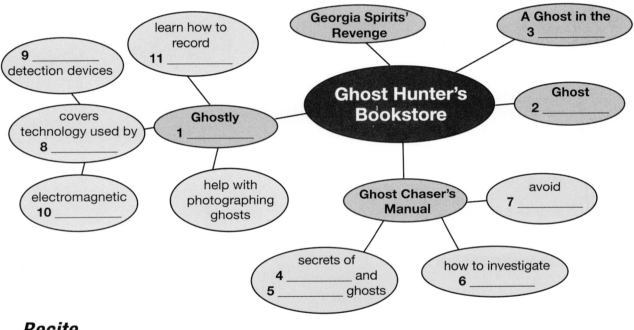

Recite

Next recite what you have learned while reading. Use your own words to recite what you remember from what you have read.

Review

During the **review** stage of SQ5R, you review the questions that you asked yourself prior to reading. **Did you find answers? Write the answers to your questions. Is there a portion of the text you did not understand well? Skim quickly through the material one more time.**

Self Check

Write a short answer to each of the following questions.

1. Have you ever used the SQ5R strategy before?

   Yes   No   I'm not sure

2. Will you practice SQ5R in your reading outside of English class?

   Yes   No   I'm not sure

3. Do you think SQ5R is helpful? Why or why not?

   _____

   _____

   _____

4. Which of the six reading passages in units 4–6 did you enjoy most? Why?

   _____

   _____

5. Which of the six reading passages in units 4–6 was easiest? Which was most difficult? Why?

   _____

   _____

6. What distractions do you face when you read? What can you do to minimize those distractions?

   _____

   _____

7. What improvements are you making as a reader? Write down one or two things that you know you can do better today than when you started this course.

   _____

   _____

8. What other improvements do you still want to make as a reader?

   _____

   _____

Review Reading 3: So, You Want to Be a Fiction Writer?

Fluency Practice

Time yourself as you read through the passage. Try to read as fluently as you can. Record your time in the Reading Rate Chart on page 240. Then answer the questions on page 115.

So, You Want to Be a Fiction Writer?

Honestly, I'm glad to hear that you're interested in becoming a fiction writer. However, I think there are a number of questions you should ask yourself before you settle on writing as a career. For
5 example, have you consciously considered why it is that you want to be a writer? Is it because you enjoy showing off, maybe? Or is it just an arbitrary choice to avoid getting a real job? Or maybe you've dreamed of creating exquisite stories ever since you
10 were an infant. Writing for a living is not an easy undertaking, and before you start, you should be sure that you are doing it for the right reasons.

An important facet of being a writer is the ability to deal with the solitude. A professional writer must be ready to spend at least five hours a day alone, often in the lonely environment of a study,
15 in front of the computer. Are you ready for this degree of isolation and confinement? At the same time, remember that writing is a craft as well, requiring sustained intensity, precision, and extended periods of concentrated effort. No watertight plot was ever created by luck. Fine writing is created through painstaking effort.

In addition to the solitude and the hard work, there is still the mysterious question of talent. How
20 can a person know whether he or she has talent or not? Well, there is no foolproof way of detecting talent, but in my experience, people who have talent for writing fiction enjoy telling stories to people around them. They love to talk about the things they've done or read, and people like listening to them. It's an exaggeration to say that all writers do this, but when I hear someone tell a good story that grabs me, I always think, "There goes a potential writer."

25 Now on to what I consider to be the heart of writing: inspiration and originality. Inspiration comes from inside, and in my opinion it grows out of having survived or overcome certain difficulties in life. People who have suffered seem to have more of a need to speak out. It has been said that happy people don't make good writers. Although this is undoubtedly exaggerated, there is a grain of truth in it. Why would a completely happy and satisfied person take on the painful task of writing?

30   Someone who wishes to do this in some way needs to do it. I believe this need is born of some kind of suffering.

   I cannot overstate the importance of originality in fiction writing. It is critical that you don't let tired old ideas and phrases creep into your writing. Each work of fiction must present something truly new. A successful work is never simply created according to a dusty old diagram or according
35   to a well-used pattern. From the first page, the reader should be greeted by a story like nothing anyone has seen before. Try to surprise your reader at every turn. Imagine making your reader say, "Wow! I never expected that to happen!"

   Well, if I haven't been able to dissuade you from becoming a writer by now, it looks like you might have made up your mind to become one. Let me give you a few tips that might help you on your
40   way to a successful writing career. First, remember that your first draft will never be perfect. It will always need work, and sometimes it will need a great deal of work. If the amount of revisions and corrections seems to be growing, don't be afraid to throw the whole thing out and begin again. The value of that first draft was to start developing and organizing your ideas. Sometimes trying to repair a heavily flawed story is worse than starting again, and it can harm the unity of the story.

45   Another technique I cannot stress enough is to write for a large audience. Make your best effort to be understood by the largest number of people you can. Remember that the most famous artists, writers, musicians, movie makers, etc., in history have been those that people of all types—rich, poor, young, old, well educated and not-so-well educated—have all been able to appreciate and enjoy.

50   When you write, put yourself in the place of the reader. Try to write stories that you would like to read yourself. If you are writing a passage only because you have to or because you can't think of anything else, your reader is certainly not going to enjoy it. When you find yourself low on inspiration, take a break, and come to back to finish writing after you've regained your inspiration and originality.

55   It's also important to remember that, as a writer, you are a kind of educator. Make sure that you are well-informed about the things you want to write about. Doing research has helped many writers to create more interesting and realistic stories.

   In conclusion, let me say that writing is different for every individual. I hope you will find the advice I've given above useful, but you will undoubtedly make new discoveries about what works best
60   for you as you pursue your new career as a fiction writer!

875 words   Time taken _____

Reading Comprehension

1 Who did the author probably write this passage for?
   a. professional fiction writers
   b. people interested in starting a career in fiction writing
   c. high school English students
   d. teachers of fiction writing

2 According to the author, which type of person might have talent for fiction writing?
   a. someone who enjoys telling stories to friends
   b. someone who has a very large vocabulary
   c. someone who likes to show off
   d. someone who likes spending hours alone

3 According to the author, what is the source of inspiration?
   a. natural talent
   b. originality
   c. suffering
   d. training

4 Which piece of advice would the author give regarding originality?
   a. Don't try to be original all the time.
   b. Don't be afraid to use a plot pattern that someone has used before.
   c. Try to be as original as you can possibly be throughout.
   d. Try to copy a successful piece of fiction.

5 How is a very flawed first draft useful in the writing process?
   a. It can usually be repaired.
   b. It is of little or no use.
   c. It usually turns out to be about half usable.
   d. It helps you develop and organize your ideas.

6 Why does the author most likely recommend writing for a large audience?
   a. Your writing may become famous and widely enjoyed.
   b. Your writing will be of a lower quality.
   c. Your writing won't take as long to write.
   d. Your writing will be popular with art critics.

7 How can putting yourself in the place of the reader help your writing?
   a. You can write stories that come from your heart.
   b. You can make your work more original.
   c. You can check whether you enjoy what you've written.
   d. You can figure out how different readers think.

8 How does the author suggest a fiction writer can write more realistic stories?
   a. by doing more research before writing
   b. by spending more time on the writing process
   c. by only writing about past experiences
   d. by using language the reader can easily understand

Time yourself as you read through the passage. Try to read as fluently as you can. Record your time in the Reading Rate Chart on page 240. Then answer the questions on page 118.

The Theory of Multiple Intelligences

What do you think about when someone says the word intelligence? You might say that it's that mysterious quality that causes people to succeed at school and in their studies. By scoring highly on intelligence tests, students have been recognized as gifted and, presumably, are sure to succeed in their studies. Experts have traditionally seen a high level of intelligence as applicable across the board to
5   most human activities, guaranteeing the possessor of high intelligence success in whatever he or she does.

In the 1980s, however, a new hypothesis about intelligence was developed. The theory of multiple intelligences was first conceived of by a Harvard University professor named Howard Gardner. His book, *Frames of Mind: The Theory of Multiple Intelligences*, postulates that the mind does not
10 possess just one kind of intelligence, but rather more than seven distinct "intelligences." Among the intelligences Gardner has indicated are linguistic, logical-mathematical, spatial, bodily-kinesthetic, musical, naturalistic, interpersonal, and intrapersonal. He has also alluded to several others and suggested that there could be many more intelligences to be discovered.

A person with a high level of linguistic intelligence is endowed with a large vocabulary and the ability
15 to use it well to express him- or herself. Gardner sees the poet as the best example of an astute user of language. In creating poems, poets make use of the full complexity of meaning and the widest range of linguistic dynamics. Naturally, someone with a high level of linguistic intelligence would excel at any of a wide variety of language-related activities including explaining, teaching, persuading others, and public speaking.

20 Logical-mathematical intelligence alludes to the skills often associated with scientists and mathematicians. Societies have been prone to associating this type of intelligence with "true" intelligence, somehow giving it a more central or significant place than other intelligences. Gardner certainly disagrees with this point of view. He sees logical-mathematical intelligence as simply one among a set of intelligences. While he asserts that it has been of exceptional importance in the history
25 of the West, he points out that it has played a more modest role in other societies.

Spatial intelligence indicates the capacity to visualize things in the mind accurately and precisely. This intelligence is therefore associated with artists, who are experts in visualizing and making intelligent use of forms and colors. A high level of spatial intelligence can also endow a person with an excellent visual memory, and perhaps even with a so-called photographic memory.

30 Yet another intelligence that has been tracked down by Gardner is musical intelligence. As you

might imagine, a person with a high level of musical intelligence excels at singing, playing musical instruments, and composing music. Gardner points out that this intelligence appears earlier than the others, as is witnessed by amazing child musicians.

The bodily-kinesthetic intelligence may surprise people, who are used to thinking of intelligence as something "inside the head." This is because it concerns excellence in using the body. People with a high level of bodily-kinesthetic intelligence might excel at building or making things, sports, dancing, or even surgery.

Another controversial intelligence which has been more recently proposed by Gardner is naturalistic intelligence. Critics have more difficulty accepting this as an intelligence than the other intelligences mentioned so far; they are more likely to see this one as an area of interest. Gardner hypothesizes that people who have a high level of naturalistic intelligence are more sensitive to nature and to their own relationship to it. For example, someone who has success at growing plants has this intelligence. A person who is successful at raising, caring for, or training animals could also be said to have a high level of naturalistic intelligence. A person with a high level of naturalistic intelligence could not only be a successful gardener, farmer, or animal trainer; that person could also make a good scientist involved in studying the natural world or a conservationist involved in protecting it.

The personal intelligences include interpersonal and intrapersonal intelligence. Intrapersonal intelligence refers to the capacity to access and control one's interior life of feelings, moods, and emotions. Someone who can accurately describe sensations of pleasure or pain, or someone who, rather than being controlled by feelings, is able to exercise restraint over them and understand them could be said to have high intrapersonal intelligence. On the other hand, people possessed of a high level of interpersonal intelligence are able to notice and understand the moods, intentions, and motivations of other people. These individuals are effective communicators who show empathy easily and work well in groups.

The novelty and the revolutionary approach of the hypothesis of multiple intelligences has resulted in several criticisms. Some have questioned the criteria that qualify something as an intelligence— something that we might otherwise simply call a talent or an ability. Others have pointed out that the existence of multiple intelligences has never been proven through scientific research. These criticisms notwithstanding, the theory of multiple intelligences has sparked fascinating debate about the value and nature of intelligence. Its applications in the field of education have led to an enrichment of educational approaches as teachers seek to reach and develop the multiple intelligences of students.

859 words   Time taken _____

Reading Comprehension

1 What is this article mainly about?
   a. how individuals can develop their intelligence
   b. a new theory of human intelligence
   c. a comparison of the value of various intelligences
   d. the reason intelligence is important

2 Which of the following is NOT an intelligence mentioned in the passage?
   a. logical-mathematical
   b. interactive
   c. interpersonal
   d. spatial

3 Which activity would a person with a high level of linguistic intelligence be most likely to excel at?
   a. visualizing images
   b. explaining ideas
   c. playing sports
   d. exercising restraint

4 Which statement is true about logical-mathematical intelligence?
   a. Some people associate it with true intelligence.
   b. It has been of little importance in the West.
   c. It includes several kinds of intelligence.
   d. It allows clear visualization of images.

5 Which intelligence would an artist who creates paintings most rely on?
   a. linguistic
   b. logical-mathematical
   c. spatial
   d. intrapersonal

6 What is unique about musical intelligence?
   a. It allows people to understand their own feelings.
   b. It has been widely criticized.
   c. It accompanies bodily-kinesthetic intelligence.
   d. It appears earlier than other intelligences.

7 How are interpersonal and intrapersonal intelligences similar?
   a. They both allow individuals to work well in groups.
   b. Restraint is an important part of both.
   c. They both involve the ability to understand moods.
   d. They both allow people to show empathy.

8 Which argument criticizing the theory of multiple intelligences has been raised by critics?
   a. It is wrongly applied to education.
   b. It has never been proven by scientific research.
   c. There are too many criteria for identifying intelligences.
   d. Ability and talents are also types of intelligences.

Getting Ready

Discuss the following questions with a partner.

1 Look at the "food pyramid" above. What food groups can you see?
2 Do you eat foods daily from each of the food groups shown? What other types of food do you eat that are not shown?
3 Do you think that in your country people, in general, have a healthy diet? Explain your answer.
4 What do you know about modern farming and food production methods? Do you think they are safe?

Unit 7

Chapter 1: Genetically Modified Food

Before You Read:
Food for Thought

Reading Skill:
Arguing For and Against a Topic

Many reading passages present two sides of an argument—one argues for, or in favor of, the topic; the other argues against it. Phrases such as "advocates of," "proponents of," and "in favor of" signal that information that supports one side of the argument will be introduced. Phrases like "opponents of," "critics of," "skeptics," or "concerns about" signal that information against the topic is coming. Also, words and phrases like "argues that," "questions," "however," "though," "in contrast," and "in spite of" signal that an opposite or different opinion is about to be introduced.

A Discuss the following questions with a partner.

1   How many meals or snacks have you eaten so far today? What foods did you eat?

2   Do you know how these foods were grown or manufactured? Describe how you think they were farmed or produced.

3   What do you understand by the term "genetically modified (GM) foods"? Are you aware of how GM foods are different from other foods? Do you know if they are available in your local supermarket?

4   Do you think that the use of modern technology in food production methods is positive or negative? Give reasons for your answer.

B These terms from the reading are frequently heard in the GM food debate. Match them with their definitions on the right.

1   advocacy groups _____
2   geneticists _____
3   genetic modification _____
4   pesticides _____
5   herbicides _____

a.   chemicals used to protect plants from insect pests
b.   organizations that support a cause
c.   chemicals used to destroy unwanted plants
d.   changing the DNA of organisms
e.   scientists who study how characteristics are passed from one generation of plants or animals to the next.

C Scan the reading for the terms and check your answers.

A Scan the reading passage below and complete the chart with information from the passage.

Genetically Modified Food

Reasons For	Reasons Against
1 _____	1 _____
2 _____	2 _____
3 _____	3 _____
4 _____	4 _____
5 _____	5 _____

B Compare your answers with a partner. Are there any other reasons you can add to your list?

C Now read the passage again and complete the comprehension exercises that follow.

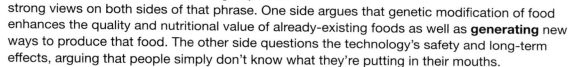

Genetically Modified Food

"What's for dinner?" It used to be that the answer to that household question was an issue for debate among family members only. But not any more. Now scientists, advocacy groups, economists,
5   trade experts, geneticists, and politicians are all discussing what should be served for dinner.

The food **fuss revolves around** one phrase: genetic modification. There are two groups with strong views on both sides of that phrase. One side argues that genetic modification of food
10 enhances the quality and nutritional value of already-existing foods as well as **generating** new ways to produce that food. The other side questions the technology's safety and long-term effects, arguing that people simply don't know what they're putting in their mouths.

The term "genetically modified" (GM) is an offspring of another term: biotechnology. A word that's been around for about thirty years, biotechnology was created in the shadow of new
15 techniques that allowed scientists to modify the genetic material in living cells.[1] Basically, that means playing around with various biological processes to produce substances that, arguably, benefit things like agriculture, medicine, and the environment.

If you know how to cut-and-paste on a computer, you've figured out genetic modification. The Canadian Food Inspection Agency describes it like this: it all begins with a cell made up of
20 chromosomes;[2] the chromosomes are made up of DNA and are organized into sections called genes; genes determine the characteristics of an organism. These genes can be "cut" from one organism and "pasted" into another. Several foods that people eat every day are products of this process, such as tomatoes that ripen on the vine[3] and maintain their **texture** and tough skin for several weeks. A potato plant developed to resist an insect known to attack it is another
25 example. In the latter case, the GM version eliminates the need for chemical pesticides.

Proponents of GM foods argue using biotechnology in the production of food products has many benefits. It speeds up the process of breeding[4] plants and animals with desired characteristics, can be used to introduce new characteristics that a product wouldn't normally have, and can improve the nutritional value of products. And, say the supporters, all of this is
30 done safely.

Groups who advocate against the use of GM foods don't see things quite the same way. They point to studies that argue GM foods could be harmful to people's health. To the groups on this side of the issue, that "could" provides more than enough reason to go forward with extreme caution, something they say isn't currently being done. GM critics say not enough time has
35 passed to study the long-term effects of the foods.

In Europe, hardly a week goes by without some headline about GM foods or, rather, "Frankenfoods"[5] as they've been called by the European media. The Church of England has entered the debate, criticizing the production of GM crops. Ever responsive to consumer demands, the European Union has taken a strong position on this issue, going so far as to
40 propose a moratorium[6] on approving GM foods. These responses are the outcome of a grassroots campaign.[7] Various scares, the best-known being mad cow disease,[8] have consumers in Europe cautious of food genetically altered to kill pests or resist herbicides.

Two British food companies have even dropped GM ingredients from their products, something the North American branches of these companies haven't done. That's not all that surprising for
45 one simple reason: there's an unmistakable split in the policies toward GM foods between the two sides of the Atlantic that some call the Atlantic Divide. Supporters argue North America's approach is more progressive, while skeptics argue it's less safe.

Whatever the case, the Atlantic Divide can be **attributed to** two things. The first is all about experience: the North American side of the Atlantic hasn't seen a scare comparable to mad
50 cow disease. The second is all about dollars: North Americans expect their food to be cheap. And while the Atlantic may divide the approach to GM foods, it doesn't stop the two sides from butting heads.[9]

The fuss over food extends to whether the manufacturing process is made known. Canada has adopted both a **mandatory** and voluntary labeling policy. According to the Canadian Food
55 Inspection Agency, mandatory labeling applies to all foods that have been changed nutritionally or **compositionally**, or to **alert** consumers of possible allergens.[10] That doesn't mean, though, that *all* GM foods will be labeled. If it can be shown through tests that the nutrition or composition of such foods remains unchanged, no special label is required. Even though labels are not required, they are allowed, but only when "truthful and not misleading." A good example
60 is the "fat free" claim made on some products. Because of the **ambiguity** surrounding voluntary labeling, it's been determined that clearer rules are needed.

The GM debate makes us consider the role technology has in our lives. What makes this debate unique is that every meal we eat is at its very core. And that fact means one thing: it's an issue that will be discussed not only around policy tables, but dinner tables as well.

This reading was adapted from *The Fuss Over Genetically Modified Food* by Leanne Hachey. Originally written for CBC News Online; http://cbc.ca/news/indepth/foodfight/hachey.html. Reprinted with permission from CBC News Online © 2002.

[1] **cells** smallest units of an organism
[2] **chromosomes** parts of a cell that contain DNA and are responsible for determining and passing on characteristics of the organism from parent to young
[3] **ripen on the vine** grow to maturity while still attached to the plant from which it comes
[4] **breeding** producing young from parents
[5] **Frankenfoods** word created by combining "Frankenstein" with "foods"; referring to the monster—created from body parts of different dead people and brought to life by a medical student named Frankenstein—that featured in the 1818 Mary Shelley novel of the same name
[6] **moratorium** a suspension of, or a ban on, something
[7] **grassroots campaign** organized effort to draw attention to an issue, usually political, at a local level
[8] **mad cow disease** cattle disease that causes deterioration of the brains of cows, a form of which can be passed to humans who eat the infected meat
[9] **butting heads** arguing as a result of opposing views
[10] **allergens** substances that cause allergies

A The questions and statements below are about the reading. Choose the correct answer for each one.

1 What is the author's purpose in writing this article?
a. to speak in favor of America's position on the GM food debate
b. to persuade the reader that Europe's position is correct on the GM food debate
c. to point out the errors in both the American and European positions
d. to inform the reader in a balanced way about both sides of the GM food debate

2 Which argument in favor of GM foods does the author NOT point out?
a. It speeds up the breeding process.
b. It can be used to introduce new characteristics.
c. It can improve the nutritional value of food.
d. It helps reduce the amount of fat in food.

3 Some people have called the disagreement between the United States and Britain over the issue of GM foods the _____ Divide.
a. genetic   b. specific   c. Atlantic   d. Pacific

4 Two things have led to the divide between the United States and Britain: _____.
a. experience and dollars   c. nutrition and labeling
b. knowledge and history   d. herbicides and pesticides

5 The GM debate makes us think about the role _____ plays in our lives.
a. nationality   b. technology   c. history   d. cuisine

B The following statements are all about the reading. Complete each one using information you have read.

1 The _____ _____ centers on one phrase: genetic modification.

2 Advocates of GM foods argue that it _____ the quality and nutritional value of foods; their opponents question the technology's _____ and _____ effects.

3 Chromosomes contain _____, which in turn is made up of genes.

4 The process of genetic modification works by _____ genes from one organism and _____ them into another.

5 The European media has nicknamed GM foods "_____."

C Critical Thinking

Discuss these questions with a partner.

1 Based on the arguments presented in the reading, do you think GM foods are safe to eat? Give reasons for your answer.

2 Does anything you have read in this passage about GM foods worry you? If so, what concerns you and why?

3 Do you think that all GM foods should be labeled, so that people can be informed about what exactly they are eating?

Vocabulary Comprehension:
Odd Word Out

A For each group, circle the word that does not belong. The words in *italics* are vocabulary items from the reading.

1	*fuss*	commotion	bother	calm
2	detracts from	centers on	turns on	*revolves around*
3	producing	resisting	*generating*	bringing about
4	finish	*texture*	aroma	appearance
5	supporters	opponents	advocates	*proponents*
6	*attributed to*	ascribed to	accredited to	spoken to
7	required	*mandatory*	voluntary	non-negotiable
8	*compositionally*	structurally	organizationally	mortally
9	warn	caution	frighten	*alert*
10	lack of clarity	security	*ambiguity*	vagueness

B Complete the sentences using the words in *italics* from A. Be sure to use the correct form of the word.

1 The new construction project in the center of town has _____ close to one hundred new jobs.

2 Sergio presented what seemed to be a clear argument, but on closer examination it was clearly full of _____.

3 Attendance at the first aid workshop is _____; all students must be there.

4 My parents don't understand what all the _____ is about computer viruses. I had to buy them some software and explain to them how and why it works.

5 Carl's a really nice guy, but his conversation usually _____ his fixation with motorbikes.

6 If you were to analyze this soup _____, you would find that it is a good source of essential vitamins and minerals the body needs.

7 Silk has a wonderfully smooth _____ that feels good against the skin.

8 _____ of stricter gun control laws have tried for years to gain more support throughout the country.

9 Jill's success can be _____ her tenacity and hard work in the office.

10 It was only after reading about food and allergies that Angelina was _____ to the possible cause of her son's illness.

A The words below can all be completed by adding the root *sist*, *stit*, or *stat*. Decide which form each word uses and write it in the space provided. Then, using your knowledge of prefixes and suffixes, write which part of speech each word is and a definition.

Vocabulary	Part of Speech	Definition
1 in_____	_____	_____
2 con_____ently	_____	_____
3 sub_____ute	_____	_____
4 per_____	_____	_____
5 _____ue	_____	_____
6 in_____ute	_____	_____
7 super_____ion	_____	_____
8 de_____	_____	_____
9 con_____ute	_____	_____

In this chapter, you read the word "resist," which means "to fight against," and "existing," which means "being," or "having life." The root word "sist," also written as "stat" and "stit," comes from the Latin word "stare," meaning "to stand," "remain," or "to last." This root is combined with prefixes and suffixes to form many words in English.

B Complete the sentences below using words from the chart. Be sure to use the correct form of each word.

1 It may seem like a silly _____, but I never walk under ladders.
2 I believe this _____ is a replica of a famous work by Rodin.
3 I really didn't want to go into the haunted house as I was too scared, but my friend _____.
4 After months of sleepless nights and constant arguing, the neighbors agreed to take action to make sure their dog _____ from barking.
5 Although this margarine tastes fine, I think it's a very poor _____ for real butter.
6 The art _____ is having a fund-raising exhibition next week. It looks interesting; we should go along.

C Now write three more sentences using the remaining words from the list in A. Share your ideas with a partner.

1 _____
2 _____
3 _____

Before You Read:
Food for Life

Reading Skill:
Identifying Meaning from Context

You can guess the meaning of important but unfamiliar words in a reading passage by using the following strategy: 1. Think about how the new word is related to the topic of what you are reading about. 2. Identify which part of speech the new word is by looking at how it fits with the other words in its sentence. 3. Look at how the word relates to the rest of the information in the paragraph surrounding it. 4. Use your knowledge of prefixes, suffixes, and word roots to identify the basic meaning of the word.

A Discuss the following questions with a partner.

1 What foods are grown in large amounts in your country?
2 Are these foods a staple of the diet in your country?
3 What foods, if any, tend to be eaten in moderation in your country?
4 Are there foods commonly eaten in your country which you know are typically not part of the diet in other countries? What are they?

B Look at the title of the reading. Scan through the reading quickly to find the answers to these questions.

1 Which countries of the world adhere to the principles of the Mediterranean diet?
2 What foods do you think are eaten in abundance in these countries?
3 Which foods do you think form the staple of the Mediterranean diet?

A The following is an extract from the reading passage. As you read through it, think about the topic of the reading, and what you already know about this topic. Pay attention to the words in bold.

> The Mediterranean region is warm and sunny, and produces large supplies of fresh fruits and vegetables almost year round that people eat many times per day. Wine, bread, olive oil, nuts, and **(1) legumes** are other **(2) staples** of the region, and the Mediterranean Sea has historically **(3) yielded** abundant quantities of fish.

B Decide which part of speech each bold word is, and write them below.

1 _____ 2 _____ 3 _____

C Circle the words in the sentence that work with or affect the bold words, and tell you the part of speech. Look at how the word relates to the rest of the paragraph. Are there any other words or phrases that give you clues to the meaning of each word? If so, circle them. Now try to identify the meaning of each word. Replace each one with a word or phrase, or write a definition.

1 _____ 2 _____ 3 _____

D Use your dictionary to check whether you have interpreted the meaning of the words correctly. Share your answers with a partner. Then read the passage again and answer the questions that follow.

Mediterranean Diet

The Mediterranean diet is based upon the eating patterns of traditional cultures in the Mediterranean region.[1] Several noted nutritionists and research projects have concluded that this diet is one of the most healthful in the world in terms of preventing such illnesses as heart disease and cancer, and increasing life expectancy.[2]

The countries that have inspired the Mediterranean diet all surround the Mediterranean Sea. These cultures have eating habits that developed over thousands of years. In Europe, parts of Italy, Greece, Portugal, Spain, and southern France **adhere to** principles of the Mediterranean diet, as do Morocco and Tunisia in North Africa. Parts of the Balkan region[3] and Turkey follow the diet, as well as Middle Eastern countries like Lebanon and Syria. The Mediterranean region is warm and sunny, and produces large supplies of fresh fruits and vegetables almost year round that people eat many times per day. Wine, bread, olive oil, nuts, and legumes are other **staples** of the region, and the Mediterranean Sea has historically yielded **abundant** quantities of fish.

International interest in the **therapeutic** qualities of the Mediterranean diet began back in the late 1950s, when medical researchers started to link the occurrence of heart disease with diet. Dr. Ancel Keys performed an epidemiological **analysis** of diets around the world (epidemiology being the branch of public health that studies patterns of diseases and their potential causes among populations). Entitled the *Seven Countries Study*, it is considered one of the greatest studies of its kind ever performed. In it, Keys gathered data on heart disease and its potential causes from nearly 13,000 men in Greece, Italy, Croatia, Serbia, Japan, Finland, the Netherlands, and the United States. The study was conducted over a period of decades. It concluded that the Mediterranean people in the study enjoyed some significant health advantages. The Mediterranean groups had lower mortality rates in all age brackets and from all causes, particularly from heart disease. The study also showed that the Mediterranean diet is as high or higher in fat than other diets, obtaining up to 40 percent of all its calories from fat. It has, however, different patterns of fat intake. Mediterranean cooking uses smaller amounts of saturated fat and higher amounts of unsaturated fat, mostly in the form of olive oil. Saturated fats are fats that are found principally in meat and dairy products, although avocados, some nuts, and some vegetable oils also contain them. Saturated fats are used by the body to make cholesterol,[4] and high levels of cholesterol have since been directly related to heart disease.

Several other studies have **validated** Keys' findings regarding the good health of people in Mediterranean countries. The World Health Organization (WHO) showed in a 1990 analysis that four major Mediterranean countries (Spain, Greece, France, and Italy) have longer life expectancies and lower rates of heart disease and cancer than other European countries and America. The data are significant because the same Mediterraneans frequently smoke and don't have regular exercise programs like many Americans, which means that other variables may be responsible. Scientists

40 have also **ruled out** genetic differences, because Mediterraneans who move to other countries tend to lose their health advantages. These findings suggest that diet and lifestyle are major factors.

The Mediterranean diet gained even more notice when Dr. Walter Willett, head of the nutrition department at Harvard University, began to recommend it. Although low-fat diets were recommended for sufferers of heart disease, groups of Mediterraneans in his studies had very high

45 intakes of fat, mainly from olive oil. Willett and others proposed that the risk of heart disease can be reduced by increasing one type of dietary fat—monounsaturated[5] fat—the type found in olive oil. Willett's proposal went against conventional nutritional recommendations to reduce all fat in the diet. It has been shown that unsaturated fats raise the level of HDL cholesterol, which is sometimes called "good cholesterol" because of its protective effect against heart disease. Willett has also

50 performed studies **correlating** the intake of meat with heart disease and cancer.

The Mediterranean diet has several general characteristics:
- The bulk of the diet comes from plant sources, including whole grains, breads, pasta, polenta,[6] bulgur,[7] and couscous, rice, potatoes, fruits, vegetables, legumes, seeds, and nuts.
- Olive oil is used generously, and is the main source of fat in the diet as well as the principal
55 cooking oil. The total fat intake **accounts for** up to 35 percent of calories. Saturated fats, however, make up only eight percent of calories or less, which **restricts** meat and dairy intake.
- Fruits and vegetables are eaten in large quantities. They are usually fresh, unprocessed,[8] grown locally, and consumed in season.
- Dairy products are consumed in small amounts daily, mainly as cheese and yogurt.
60 - Eggs are used sparingly, up to four eggs per week.
- Fish and poultry are consumed only one to three times per week, with fish preferred over poultry.
- Red meat is consumed only a few times per month.
- Honey is the principal sweetener, and sweets are eaten only a few times per week.
- Wine is consumed in moderate amounts with meals (one to two glasses daily).

This reading was adapted from *Mediterranean Diet*. From *The Gale Encyclopedia of Alternative Medicine* by Douglas Dupler, © The Gale Group, 2001. Reprinted by permission of The Gale Group.

[1] **Mediterranean region** area surrounding the Mediterranean Sea incorporating Spain, southern France, Italy, Greece, Portugal, Sardinia, Sicily, and countries along the northern African coast
[2] **life expectancy** the average age to which a person is expected to live
[3] **Balkan region** area of southeast Europe including Albania, Bulgaria, northern Greece, southeast Romania, western Turkey, and Yugoslavia
[4] **cholesterol** substance found in animal tissue and other foods that affects levels of fat stored in the human body
[5] **monounsaturated** type of saturated fat that has only one bond in its carbon chain
[6] **polenta** thick porridge-type meal made of cornmeal boiled with water
[7] **bulgur** dried cracked wheat
[8] **unprocessed** not treated or altered in any way; in a natural state

A Choose the best answer for each question or statement below. Compare your answers with a partner.

1 The Mediterranean region produces large amounts of _____ all year round.
   a. red meat and wine
   b. fruits and vegetables
   c. nuts and olive oil
   d. fish and dairy products

2 International interest in the Mediterranean diet began _____.
   a. thousands of years ago
   b. in the 1950s
   c. in the 1970s
   d. in the 1990s

3 The Mediterranean diet has different patterns of fat intake as the cooking uses _____.
   a. more meat and less dairy products
   b. more nuts and less olive oil
   c. less saturated fat and more unsaturated fat
   d. more avocados and less vegetable oil

4 A World Health Organization study showed that people from Spain, Greece, France, and Italy _____.
   a. exercise more than Americans
   b. experience health advantages by moving overseas
   c. live, on average, shorter lives than Americans
   d. have lower rates of cancer and heart disease

5 Medical studies have linked the Mediterranean diet to _____.
   a. a lower life expectancy
   b. cancer and smoking
   c. patterns of lung disease in men
   d. lower levels of heart disease

B The following questions are all about the reading. Answer each one using the information you have read. Try not to look back at the reading for the answers.

1 Why has the Mediterranean diet attracted the attention of nutritionists?
2 What did a scientific study discover about the health of people who moved away from the Mediterranean region?
3 What type of fat did Dr. Willett recommend increasing in the diet?
4 Does the Mediterranean diet consist of mostly plant or mostly animal products?
5 What is the main source of fat in the Mediterranean diet?

C Critical Thinking

Discuss these questions with a partner.

1 How does the Mediterranean diet sound to you? Would you be able to eat that way all the time?

2 What are the main sources of fat in your diet? What percentage of your diet is from fat?

3 How is your diet similar to or different from the Mediterranean diet?

Vocabulary Comprehension:
Words in Context

A Look at the following target vocabulary items from the reading. Use the context of the items within the passage to work out the meaning of each one.

> adhere to   staples   abundant   therapeutic   analysis
> validated   ruled out   correlating   accounts for   restricts

B Read the paragraph below and fill in the blanks using the vocabulary items from A. Be sure to use the correct form of each word.

Get in Shape; Walk It Off!

Do you (1)_____ an exercise program or have you (2)_____ working out? Lack of exercise (3)_____ a large percentage of ill health. Did you know that incorporating a daily routine of walking into your schedule can help you stay in shape? There are many reasons to walk: First of all, it's (4)_____. While you are walking, you can work on your mind, as well as your body. Doctors are consistently (5)_____ healthy bodies with healthy minds. This has been (6)_____ with statistical research studies. Clearing the mind and walking off your worries can have positive effects on your health. Furthermore, walking means you are not (7)_____ to exercising in the confines of a gym—you can walk at any time. There is also no need for (8)_____ exercise equipment, weights, or clothing. Many people have started "walking clubs" at their workplace. During lunch, or for thirty minutes in the morning, a group may get together to walk a few blocks around the neighborhood they work in. This is a great way to keep you motivated and on track. Finally, as well as using exercise to get in shape, give your diet a careful (9)_____. What foods are the (10)_____ of your diet? Start replacing those fattening mid-morning snacks with fruit—it's just as filling, but with half the calories and fat! So tomorrow when you wake up, strap on those sneakers, pick up some fruit, and start to walk it off—it's easy!

C Answer these questions. Share your answers with a partner.

1 What are some good eating habits that you try to *adhere to*?
2 What are the *staple* foods of your own diet?
3 If you could eat an *abundant* amount of any food, what would it be, and why?
4 Take a moment to *analyze* your lifestyle. Would you say it is healthy or unhealthy? What changes do you need to make, if any, to make it better?

A Study the words in the chart below. What do you think they mean? Use your knowledge of prefixes, suffixes, and the roots *mono*, *dec*, *cent*, and *mill* to try to work out the meaning of each word.

Noun	Verb	Adjective
monologue decathlon decibel percentage century centenarian millipede	monopolize decimate	monotonous centennial millennial

Vocabulary Skill:
Numerical Root Words *mono*, *dec*, *cent*, and *mill*

In this chapter, you read the word "monounsaturated," which contains the root "mono," meaning "single" or "one." There are several roots in English that correlate to numbers. For example, "dec" or "deci" means "ten," "cent" or "centi" means "one hundred," and "mill" or "milli" means "one thousand."

B Complete the sentences below using the vocabulary from A. Be sure to use the correct form of each word.

News in Brief

Biologists have discovered a new breed of **(1)**_____. The discovery was made when lettuce farmers reported that this year's crop had been **(2)**_____ by an insect. A high **(3)**_____ of the farms affected are in the southern United States.

A group of **(4)**_____ attended a dinner party with the President last night. The dinner was held as part of the President's agenda to provide recognition for citizens who have lived through the last **(5)**_____, and in doing so contributed to the country's economic growth and development. The President gave a **(6)**_____ on this topic during the evening which was met with indifference from some of the older folks; a couple said they found his speech **(7)**_____, while others complained that his talk was so long he ended up **(8)**_____ the evening!

World class athlete Guy Simpson won gold in the **(9)**_____ event at the World Games in Athens yesterday. As Simpson received his medal, the cheer from the crowd was so loud it reached new **(10)**_____ levels, and drowned out the national anthem!

A leading politician has proposed a new sporting event to be held once every one hundred years. The **(11)**_____ Games, as they would be known, would be held to honor athletes at the peak of their career at the time of the games. While some people have denounced the idea as ridiculous, others have taken it one step further and proposed that the games that fall on the thousand year anniversary of the start of the games be named the **(12)**_____ Games! It seems, for some, the Olympics just aren't good enough.

Real Life Skill:
Understanding Punctuation

Formal academic and business writing uses a number of specialized punctuation marks. Knowing the meanings of these marks, and how and why they are used, will enable you to understand the exact meaning of what you are reading, and how you should read it. They are also important to know when writing in English formally, or for academic purposes.

A Match each punctuation mark with its function and description of how it works.

Punctuation mark
1   [ ] square brackets _____
2   ( ) parentheses _____
3   . . . ellipsis _____
4   – dash _____
5   - hyphen _____
6   / slash or virgule _____
7   & ampersand _____
8   ' ' single quote marks _____
9   : colon _____
10   ; semi-colon _____
11   * asterisk _____

Function
a. shows two alternatives
b. separates ideas in a sentence or used before a list
c. shows that words or letters were left out
d. shows separate information inside a sentence
e. connects two closely related sentences
f. refers to a note at the bottom of the page
g. shows a quotation inside another quotation
h. a symbol for *and*
i. adds information to explain the first clause of a sentence
j. combines two closely connected names or words
k. shows words that were not originally in the text but added later by the editor

B Use the marks above to punctuate the sentences below.

1 The reporter stated that "The man accused of the crime stood up in court and shouted not guilty at the judge."
2 Many new forms of communication were introduced during the twentieth century fax, e-mail, and cell phones.
3 One of the leading companies in the pharmaceutical industry is Palmer Jackson.
4 She put on the dress, then looked at herself in a full length mirror.
5 We accept payment by credit card, also by check money order.
6 Good nutrition is important for athletes it's also vital for the rest of us.
7 Joyce yelled, "If you don't stop that right now, I'll   "
8 John gave all of his own money to Fred why I'll never know.
9 A police report recently released shows a disturbing increase in the incidence of violent crime in city centers. See note 1.

What Do You Think?

1 What are some of the most important traditional principles of eating in your culture?
2 Are you aware of the mortality rates in your country for heart disease and cancer? Do you think there is any aspect of diet and lifestyle that people in your country could change in order to reduce the number of deaths related to these diseases?
3 As you get older, do you think you will become more conscious of what you eat? Why?
4 There is a saying in English: "You are what you eat." What do you understand this saying to mean? Do you think this is true? Explain your answer. Is there a similar saying in your native language?

1. _____
2. _____
3. _____

4. _____
5. _____
6. _____

7. _____
8. _____
9. _____

Getting Ready

Discuss the following questions with a partner.

1 Can you name all the planets in the solar system? Label the picture above.
2 What other objects or bodies exist in the solar system?
3 Do you believe that there are life forms, either basic or intelligent, on other planets?
4 Do you think that one day humans may inhabit other planets? Why or why not?

Chapter 1: Near-Earth Objects: Monsters of Doom?

Before You Read:
Avoiding Asteroids

A Discuss the following questions with a partner.

1 Do you ever watch science fiction or adventure movies about space?
   Do you think any of the events portrayed in those films could happen?
2 Do you think there are any objects in space that pose a danger to Earth?
3 Do you think that if a large object were on a collision course with Earth, we
   would have the power to prevent the collision and the devastation that would
   follow? Explain the reasons for your answer.

B The terms from the reading on the left are things found in space. Match
   them with the definitions. Then scan the reading to check your answers.

1 asteroid _____
2 comet _____
3 crater _____
4 meteoroid _____
5 space probe _____

a. an object circling the sun that usually has a "tail"
b. a device sent into space to collect information
c. a large rock in space that orbits the sun
d. a large hole where an object has hit a planet's surface
e. an object which enters the earth's atmosphere and
    descends in a fiery ball

Reading Skill:
Understanding
Inference

Information in a
reading passage
can be found in two
ways: by what is
stated directly and
written clearly on
the page, or by what
we can infer. When
we infer, we use the
information that is
stated directly to
draw conclusions
about events, or the
writer's opinion or
purpose. Knowing
how to infer can
help you to better
understand the
writer's purpose and
ideas. It is a useful
skill to know when
reading for pleasure,
and can help you
better understand
reading passages in
exams.

A Read through each of the following statements carefully. Scan through
   the reading passage and decide if each statement is stated (S) or inferred (I).
   Check (✔) the correct column.

		S	I
1	If asteroid XF11 hit the earth, it would destroy much of the planet and its inhabitants.		
2	Brian Marsden was very embarrassed about his mistake.		
3	Asteroids vary widely in shape and size.		
4	Isaac Asimov is a writer of science fiction stories.		
5	If all the asteroids were joined together, there may be enough material to form a planet.		
6	Earth will most probably be hit by an NEO in the future.		
7	Earth is scattered with evidence of previous NEO impacts.		
8	Public concern about XF11 probably helped boost attendance at two Hollywood disaster movies.		

B Check your answers with a partner. Discuss the reasons for your answers
   by making reference to the relevant parts of the reading.

C Now read the passage again and answer the questions that follow.

Near-Earth Objects: Monsters of Doom?

A meteoroid impact

In March of 1998, astronomer Brian Marsden at the Harvard-Smithsonian Astrophysical Observatory issued a **spine-chilling** announcement. Based on eighty-eight days of observing asteroid 1977 XF11,
5 he calculated that this massive rock would come **perilously** close to Earth in 2028. It could miss us by a mere 30,000 miles[1]—only about one-eighth our distance from the moon. Almost a mile wide, if the rock struck Earth the devastation would be too awful
10 to **contemplate**.

The next day, Marsden was humbly apologizing. NASA's Jet Propulsion Laboratory located a photo of XF11 that permitted a more precise calculation of its path. On its 2028 crossing of the Earth's orbit, it will miss us by 600,000 miles, about two-and-a-half times the average distance between Earth and the moon.

15 Near-Earth Objects (NEOs) is a contemporary term for massive objects that periodically cross Earth's orbit, and in doing so come close to our planet. They include asteroids, meteoroids, and comets. The word "asteroid" is Greek for "star-like," so named because early telescopes[2] could see them only as points of light. Two large asteroids have since been photographed up close by space probes. They resemble misshapen potatoes, their surfaces covered with craters like the surface of
20 our moon. Almost all asteroids are confined to the asteroid belt,[3] but many wander far beyond the orbit of Jupiter, and others **plunge** inward past the orbit of Venus. Larger asteroids are spherical, but smaller ones are extremely irregular. It is estimated that more than a thousand asteroids are at least a mile wide. Perhaps a dozen are three or more miles wide. There is no lower limit to asteroid size because they grade down to tiny rocks and particles of dust, but no asteroid is big enough to hold
25 an atmosphere. It is these large NEOs that pose a monstrous threat to humanity if they come close to Earth or hit it.

What produced the asteroids? The writer Isaac Asimov posed the once-popular science fiction idea that asteroids are **remnants** of a small planet whose inhabitants discovered nuclear energy and blew their world to smithereens.[4] But not even a nuclear explosion would be great enough to form
30 the asteroid belt. The prevailing scientific view is that asteroids are material that failed to **coagulate** into a planet. There is no doubt that eventually Earth will be struck by a massive NEO because such events have occurred in the past. The most recent was the 1908 crash of a large NEO in the Tunguska River valley of central Siberia. It flattened trees for many miles around and killed a herd of reindeer. Earth is spotted with dozens of visible craters that **testify** to similar impacts, and there
35 surely are thousands of craters that vanished long ago from erosion.[5] It is widely believed that the impact of a giant NEO caused a mass extinction of life that included the dinosaurs, 65 million years ago.

In 1937 the asteroid Hermes, half a mile wide, missed us by about twice the distance between Earth and the moon. In 1989 an asteroid called Asclepius, also about half a mile across, came even
40 closer. In 1991 a small asteroid about 30 feet[6] wide missed the earth by less than half the distance

to the moon. The latest near miss was in 1996 when JA1, a third of a mile wide, set a record for large asteroids by missing us by a mere 280,000 miles, only 40,000 miles longer than the distance between Earth and the moon.

45 Disasters caused by NEOs striking Earth are common themes in early science fiction and some modern disaster movies. Sci-fi writer H. G. Wells pioneered the theme. His short story "The Star," for example, is a vivid account of devastation caused by a mammoth NEO. In the story, an asteroid from the outskirts of the solar system is shifted from its orbit and collides with Neptune. The two **coalesce** to form a flaming "star" that almost demolishes the Earth before it plunges into the sun.

50 On the movie screen, New York City has twice been destroyed by NEOs. It was demolished in the **dreary** 1979 film, *Meteor*. In the 1951 film, *When Worlds Collide*, a wandering star called Ballus flattens the city with a gigantic tidal wave. The XF11 scare was also great publicity for two disaster movies about NEO impacts: *Armageddon* and *Deep Impact*.

55 If some time in the future an asteroid is determined to be on a near collision course with Earth, what can be done to prevent disaster? One suggestion, not overlooked in science fiction, is to attach a nuclear bomb to the rock that will blow it into a harmless orbit. In fact, early science fiction envisioned using cannonballs[7] to deflect comets. The danger of bombing an asteroid is that this could produce fragments that would hit the earth, causing even more damage than the intact rock. Better techniques for diverting an asteroid may be landing a rocket engine on it to **nudge** it away, or attaching a large solar sail to let the sun's radiation do the nudging.

60 Perhaps those sci-fi movies and Hollywood blockbusters aren't quite so farfetched after all.

This reading was adapted from *Near-Earth Objects: Monsters of Doom?* by Martin Gardner.
Reprinted with permission of the *Skeptical Enquirer* © July–August 1998.

[1] **miles** one mile equals approximately 1.6 kilometers
[2] **telescopes** instruments used to view distant objects more closely
[3] **asteroid belt** a strip or band of asteroids, situated between Mars and Jupiter, that orbits the sun
[4] **smithereens** tiny pieces or fragments
[5] **erosion** the wearing away of a surface, usually rock, by the action of wind or water
[6] **feet** one foot is equal to approximately 0.3 meters
[7] **cannonballs** heavy metal balls fired from cannons (very large tube-shaped guns)

A The following questions are all about the reading. Answer each one using the information you have read. Try not to look back at the reading for the answer.

1 Where does Brian Marsden work?
2 What did NASA use to recalculate the path of XF11?
3 Where does the word "asteroid" come from? What does it mean?
4 What is the accepted scientific view of how asteroids are formed?
5 What suggestions does the passage give for preventing an asteroid from colliding with Earth?

B Decide if the following statements about the reading are true (T) or false (F). If you check (✔) false, correct the statement to make it true.

	T	F
1 Brian Marsden apologized for making a mistake about an NEO.		
2 The most recent NEO impact was in 1950.		
3 Some people believe the dinosaurs were killed off by an NEO.		
4 In its history, New York City was twice damaged by NEOs.		
5 Bombing an asteroid is not the best way of stopping it from hitting the earth.		

C Critical Thinking

Discuss these questions with a partner.
1 Have you seen any of the movies mentioned in the reading? If so, what did you think of them?
2 Do you think that government space agencies such as NASA already have plans for when an NEO collides with Earth? Give reasons for your answer.
3 If an asteroid were known to be on a collision course with Earth, and would hit in one week, what things would you want to do in that week?

Vocabulary Comprehension:
Word Definitions

A Look at the list of words from the reading. Match each one with a definition on the right.

1 spine-chilling _____
2 perilously _____
3 contemplate _____
4 plunge _____
5 remnants _____
6 coagulate _____
7 testify _____
8 coalesce _____
9 dreary _____
10 nudge _____

a. to cause a liquid to transform into a solid or semi-solid mass
b. to move forward or downward suddenly or violently
c. to grow or bond together to form a whole
d. to provide or serve as evidence
e. extremely frightening; eerie
f. dangerously
g. dull; boring
h. to push gently
i. to think about or consider carefully
j. smaller pieces of something left over from a larger piece

B Complete the paragraph using the vocabulary from A. Be sure to use the correct form of each word.

Meteorite Dream

Many years ago, my parents took me to the Museum of Natural History in New York City. That's where I saw my first meteorite—a meteorite that inspired a **(1)**_____ dream!

In this dream I was walking alone, at night, in a large canyon. I could see a bright light in the sky that gradually approached the canyon. Suddenly, the light was right above me and a deafening sound filled the air. Numerous rocks **(2)**_____ down from the sky and hit the floor of the canyon, **(3)**_____ close to me. I leaped out of the way, and hid behind a boulder to avoid being hit by **(4)**_____ from each one that shattered on the ground. I was terrified; my whole body was frozen. As I crouched behind the boulder, I noticed spots of silver liquid that had landed on the ground. I watched in horror as the liquid began to **(5)**_____ into a shape—it was forming some kind of spacecraft! I heard a noise and looked across the canyon to see the rocks move toward each other and **(6)**_____ into larger shapes. Gradually, much to my shock, they began to resemble humans! I crouched lower behind the boulder and **(7)**_____ what to do next. Would these "humans" know I was there? How could I escape? My heart was pounding and I was sweating with fear; I made a run for it. As I raced across the canyon, dodging boulders and leaping over rocks, I felt a heavy hand on my left shoulder, and heard a loud voice calling my name.

I opened my eyes to see my mother standing over me, **(8)**_____ me to wake me up. "Come on, breakfast's ready," she said, as I stared up at her in surprise. "What on earth were you dreaming about?" Over breakfast I told her about my dream. "Well, you certainly don't have **(9)**_____ dreams," was her only comment, as she laughed at my story. After breakfast, I picked up the paper to read that the previous day a woman had **(10)**_____ to the FBI that she saw large rocks fall out of the sky and land in a canyon near her home. According to her report, a few minutes later, aliens emerged from the canyon and walked off into the distance.

Had my nightmare been just that—a bad dream—or was it real?

A For each word below, study the different parts. Then, write the part of speech and a simple definition. Use your dictionary to help you. Share your ideas with a partner.

Vocabulary Skill:
The Prefix *mis-*

Vocabulary	Part of Speech	Definition
1 misconception	_____	_____
2 unmistakably	_____	_____
3 misbehavior	_____	_____
4 miscommunication	_____	_____
5 misdemeanor	_____	_____
6 mismanage	_____	_____
7 mispronounce	_____	_____
8 misfit	_____	_____
9 misfortune	_____	_____
10 misrepresent	_____	_____

In this chapter, you read the word "misshapen," meaning "badly shaped" or "deformed." This word uses the negative prefix "mis-," which means "bad" or "wrong," with the word "shapen." "Mis-" is combined with many roots to form other words in English.

B Complete each sentence using the words from A. Be sure to use the correct form of each word.

1 As a result of so many years of being _____, the company went bankrupt.

2 I get so tired of people _____ my name. I always ask people how to say their name correctly.

3 Jean and I ended up not talking as a result of our _____. I said one thing, but she took it completely the wrong way.

4 I find that many people who have not traveled outside of their own countries have huge _____ about what goes on in other parts of the world.

5 The actor's real words were _____ in the press, and he was made to sound like a terrible person.

6 Although it was only for a _____, Alicia was still taken to the police station and cautioned.

7 Although Allison has warned her children many times about their _____, they don't seem to take much notice of her.

8 The teachers say that Paulo is very gifted and really too intelligent for other children his age. That's why he comes across as such a _____ in school.

9 It was a terrible _____ that Alexander broke both his legs on his skiing trip.

10 There is no question about it—I heard _____ the sound of breaking glass come after that flash in the sky.

Chapter 2: Life on Mars Likely, Scientist Claims

Before You Read:
The Red Planet

Discuss the following questions with a partner.

1 What do you know about the planet Mars? Do you know if it contains any signs of life?
2 How much do you know about the exploration of Mars by humans so far?
3 Do you think that living creatures from Earth could survive on Mars?
4 Is there any way that humans could make use of Mars in the future?

Reading Skill:
Scanning

When we need to read something to find specific information, we move our eyes very quickly across the text. When we "scan" like this, we do not read every word or stop when we see a word we do not understand; we read quickly and pause only to find the particular information we are looking for.

A Read these statements about the exploration of Mars and decide if each statement is true (T) or false (F).

		T	F
1	NASA has sent two robots to explore the surface of Mars.		
2	Gilbert Levin is a scientist who works for NASA.		
3	Spirit and Opportunity are the names of spaceships.		
4	NASA also sent two astronauts to explore Mars.		
5	There seems to be evidence of water on Mars.		
6	If there is water on Mars, then there is sure to be life there.		
7	NASA could send robot ships to go and get material from the surface of Mars.		
8	Life from Mars could be potentially dangerous to life on Earth.		

B Scan the reading to find out if the statements above are really true or false.

C Read the text again; then answer the questions that follow.

Life on Mars Likely, Scientist Claims

DENVER, COLORADO—Those twin robots hard at work on Mars have transmitted **teasing** views that reinforce the prospect that microbial[1] life may exist on the red planet.

5 Results from NASA's Spirit and Opportunity rovers are being looked over by a legion of planetary experts, including a scientist who remains steadfast that his experiment in 1976 proved the presence of active microbial life in 10 the topsoil of Mars. "All factors necessary to constitute a habitat for life as we know it exist on current-day Mars," explained Gilbert Levin, executive officer for science at Spherix Incorporated of Beltsville, Maryland.

Provocative find

15 Levin has a long-standing interest in time-weathered Mars and the promise of life today on that distant and dusty world. NASA's 1976 Viking mission to Mars was geared-up to look for possible Martian life. And it was Levin's Labeled Release experiment that made a provocative find: The presence of a highly reactive agent[2] in the surface material of Mars. Levin concluded in 1997 that this activity was triggered by living micro-organisms **lurking** in the Martian soil—a judgment he 20 admits has not been generally accepted by the scientific community.

Now roll forward to the present. Consider the findings of Spirit and Opportunity, the golf-cart sized robots wheeling over Mars at Gusev Crater[3] and Meridiani Planum.[4] "Those rovers have been absolutely sensational, pouring out thousands of images. Those images have lots of information in them. And I've tried to **deduce** something in there relative to life . . . and I think I 25 found a lot," Levin told *SPACE.com*.

Squeezed out of the soil

In **perusing** rover imagery, Levin reports there is clear evidence for liquid water existing under Martian environmental conditions. "The images should be reviewed against the background of surface temperatures as varying from below to above freezing reported by both Spirit and 30 Opportunity," he explained.

Levin points to the potential for mud puddles on Mars, showing an image of clearly disturbed Martian soil after rover airbags bounced across Mars' surface. Possible standing water and sinkholes[5] can also be seen in rover imagery, according to his analysis. In some pictures, the often-discussed "blueberries," tiny spheres of material, disappear as if submerged underneath 35 mud-like surroundings, he added.

Then there are tracks left by the machines as they roll across the Martian terrain. Self-taken shots by the robots show what Levin said appears to be water squeezed out of the soil which then freezes into a whitish **residue** left in embedded tread marks.

Similarly, Levin added, are images taken by Opportunity of the results from an operation of the robot's Rock Abrasion Tool, or RAT. The center of that particular RAT hole is largely white, possibly indicating the formation of frost since the hole was drilled, he noted.

Organisms there now?

"The evidence presented strongly indicates the presence of liquid water or **moisture** at the Mars Exploration Rover sites," Levin reported at the SPIE meeting. "Mars today could support many forms of terrestrial[6] microbial life."

Other scientists are cautious to point out that the presence of water does not guarantee life. Rather, it means one crucial ingredient exists.

There is clear evidence for frost or ice on Mars, the former Viking experimenter stated. At some point of the day—when temperatures climb above freezing—there's going to be moisture ". . . and that's enough to support micro-organisms," he said. None of the many new findings about Mars revealed by Spirit and Opportunity, Levin concluded, conflict with, or render **untenable**, his long-held belief that the Viking Labeled Release experiment in 1976 detected living micro-organisms in the soil of Mars.

"I contend that today you could take a great many Earth micro-organisms, put them on Mars, and they'd grow," Levin said. "And I think there are organisms there now. They may have come from Earth. They may have originated on Mars. They may have come from a third place that populated both Mars and Earth." Rocks can be kicked up from one planet by an asteroid impact, drift through the vacuum of space for eons, then land on the other. Other studies have shown that these rocks could potentially transport life, in a **dormant** phase, from one planet to the other. Levin said that he thinks the "greatest speculation" would be to say there can be *no* life on Mars.

Moon used as Earth bio-shield

If indeed Mars is rife with life, care should be taken in hauling back to Earth specimens of rock and surface materials from the red planet. NASA has indicated that, in the next decade, robotic craft could be **dispatched** to gather and return to Earth select samples of Mars for detailed laboratory study. Could those bits of Mars, perhaps **laden with** Martian microbes, act as dangerous cargo? As a precaution, Levin advocates a kind of bio-shield strategy for Earth—using the Moon.

The new NASA vision to re-establish a human presence on the Moon is good timing, Levin said. "Bring samples of Mars not to Earth but to the Moon," he said. "There we would have built a scientific laboratory in which scientists could examine the samples and determine whether or not there is a hazard."

This reading was adapted from *Life on Mars Likely, Scientist Claims* by Leonard David.
Reprinted with permission from Imaginova Corp © 2004.

[1] **microbial** having to do with viruses, bacteria, and other forms of life too small for the human eye to see
[2] **highly reactive agent** a substance which interacts readily with other substances
[3] **Gusev Crater** a 145-kilometer-wide crater in the surface of Mars
[4] **Meridiani Planum** a large plain on the surface of Mars
[5] **sinkholes** pits in a planet's surface created by underground water
[6] **terrestrial** related to the Earth

A **How much do you remember from the reading? Choose the best answer for each question or statement. Compare your answers with a partner.**

1 What is the article mainly about?
   a. recent findings on Mars and their implications
   b. how to utilize life on Mars
   c. efforts to disprove that there is life on Mars
   d. plans for humans to visit Mars in the near future
2 What do most other scientists in the scientific community think about Levin's belief that micro-organisms exist in the soil of Mars?
   a. They agree with him.
   b. They do not accept it.
   c. They had previously confirmed it.
   d. They think it will probably be proven true.
3 Which of the following is NOT cited as evidence for water on Mars?
   a. whitish residue in tread marks
   b. "blueberries" disappearing
   c. the white center of RAT holes
   d. rocks kicked up from a planet
4 According to some scientists, water on Mars _____.
   a. could be brought to the Moon
   b. came from the Earth
   c. would not guarantee that there is life there
   d. allows Martian life to live on Earth
5 Why might material from Mars be brought to the Moon?
   a. to be analyzed by scientists in a safe environment
   b. to test robotic craft
   c. to be used as building material for a kind of bio-shield
   d. to be used as building material for a Moon base

B **The following statements are all about the reading. Complete each one using information you have read.**

1 The purpose of the 1976 Viking mission was to look for _____.
2 The Mars rovers Spirit and Opportunity are about the size of a _____.
3 Spirit and Opportunity have sent many _____ back to Earth.
4 The temperature on Mars ranges from below to above _____.
5 NASA has a new vision of re-establishing a human presence _____.

C Critical Thinking

Discuss these questions with a partner.
1 Does the question of whether or not there is life on Mars seem important to you? Why or why not?
2 Gilbert Levin claimed that if we put micro-organisms from Earth on Mars, they would grow. Do you think we should try to do this? Explain your answer.

Vocabulary Comprehension:
Odd Word Out

A For each group, circle the word that does not belong. The words in *italics* are vocabulary items from the reading.

1	*teasing*	intriguing	tantalizing	discouraging
2	digging	*lurking*	hiding	skulking
3	conclude	imagine	*deduce*	figure out
4	looking through	skimming	interpreting	*perusing*
5	*residue*	remainder	vestiges	deficiency
6	humidity	*moisture*	aridity	wetness
7	unassailable	indefensible	*untenable*	unsound
8	inactive	sleeping	transient	*dormant*
9	*dispatched*	launched	sent	deterred
10	loaded with	*laden with*	longing for	full of

B Complete the sentences below using the words in *italics* from A. Be sure to use the correct form of each word.

1 The townspeople didn't mind living on the slopes of the volcano; it had been _____ for hundreds of years.

2 On Thanksgiving Day, our relatives were greeted by the sight of a long table _____ all their favorite foods.

3 Nearly dying of thirst, Satea saw the _____ sight of a stream, but he soon realized it was just his eyes playing tricks on him.

4 The crocodile _____ by the river bank waiting for its next victim.

5 All the hospitals in the city _____ every available ambulance to the scene of the airplane crash.

6 While waiting in the dentist's office, Mimi _____ several magazines.

7 During the difficult operation, the nurse periodically wiped the _____ from the doctor's forehead with a cloth.

8 The scientist saw that the overwhelming proof against his theory made his position _____, so he formulated a new hypothesis.

9 Because of the crumbs and chocolate all over her face, it was easy to _____ that Samantha had taken the cookies from the cookie jar.

10 After mopping up the spilled chemicals, there was still a sticky _____ on the laboratory floor.

A For each word, study the different parts. Then write the part of speech and a simple definition for each one. Use your knowledge of prefixes and suffixes and your dictionary to help you. Share your ideas with a partner.

Vocabulary Skill:

The Root Word *vac*

Vocabulary	Part of Speech	Definition
1 void	_____	_____
2 devoid	_____	_____
3 evacuate	_____	_____
4 vacant	_____	_____
5 vanish	_____	_____
6 avoid	_____	_____
7 vacation	_____	_____
8 vacuous	_____	_____

In this chapter, you read the word "vacuum," which means "an empty airless space." This word is formed from the Latin "vacuus" or "vacare," meaning "to be empty." Variants of this root are "void" or "van," which share the same meaning. These roots are combined with prefixes and suffixes to form many words in English that have a similar meaning.

B Now complete each sentence using the words from A. Be sure to use the correct form of each word.

1 As soon as the earthquake started, everyone was ordered to _____ the building.
2 I've just been told by my tutor that my essays can only be described as dull, boring, and _____.
3 Although he has many hobbies, the _____ that was left in my grandfather's life when my grandmother died has never been filled.
4 Troy is such a serious person; he comes across as being completely _____ of any sense of humor.
5 It is an incredibly interesting country to travel to, but you must remember to _____ drinking the tap water or you'll become ill.
6 I have to finish this report by Friday as I'm leaving for a two-week _____ to Barbados on Saturday afternoon.
7 This apartment will only be _____ from next month. Until then, someone will be living here.
8 In scary movies, someone always _____; that event is so predictable!

C Write two sentences of your own using any two words from the chart in A.

1 _____
2 _____

Real Life Skill:
Remembering What You Read

Scientists have used discoveries about how memory works to develop mnemonic techniques for more effective study. One of these techniques, called "SQ3R," is a five-step method to help students understand the content of a reading, and retain it in their memory for exams. The combination of reading actively, writing, and speaking uses more areas of the brain, and processes the information more effectively.

A Read the name of each step of the SQ3R method; then match each one with its description.

Step 1: Survey _____   Step 2: Question _____   Step 3: Read _____

Step 4: Recite _____   Step 5: Review _____

a. Using your notes with the questions and answers, go over the material within twenty-four hours of the first time you prepare it. Review it again after one week. Continue to go over your notes regularly until your exam.

b. Go through the reading again, slowly and carefully, finding and writing down the answers to each of your questions.

c. As you skim through the reading, write down a number of questions that you think it will answer. For example, if the introduction says, "Cell phones have changed our world in several ways," one question might be: What are some ways that cell phones have changed the world?

d. Skim quickly through the reading to find its main ideas and purpose. Look at any titles, pictures, the introduction and conclusion, and the first and last sentence of each paragraph.

e. After you have written the answers to all of your questions, read each question and answer aloud. This will help to fix the material in your memory.

B Choose one of the readings in this book. It can be from this unit, from an earlier unit, or from a unit you have not studied yet. Imagine you are using the SQ3R approach to study the material in that reading for an exam. Write three or four questions you would use to help you retain the information.

1 _____?

2 _____?

3 _____?

4 _____?

What Do You Think?

1 The scientist Stephen Hawking said that humans must go into space in order to survive. Do you agree or disagree? Explain your reasons.

2 Do you think that governments can justify spending billions of dollars on space exploration, or should that money be put to better use on Earth? Explain your answer.

3 Which planet, if any, do you think should be explored next? Why?

4 Some extreme skeptics believe that humans never landed on the moon, and it was all a hoax. What do you think?

Getting Ready

Discuss the following questions with a partner.

1 What types of energy generation are shown in the pictures above?
2 What are some advantages and drawbacks of the energy generation methods shown?
3 What types of energy generation does the country you are living in rely on?
4 What do you think humans will use for energy in the far future?

Chapter 1: Biomass: Let's Set the World on Fire

Reading Skill:
Identifying Fact Versus Opinion

A fact is something that can be checked and proven. An opinion is one person's personal belief or feeling about something. In writing, opinions are often expressed using words and phrases like "in my opinion," "believe," and "should," or speculative language such as "could," "might," and "may." Being able to distinguish between fact and opinion is an important reading skill, as much of what we read can be a mixture of both. Using this skill can help you to better understand a reading, become a more critical reader, and put the information you have read to good use.

A Answer the following questions.

1 What do you understand by the term "global warming"?
2 What are considered to be the main causes of global warming?
3 How are scientists or government members in your country working to address the issue of global warming? Do you think they are doing enough?
4 What other action can, or should, be taken to further address this issue either globally or in your country?
5 What do you understand by the term "alternative energies"? Name some types of alternative energies. How can the use of these energies help in addressing the issue of global warming?

B Discuss your answers with a partner.

A Read each of the following statements. Check (✔) F if you think the statement expresses a fact, or O if you think it expresses an opinion. Underline the words that helped you determine your answer.

		F	O
1	Fossil fuels are getting harder to find.		
2	Nuclear power has proven to be prohibitively expensive.		
3	Solar panels require eight years of use to replace the conventional energy used to manufacture them.		
4	In time, the fossil fuel waves may come to be seen as something of a historical blip.		
5	Power generation produces twice as much heat as electricity.		
6	Bioenergy power stations could be located near the settlements they would serve.		
7	Farmers could transform themselves into energy heroes by changing their crop.		
8	Ravaged rural economies would be boosted by the creation of tens of thousands of new jobs in forestry, transportation, and power plant operation.		

B Compare your answers with a partner. Scan through the passage to find where the information in each statement above is mentioned, and check your answers.

C Now read through the passage and complete the comprehension exercises that follow. Underline any other facts and opinions you find as you are reading.

Biomass: Let's Set the World on Fire

If coal, oil, and gas are just the residues of plants that once lived above ground, then why not burn plants on the surface? With ready access to abundant sources of food in many countries
5 of the world, there is a smaller need to **devote** vast territories of farmland to food production. In contrast, the demand for energy has no limits.

The **fossil fuels** on which we have come to depend are growing harder to find, and therefore
10 more expensive. The latest findings on global warming suggest that the diversion of the Gulf Stream[1] and the melting of polar ice caps[2] may be among the least of the environmental problems ahead of us. Once methane[3] bubbles up from the sea and the forests catch fire, releasing yet more carbon instead of absorbing it, warming may
15 increase to a level at which human life will become impossible, anywhere on the planet.

We know we must replace coal, oil, and gas with renewable sources of energy. But how? The answer used to be "go nuclear," but nuclear power has proved prohibitively expensive. Hydropower sounds clean, but you have to flood entire valleys for it to work. Much is heard of wind, wave, and solar power. Unfortunately, **intermittent** energy sources need to be backed up by conventional power, for
20 the wind does not always blow, and the sun does not always shine. Even more problematic is the manufacture of the hardware that such sources of power require. This can use up almost as much energy as they generate. Put a solar panel[4] on your roof, and it will take the first eight years of its use to replace the conventional energy that was needed to make the panel.

The hard truth is that since humans first discovered fire, we have found no energy source that begins
25 to **measure up to** nature's hydrocarbons.[5] Yet coal, oil, and gas are formed from the mineral residue of plants that once lived above ground. Suppose that, instead of **extracting** and burning fossil fuels, we burned plants growing on the surface. And suppose we constantly replanted the areas from which we harvested this living fuel, and then burned the replacement plants. Suddenly things would be very different. **Scarcity** would disappear, as fuel became endlessly renewable. So, too, would
30 the threat to the climate. Carbon would be released when the first plants burned, but an equivalent amount of carbon would be re-absorbed by the replacement plants. In effect, the same carbon would go around and around, as we extracted the energy we need by burning it over and over again.

What a good idea! And it is the same good idea that humanity relied upon until quite recently. In time, the fossil fuel waves—first coal, then oil, and now gas—may come to be seen as something of
35 a historical **blip**, just like so many other twentieth-century phenomena. But could we really meet our energy needs today by burning plants? We could.

A ton of straw,[6] when biologically converted from cellulose[7] to bioethanol,[8] will produce 300 liters of vehicle fuel. Two tons of dry wood will produce as much electricity as one ton of coal, oil, or gas. Not as good, you may think, but there is more to the story. Power generation produces twice as
40 much heat as electricity. At present, however, electricity is produced in huge power stations sited for easy access to fossil fuel supplies. These stations cannot use the heat that they produce so it is simply wasted. Up to 20 percent of the electricity these stations produce is also wasted through

overproduction to meet demand peaks, and friction during the long-distance journeys around grids.[9]

Plants, however, can grow anywhere, so bioenergy power stations could be located near the
45 settlements they would serve. Biofuel could be fed into furnaces as demand required. Numerous
small generating stations could capture the heat they gave off and pipe it to surrounding
communities. Power plants such as these can burn any kind of biomass. Wood produced from the
short-rotation cutting back[10] of fast-growing trees works best, but long grasses will also do. All you
need is the land to grow the plants. Where would that come from?

50 Before the era of mass fossil fuel use, Britain devoted about one-third of its land surface to
growing fuel. Recovery of that land, together with existing woodland, for biomass production could
enable Britain to meet its entire electricity needs, and much of its heat energy besides. The **fiscal**
restructuring of its energy market would **swiftly** direct energy distributors toward the new fuel of
choice.

55 Farmers could transform themselves into energy heroes merely by changing their crop.
Conservationists would see tree cover in places like Britain, currently lower than almost anywhere
else in Europe, return at last to respectable levels. The **ravaged** rural economies in many countries
would be boosted by the creation of tens of thousands of new jobs in forestry, transportation, and
power plant operation.

60 Will it happen? Saving the world may not be a priority among nations, but it should be.

This reading was adapted from *Let's Set the Countryside on Fire (Alternative Energy Sources)*
by David Cox © 2001 New Statesman, Ltd. All rights reserved. Published in *New Statesman's Supplement*.

[1] **Gulf Stream** a warm ocean current that flows from the Gulf of Mexico through the Straits of Florida then north
      and northeast to merge with the North Atlantic Ocean
[2] **polar ice caps** the areas above the north and south poles of the Earth that are permanently covered with ice
[3] **methane** an odorless, colorless, flammable gas used as a fuel
[4] **solar panel** flat board containing a group of connected cells that absorb sunlight to produce energy
[5] **hydrocarbons** organic materials that contain only carbon and hydrogen, e.g., methane
[6] **straw** grain stalks used as animal bedding and food or for weaving into mats and baskets
[7] **cellulose** the main substance of the cell walls of most plants
[8] **bioethanol** a type of liquid, which can be used as fuel, produced from biofuel (processed plants)
[9] **grids** networks of cables and power stations used to transmit electricity
[10] **short-rotation cutting back** process of harvesting plants that grow and mature quickly enough to be able to be
      harvested and replanted in a short space of time, usually a few years

A How much do you remember about the reading? For each question or statement, choose the best answer.

1 Which statement best expresses the author's attitude to alternatives to fossil fuels?
   a. He favors hydro, wind, and solar power.
   b. He favors the use of plants to produce energy.
   c. He thinks we should continue using fossil fuels.
   d. He feels nuclear energy is the most promising.
2 Coal, oil, and gas are formed from _____.
   a. the sun heating the earth
   b. unknown underground processes
   c. the mineral residues of plants
   d. mainly prehistoric animals and dinosaurs
3 Which of the following is NOT mentioned as a danger involved with global warming?
   a. Arctic and Antarctic animals will die out.
   b. The Gulf Stream will be diverted.
   c. The polar ice caps will melt.
   d. Forests will catch fire.
4 How are plants superior to fossil fuels as fuel?
   a. They can be turned into gas.
   b. They are renewable.
   c. They release carbon when burned.
   d. They contain more energy by weight.
5 The author believes that biomass production could turn farmers into _____.
   a. businessmen
   b. economists
   c. scientists
   d. heroes

B Decide if the following statements about the reading are true (T) or false (F). If you check (✔) false, correct the statement to make it true.

	T	F
1 The author is of the opinion that we have no choice but to replace fossil fuels.		
2 Fossil fuels are becoming easier to find.		
3 Over 20 percent of the energy from electrical power plants is wasted due to mismanagement.		
4 The carbon dioxide released from burning plants would be reabsorbed by humans.		
5 Before fossil fuels came into use, one-third of Britain's land was devoted to growing fuel.		

C Critical Thinking

Discuss these questions with a partner.
1 Do you think that the ideas for producing alternative, renewable energy in the reading are realistic or idealistic? Explain your answer.
2 Some people think that global warming is the most serious environmental issue facing humans today. Do you agree? Why or why not?
3 The last sentence of the reading passage states that saving the world should be a priority among nations. Do you agree with this? Explain your answer.

Vocabulary Comprehension:
Words in Context

A Look at the following target vocabulary items from the reading. Use the strategies outlined on pages 66 and 126 to work out the meaning of each one from its context in the passage.

> devote   fossil fuels   intermittent   measure up to
> extract   scarcity   blip   fiscal   swiftly   ravaged

B Read the paragraph below and fill in the blanks using the vocabulary items from A. Be sure to use the correct form of each word.

Building Environmental Awareness

We are living in an era when environmental issues such as global warming are of great concern. The burning of **(1)**_____ that are **(2)**_____ from the Earth has resulted in huge amounts of carbon being released into the atmosphere. At the same time, forests are being **(3)**_____ by fires, meaning there are fewer trees available to absorb the carbon and recycle it into oxygen. In addition, our waterways are constantly being polluted by chemical residues from industry, and household detergents. The future safety of our water supply is uncertain and some countries may soon be faced with a(n) **(4)**_____ of clean water.

Some people believe this is just a climatic **(5)**_____ in the history of the Earth; others believe that people around the world need to **(6)**_____ more time and energy to environmental awareness. They believe that **(7)**_____ solutions are not the answer and that governments need to act **(8)**_____, and work continuously, to encourage people everywhere to take responsibility for the future of our planet. One obvious way to start cleaning up the planet would be to find alternative sources of fuel that **(9)**_____ the reliability of natural gas, petroleum, coal, and other fuels we have become dependent on. This could be prudent from a **(10)**_____ point of view as well; these fuels continue to rise in price with no ceiling in sight.

A For each word, study the different parts. Then write the part of speech and a simple definition. Use your knowledge of prefixes and suffixes, as well as your dictionary, to help you. Share your ideas with a partner.

Vocabulary	Part of Speech	Definition
1 emission	_____	_____
2 messenger	_____	_____
3 missive	_____	_____
4 submit	_____	_____
5 missile	_____	_____
6 permit	_____	_____
7 dismiss	_____	_____
8 remittance	_____	_____

B Complete the sentences below using the words from A. Be sure to use the correct form of each word.

1 After working on their project for months, it was finally good enough for the team of architects to _____ to their clients.
2 Many countries have strict regulations in order to control exhaust _____ from motor vehicles.
3 The defendant's _____, in which he apologized to the families of the victims of his crimes, was not well received; they wanted to hear a spoken apology.
4 Around the world, it is becoming increasingly common for smoking not to be _____ inside buildings.
5 Disorderly conduct led to the immediate _____ of the employee.
6 Many agree that world leaders must work together to prevent the continued development of nuclear _____, and other weapons of mass destruction.
7 Hiro will be able to pay his tuition when he receives a cash _____ from home.
8 The _____ arrived exactly on time with the envelope tucked safely under his jacket.

Vocabulary Skill:
The Root Word *mit*

In this chapter, you read the word "intermittent," which means "stopping and starting at intervals." This word is formed from the root "mit," also written as "mis," or "mes," which comes from the Latin word "mittere," meaning to "send," "let go," or "allow." This root is combined with prefixes and suffixes to form many other words in English.

Chapter 2: A Long Road to Cleaner Energy Sources

Before You Read:
Alternative Energies

A Answer the following questions.

1 Name some modern inventions that are causes of environmental pollution.
2 What is the "greenhouse effect"? Can you name any "greenhouse gases"? Do you know what role these play in global warming?
3 What other reasons are you aware of, besides global warming, for finding alternative energy sources?
4 In the future, do you think we will be able to use the same energy source to power cars as we do now? Why or why not?

B Compare your answers with a partner.

Reading Skill:
Previewing

Previewing is something good readers do when they first encounter new reading material. They ask themselves questions like these: *What is this about? What kind of text is this? What do I already know about it?* Previewing can involve skimming, scanning, and predicting to help us get acquainted with the reading passage.

A Take one minute to preview the reading passage. Think about the title, the subtitles, scan the passage for interesting information, and skim the beginning and ending paragraphs.

B Now discuss these questions about the reading passage with a partner.

1 What do you think the passage is about?
2 Where could you find this kind of an article?
3 What do you already know about this subject?
4 What interesting points did you notice?
5 Do you think you'll enjoy reading the passage?

C Try to predict which of the following topics will be discussed in the article. Check (✔) the ones you think you will read about.

☐ alternative energy sources   ☐ the need to increase coal production

☐ the latest luxury cars   ☐ cars that run on hydrogen fuel

☐ limited fossil fuel supplies   ☐ obstacles to hydrogen fuel technology

D Now read through the passage; then answer the questions that follow.

A Long Road to Cleaner Energy Sources

People waste energy constantly, even if unintentionally. According to the Texas Transportation Institute, drivers in the Washington area burn, on average, one quart[1] of fuel per person each workday just sitting in traffic jams. This waste has some serious **side effects**. That beautiful red and pink sky you sometimes see as the sun sets can be attributed to clouds of nitrogen oxides,[2] and other pollutants[3] from emissions, **mucking up** the atmosphere. Surely better, cleaner, and more efficient alternative energy sources must exist.

What is meant by the term "alternative energy source"?

When we think of energy, or fuel, for our homes and cars, we think of petroleum,[4] a fossil fuel processed from oil removed from the ground, of which we know there is a limited supply. But alternative fuels can be many things—the wind, sun, and water can all be used to create fuel. These alternative energies also share the distinction of being what we call renewable resources. Natural gas, propane,[5] and octane[6] can also be used to create energy, but they are not renewable, in that once they are consumed they are gone.

Is the threat of running out of petroleum real?

It has taken thousands, if not millions, of years to create the natural stores of petroleum we have now. We are using what is available at a much faster rate than it is being produced over time. The real controversy surrounding the amounts of petroleum we have is how much we need to keep **in reserve**, for future use. Most experts agree that by around 2025, the amount of petroleum we use will **reach a peak**, then production and availability will begin to seriously decline. This is not to say there will be no petroleum at this point, but it will become very difficult, and therefore expensive, to harvest.

Is that the most important reason to develop alternative fuel and energy sources?

There are two very clear reasons to do so. One is that whether we have sixty or six hundred years of fossil fuels left, we have to find other fuel sources eventually, so the sooner we start, the **better off** we will be. The other big argument is that when you burn fossil fuels, you release substances that have been **literally** trapped in the ground for a long time, which leads to some long-term negative effects, such as global warming and the greenhouse effect.

What are hydrogen fuel cells?

A fuel cell works like a battery in that it produces electricity. Unlike a battery, however, it does not store electricity; therefore, it needs a constant source of fuel. In a hydrogen fuel cell vehicle, for example, that fuel source is pressurized[7] hydrogen gas.

Where does hydrogen fuel come from?

Hydrogen is not a source material that you can extract, like oil. Instead, it is a byproduct of something else. One of the most readily available sources for hydrogen is natural gas. However, this leads us back to the problems associated with fossil fuels. Processing natural gas into hydrogen still creates carbon emissions (such as carbon dioxide), which are leading sources of greenhouse gases. The amount of carbon emissions created in this process is significantly less than emissions created in petroleum use, though.

Does hydrogen work like fossil fuels?

Most people are familiar with the electrolysis[8] of water where electricity is used to break water into hydrogen and oxygen. When children do this experiment in a lab, they usually burn the hydrogen gas, creating a very loud bang that results from the release of energy in hydrogen combustion.[9] The fuel cell takes that experiment, but works it backward. Instead of breaking down water into hydrogen and oxygen, the hydrogen and oxygen are combined to create electricity, and the byproducts are heat and water.

Will hydrogen work just like gasoline in our cars, and give us the same speed performance?

The power needed for our current vehicles is created when gasoline and air are combined to create combustion. As the **aforementioned** experiment shows, this same type of energy can be produced using hydrogen as fuel. The difficulty of **mass-producing** cars powered by hydrogen fuel cells is that hydrogen is a pressurized gas, not a liquid product like gasoline. One of the biggest **obstacles** is in developing easy-to-use "hydrogen stations," similar to our present-day gas stations. But because a hydrogen fuel cell car will produce zero emissions, they represent a comparatively positive impact on the environment.

What is stopping the development of more hydrogen fuel cell vehicles?

One of the main issues is the cost of the technology development. It will be some time before a hydrogen fuel cell vehicle will be available at a reasonable price. A second issue is the problem of creating a system of accessible hydrogen stations where drivers can refuel. There is also the physical problem of developing hydrogen fuel in an easy-to-deliver form. Two possibilities are a **compressed** gas, or a liquid that would need to be kept at a temperature of 20 degrees Kelvin[10] above absolute zero,[11] or minus 250 degrees Celsius. This sounds dangerous, but work is being done to make this environmentally friendly fuel as safe as gasoline.

This reading was taken from *Facing a Long Road to Cleaner Energy Sources* by Joseph Szadkowski, published March 14, 2002, in *The Washington Times*. Adapted with permission of *The Washington Times*. Copyright © 2002 News World Communications, Inc. Reprinted with permission of *The Washington Times*.

[1] **one quart** a unit of liquid measure equal to ¼ gallon or .946 liter
[2] **nitrogen oxides** chemically symbolized as NO_x; a group of colorless, odorless gases, all containing nitrogen and oxygen, which form as a byproduct of burning fuel, and act as environmental pollutants
[3] **pollutants** waste materials that cause harm to living organisms, and contaminate soil, air, and water
[4] **petroleum** a thick, flammable mixture of liquid, gas, and solid hydrocarbons extracted from the earth, processed, and separated into various substances and used to power cars, for heating, light, etc.
[5] **propane** a colorless gas found in natural gas and petroleum, used as a fuel
[6] **octane** a group of hydrocarbons found in petroleum and used as a fuel
[7] **pressurized** put or stored under a greater than normal pressure so as to allow a rapid, steady release
[8] **electrolysis** a chemical change caused by an electric current
[9] **combustion** a chemical change, usually induced by burning, that produces heat and light
[10] **Kelvin** a unit of absolute temperature, each unit being equal to one Celsius degree
[11] **absolute zero** the temperature at which there is absolutely no heat; equal to –273.15°C or –459.67°F

A How much do you remember from the reading? Choose the best answer for each question or statement.

1 Why is the reading passage entitled "A Long Road to Cleaner Energy Sources"?
   a. because cleaner energy sources allow vehicles to run longer
   b. because cleaner energy sources are likely to be used by vehicles on roads
   c. because it may take a long time before cleaner energy sources are available
   d. because cleaner energy sources will be used for a long time
2 The writer claims that drivers stuck in traffic jams in _____ waste, on average, one quart of fuel per day.
   a. Texas
   b. the Transportation Institute
   c. the mud
   d. the Washington area
3 An "alternative energy source" is _____.
   a. renewable
   b. in limited supply
   c. processed from natural gas
   d. processed from oil
4 After 2025, petroleum will become increasingly expensive to _____.
   a. burn   **b.** harvest   **c.** transport   **d.** store
5 One reason for developing alternative fuel sources is _____.
   a. to use less energy
   b. to save money
   c. to protect the environment
   d. to drive more efficiently

B Complete the sentences with information from the reading. Write no more than three words for each answer.

1 Around 2025, most experts agree that petroleum use will _____.
2 Hydrogen fuel cells are energy sources fed by pressurized _____.
3 The most common source of hydrogen is _____.
4 The advantage of using hydrogen fuel over fossil fuel is that it creates zero
   _____.
5 The development of hydrogen fuel cell vehicles is slow because of the cost of _____.

C Critical Thinking

Discuss these questions with a partner.
1 What do you imagine a hydrogen-powered vehicle would look like?
2 Can you envisage how one of these vehicles would work, and how refueling stations would work?
3 Do you think that the concept of using hydrogen fuel cells is a realistic one? Why or why not?

Vocabulary Comprehension:
Word Definitions

A Look at the list of words and phrases from the reading. Match each one with a definition on the right.

1 side effects _____
2 mucking up _____
3 in reserve _____
4 reach a peak _____
5 better off _____
6 literally _____
7 aforementioned _____
8 mass-producing _____
9 obstacles _____
10 compressed _____

a. attain the highest level of usage or intensity
b. state of being more prosperous than before
c. pressed together so as to use less space
d. secondary effects of something, usually unpleasant
e. in the strictest sense; having the most exact meaning
f. manufacturing in large quantities
g. things that prevent or hinder progress
h. for use if and when needed
i. discussed above, or earlier
j. damaging; ruining

B Complete the paragraph using most of the vocabulary from A—there is one word that is not used. Be sure to use the correct form of each word.

Protect the Environment; Protect Ourselves

Have you ever considered how environmental pollution might be affecting our bodies? Pollutants in the air can **(1)**_____ be absorbed by our skin, or inhaled through our noses. The **(2)**_____ of this can be very obvious, for example, pimples and skin complaints. Other people suffer from serious bronchial disorders such as asthma, especially those who live in industrial cities where smoke and gases can be seen coming out of factory chimneys, and **(3)**_____ the atmosphere daily. At certain times, when emissions from these factories **(4)**_____, people can become very ill, and must ensure they have plenty of medication **(5)**_____. Although drug companies now **(6)**_____ various medications to deal with both of the **(7)**_____ conditions, many people say the only way they can be **(8)**_____ health-wise is by moving out of the city, and into an area with fewer factories. Of course, this is not always possible, one obvious **(9)**_____ being finding employment in another area.

A For each word, study the different parts. Then write the part of speech and a simple definition. Use your knowledge of word roots, suffixes, and your dictionary to help you. Share your ideas with a partner.

Vocabulary Skill:
The Prefix *ob-*

Vocabulary	Part of Speech	Definition
1 opponent	_____	_____
2 obstruct	_____	_____
3 optimistic	_____	_____
4 objectionable	_____	_____
5 oppression	_____	_____
6 obligatory	_____	_____
7 obnoxious	_____	_____
8 observatory	_____	_____
9 obtrusive	_____	_____
10 obviously	_____	_____

In this chapter you read the word "obstacle," which begins with the prefix "ob-," meaning "toward" or "against." This prefix, also written as "op-," is very common and is used with nouns, verbs, adjectives, and adverbs to form many words in English.

B Complete each sentence below using the words from A. Be sure to use the correct form of each word. More than one answer may be possible.

1 Francesca seemed to be unaware that her moody behavior every morning was considered to be quite _____ by everyone else in the office.

2 Misha _____ had to move to another apartment after the building she was living in caught fire.

3 Even though Sebastian was beaten by his _____ in the tennis finals, he remains _____ about his chances of winning the golf tournament.

4 Our new house will have an _____ on the top floor so we can study the stars.

5 The witness was fined for providing the police with the wrong information, and in doing so _____ the course of justice.

6 Some of Karl's colleagues find his approach to dealing with problems to be highly _____; others think he is trying to be helpful.

7 In order to apply to this university, it is _____ that you attend an interview.

8 As a result of his _____ manner, Jim only lasted one afternoon working as a waiter.

9 After many years of tolerating government _____, the people voted for a leader who promised them the freedom of a true democracy.

Real Life Skill:
Using a Thesaurus

A thesaurus is a vocabulary reference book that gives lists of synonyms (words that have similar meanings), and antonyms (words that have opposite meanings). It also contains groups of words related to important concepts. A thesaurus is a useful tool to help expand and enrich your vocabulary, and give more variety to your writing. However, as it does not contain definitions, you should always check the exact meaning and nuance in your dictionary before using a new word.

A Look at the following sentence. Then read the entries from a thesaurus.

One of the biggest *obstacles* in developing alternative energy sources is the lack of government support.

obstacle *noun* bar, barricade, barrier, hindrance, impediment, obstruction, snag. See DIFFICULTY, OPPOSITION. *Ant:* See AID, COOPERATION
opposition *noun* **1.** resistance, rivalry. See RESIST. **2.** antagonism, contradiction, contrariness. *Ant:* See SUPPORT
difficulty *noun* **1.** hardship, rigor. *Ant:* See EASY. **2.** clash, conflict, confrontation, contention, discord, dissent, faction, disharmony, war. See CONFLICT

B Use the thesaurus entries to rewrite the sentence, substituting two different words for *obstacle*. Use your dictionary to check the exact meaning and nuance of the words you chose.

1 _____

2 _____

C Read the following sentence, then look at the thesaurus entry beneath it.

More investment would ensure the *swift* development of new sources of energy.

swift *adjective* expeditious, fast, fleet, quick, rapid, speedy. See FAST
fast *adjective* **1.** brief, hasty, hurried, quick, short, speedy, swift. **2.** clinging, firm, secure, tenacious, tight. See FREE, TIGHTEN

D Circle all the words in the thesaurus entry that can be used in place of the word *swift* in the sentence. Use your dictionary to check your answers. Share your ideas with a partner.

What Do You Think?

1 Do you think large companies are doing enough to prepare for the day when there will be no more petroleum?
2 What are some interesting examples of alternative energies you have seen where you live?
3 Do you tend to waste energy? If yes, how? If no, how are you careful to save it?
4 Are you optimistic or pessimistic about the future of energy? Explain your answer.

Fluency Strategy: *PARCER*

The reading fluency strategy **PARCER** helps you break a reading into smaller parts in order to help you increase your comprehension. PARCER stands for: **P**review, **A**sk, **R**ead, **C**heck, **E**valuate, and **R**elate.

Preview

Preview "Trans Fats in Trouble" by reading the first paragraph, the first sentence in paragraphs 2–4, and the final paragraph.

Trans Fats in Trouble

There is a great deal of fuss revolving around *trans fats* these days. Much of this can be attributed to a 2006 medical study, validated by the medical community, correlating a high intake of trans fats with a greater chance of heart disease. In studies, trans fats have also been linked to obesity, cancer, and other health conditions, although this has been neither proven nor ruled out by the scientific community.

Compositionally, trans fats are slightly different than other fats.

Some countries have begun to restrict the use of trans fats.

A trans fat ban in New York's 24,000 restaurants has been generating a lot of interest.

While there are some examples of companies voluntarily restricting trans fats, it doesn't appear that restaurants in New York are willing to switch on their own. By contrast, restaurants in the small city of Tiburon, California, voluntarily agreed to eliminate oils containing trans fats. Philadelphia, like New York, has resorted to the law to eliminate trans fats from the city's kitchens. States considering banning trans fats in the future include Massachusetts, Maryland, California, and Vermont.

Ask

Ask yourself what questions you have after previewing "Trans Fats in Trouble." Make a list of the questions.

1 _____

2 _____

3 _____

Read

After you have previewed the text and asked questions, you are now ready to read.

Trans Fats in Trouble

There is a great deal of fuss revolving around *trans fats* these days. Much of this can be attributed to a 2006 medical study, validated by the medical community,
5 correlating a high intake of trans fats with a greater chance of heart disease. In studies, trans fats have also been linked to obesity, cancer, and other health conditions, although this has been neither
10 proven nor ruled out by the scientific community.

Compositionally, trans fats are slightly different than other fats. They are created in a process that is more than 100 years old, whereby oil is chemically changed through heating and by the addition of hydrogen atoms. The resulting oil is called *hydrogenated oil*, and it contains a high
15 level of trans fats. Hydrogenated oil lasts longer than natural oil and, because it melts at a higher temperature, is more useful in baking and frying. Until recently, trans fats have been abundant in staples such as bread products, including donuts, cookies, and crackers. They give food a rich flavor and texture, but are much cheaper than butter.

Some countries have begun to restrict the use of trans fats. Denmark was the first, in March of
20 2003, to restrict hydrogenated oils in foods. Later that year, Canada introduced similar legislation controlling hydrogenated oils. In 2005, the Canadian government made it mandatory to list amounts of trans fats on food labels. The United States also requires such labeling to alert consumers to the presence of trans fats.

A trans fat ban in New York's 24,000 restaurants has been generating a lot of interest.
25 Restaurants will be forced to adhere to strict rules concerning trans fats; no more than one half gram will be allowed in any food product. Proponents of the ban say trans fats account for 18,000 deaths of people under 65 every year. Critics of the law feel that the government shouldn't intrude into what should be an issue of personal freedom and choice. In addition, some of the alternatives to hydrogenated oils, for example palm oil, are also considered to be
30 unhealthy.

While there are some examples of companies voluntarily restricting trans fats, it doesn't appear that restaurants in New York are willing to switch on their own. By contrast, restaurants in the small city of Tiburon, California, voluntarily agreed to eliminate oils containing trans fats. Philadelphia, like New York, has resorted to the law to eliminate trans fats from the city's
35 kitchens. States considering banning trans fats in the future include Massachusetts, Maryland, California, and Vermont.

Check

Check your reading comprehension by answering the following questions.

1 What is the author's main purpose in writing this article?
  a. to warn readers not to eat trans fats
  b. to inform readers about a movement against trans fats
  c. to explain why trans fats aren't very dangerous
  d. to convince readers to join the fight against trans fats

2 Which health condition have trans fats not been linked to?
  a. heart disease
  b. obesity
  c. cancer
  d. eye disease

3 Which statement is NOT true about hydrogenated oils?
  a. They can be used to make bread.
  b. They are often used to fry foods.
  c. They are more expensive than butter.
  d. They are chemically changed through heating.

4 Where were trans fats first restricted?
  a. Denmark
  b. Canada
  c. New York
  d. Philadelphia

5 Which argument do critics of New York's trans fat ban make?
  a. Trans fats account for 18,000 deaths per year.
  b. Restaurants can't find alternative oils.
  c. The government shouldn't limit individuals' freedom of choice.
  d. Palm oil is actually a kind of hydrogenated oil.

6 Where did restaurants voluntarily stop using trans fats?
  a. Denmark
  b. Tiburon
  c. Chicago
  d. Canada

7 What is probably true about the movement to restrict trans fats in the United States?
  a. The movement seems to have come to a stop.
  b. Only cities and not states are considering restricting trans fats.
  c. Bans are being considered in more areas.
  d. Most places have already banned trans fats.

Evaluate

Now, evaluate how well you understood by correcting the answers to the reading comprehension questions. For each question you miss, review why you missed it.

Relate

In the final stage of PARCER, you relate what you read to what you already know about the topic. Make notes below showing what you already knew about this topic. Discuss the reading with a partner, and talk about what else you know about the topic.

Self Check

Write a short answer to each of the following questions.

1. Have you ever used the PARCER strategy before?

   Yes   No   I'm not sure

2. Will you practice PARCER in your reading outside of English class?

   Yes   No   I'm not sure

3. Do you think PARCER is helpful? Why or why not?

   _____

   _____

4. Which of the six reading passages in units 7–9 did you enjoy most? Why?

   _____

   _____

5. Which of the six reading passages in units 7–9 was easiest? Which was most difficult? Why?

   _____

   _____

6. What do you know now that you didn't know before studying units 7–9?

   _____

   _____

7. What else would you like to know about any of those topics?

   _____

   _____

8. How will you try to improve your reading fluency from now on?

   _____

   _____

   _____

Review Reading 5: *Changes in the Solar System*

Fluency Practice

Time yourself as you read through the passage. Try to read as fluently as you can. Record your time in the Reading Rate Chart on page 240. Then answer the questions on page 169.

Changes in the Solar System

It would certainly be reassuring to think that our solar system has always been and will always continue to be the same. It can be surprising,
5 worrying, and even spine-chilling to contemplate past and future changes involving the sun and the planets. Since the present solar system coalesced about 4.6 billion years ago,
10 many physical changes, and also changes in our understanding, have taken place.

At the heart of our solar system is the sun. At its birth, the sun shone with about only 40 percent of its current strength. Scientists have deduced that the sun is about halfway through
15 its long life. As the sun gradually increased in power, it brought about dramatic changes in some of the planets near it, with the exception of the first planet Mercury, whose dreary surface has always been nearly without moisture, as images sent back to Earth from the Mariner 10 space probe testify to.

The second planet from the sun is Venus. Lurking beneath its constant cover of clouds is
20 a deadly environment of 460 degrees Celsius and pressure that is 90 times that of Earth. It has an atmosphere that is laden with poisonous chemicals. However, scientists now think that it might not always have been that way. Venus might once have been covered in oceans, with reasonable temperatures and may even have supported life. As the young sun grew in strength, it could have heated Venus up, causing more and more water vapor to be
25 released into the atmosphere. This could have accelerated the warming process through the "greenhouse effect." The greenhouse effect can warm up a planet in the same way that the glass roof and walls of a greenhouse make the inside of the house warmer than the outside. Water vapor and other gases act as windows of glass around a planet, causing it to heat up. According to this theory, the heat had caused all the water on Venus to disappear, and the sun
30 continued to heat the planet until today, when the possibility of life on the surface of Venus is completely untenable.

Earth, the third planet from the sun, has also undergone changes over the course of the life of the solar system. Up until 650 million years ago, there were long periods of time when the water on the surface of the Earth was frozen into a sheet of ice with few openings to the oceans below. At other times, due to the placement of the continents, there was almost no ice, not even at the north or south poles.

As the sun continues to get hotter over the long term, the Earth will continue to heat up as well. As temperatures are nudged slowly upward, more water vapor will be released into the atmosphere, creating a more potent greenhouse effect. In about 500 million years, scientists expect temperatures to be perilously high and out of control, and Earth will follow the same path as Venus.

Mars, the fourth planet from the sun, is naturally cooler than Earth. Nighttime temperatures plunge to well below minus 100 degrees Celsius. Robots dispatched to Mars have sent back images that suggest there could be water on Mars. Some scientists believe that there were once oceans on Mars. They think that Mars was once warmed by the greenhouse effect, thanks to gases from its now dormant volcanoes. Scientists have suggested releasing greenhouse gases into the atmosphere of Mars in order to warm it up. Some have estimated that such a transformation of Mars could be achieved in just several hundred years.

Because of the great distances involved, we know less about the remaining planets in our solar system: Jupiter, Saturn, Uranus, and Neptune. Some of them have been perused by space probes that have sent back teasing images that have opened scientists' eyes to some new facts. For example, when the probe Voyager II flew by Jupiter's moon Io, it sent back images of seven active volcanoes. They were the first active volcanoes found anywhere other than on Earth. An additional ring was discovered around Saturn, and a new ring was discovered around the planet Uranus. At least one new moon was discovered orbiting Saturn as well.

Schoolchildren have long been taught that Pluto, discovered in 1930, was the ninth and final planet of the solar system. Well, in 2007, scientists decided to demote Pluto from the status of planet to that of "dwarf planet." It was recently discovered that Pluto is actually much smaller than had been previously thought. Other objects that are Pluto's size have never been called planets. Additionally, Pluto's strange orbit is not at all similar to that of the other eight planets. This will result in a slight change in many textbooks on the subject of the solar system.

To sum up, it seems that physical changes to our solar system take place gradually, over millions of years. However, in the realm of human perception, we have recently seen volcanoes on Io and a moon of Saturn "appear" and watched a planet "disappear" in our own lifetime. The solar system has always been and will probably always be an exciting and dynamic place that is full of surprising changes.

866 words   Time taken _____

Reading Comprehension

1 What is the author's purpose in writing this article?
  a. to warn the reader about coming changes
  b. to convince the reader to help prevent changes
  c. to inform the reader about a variety of changes
  d. to amuse the reader with humorous stories of changes

2 Which statement about the sun is true?
  a. It is stronger now than it used to be.
  b. It is 40 percent weaker now than it used to be.
  c. It is most of the way through its life.
  d. It was strongest when it was first created.

3 Which of these statements about Venus is a theory and not a proven fact?
  a. It has temperatures of 460 degrees Celsius.
  b. It used to have oceans on it.
  c. It is the second planet from the sun.
  d. Its surface has 90 times the pressure of Earth's atmosphere.

4 Which of these can be a cause of the greenhouse effect?
  a. glass in the atmosphere of a planet
  b. too little heat coming from the sun
  c. heat coming from underground
  d. water vapor in the atmosphere of a planet

5 Which planet was described as being almost completely covered in ice in the past?
  a. Mercury
  b. Venus
  c. Earth
  d. Mars

6 Why was Mars once warmer than it is today?
  a. It was warmed by the greenhouse effect.
  b. It was warmed by large oceans.
  c. It used to be closer to the sun.
  d. It was warmed by heat from volcanoes.

7 What piece of information was not mentioned as being learned from space probes?
  a. Io has active volcanoes.
  b. Uranus has a ring.
  c. Saturn has an additional moon.
  d. Pluto is not a planet.

8 What is probably true about a dwarf planet?
  a. It is warmer than an actual planet.
  b. It is smaller than an actual planet.
  c. It is older than an actual planet.
  d. It moves more quickly than an actual planet.

Review Reading 6: Green Energy

Fluency Practice

Time yourself as you read through the passage. Try to read as fluently as you can. Record your time in the Reading Rate Chart on page 240. Then answer the questions on page 172.

Green Energy

Many people are concerned with the world's continued dependence on petroleum and coal as energy sources. They are not "green" sources of energy, because they do not burn cleanly and
5   tend to muck up the environment with smoky residues. Also, they are not renewable, meaning that once they are used up, they are gone, and this will inevitably lead to scarcity. Another unfortunate side effect is the production of a
10 great deal of carbon dioxide, a gas which contributes to global warming through the greenhouse effect. For these and other reasons, people are devoting themselves to finding renewable, sustainable, green sources of energy.

One such green source of energy is solar power from solar panels. Solar panels are devices that
15 can absorb energy directly from the sun and convert it to electricity. Solar energy is useful in places without access to electric power lines, for example, in places far away from cities and towns or in space. There are, however, certain drawbacks. On Earth, the power is intermittent, because the sun doesn't shine at night. Also, solar energy doesn't measure up to other sources of energy in terms of power.

20 People in rural areas of China's Xinjiang Province are finding solar energy to be an excellent alternative to coal. Many of the shepherds there move from place to place with their sheep, far from electric power lines. Several large companies are helping people to buy solar panels. They are small and light, so they are easy to travel with. They also provide enough energy to run a small heater, a radio, a TV, or a couple of light bulbs. China currently uses two billion tons of coal annually; this is
25 equal to the coal use of India, Russia, and the United States combined. Green energy sources such as solar power are being welcomed as a way of cutting down on air pollution.

Gasoline is a petroleum-based fuel that is hard to imagine giving up. It is literally the lifeblood of modern society. People do not want to give up driving automobiles, and this has been a major obstacle to ending the world's gasoline addiction. Unfortunately, some analysts fear that world oil

30　production will soon reach a peak and then go into a sharp decline. Butanol, ethanol, and biodiesel are fuels made from plants. They are renewable, green alternatives to gasoline. They can be made from a variety of plants, including corn, soybeans, and others. Many people feel they can help ease the world's gasoline addiction. Others are concerned that corn and soybeans that could be used to feed the world, will instead be dedicated to making automobile fuel.

35　Several automobile manufacturers are now mass-producing so-called "flex-fuel" cars that can burn a variety of fuels in addition to gasoline. Nearly 20 percent of all new cars sold in Brazil are of the flex-fuel type. Drivers claim that they are better off with a flex-fuel car, as they are able to save a significant amount of money at the gas pump. The car can run entirely on, for example, ethanol, although it also keeps a small tank of gasoline in reserve to help start the car on cold days. Most
40　filling stations in Brazil offer both gasoline and ethanol. In other countries, green fuel can still be hard to find, so flex-fuel cars are still just a blip on the radar.

At present, little more than one percent of the world's power needs are met by wind power. Wind power is produced by wind farms: large areas on land or sea with evenly spaced turbines. Turbines are similar to windmills, usually with three arms that spin swiftly when the wind blows and thereby
45　create energy. Wind energy is clean and renewable. It does have certain drawbacks, however. It is generally very expensive to set up a wind farm. Wind farms can involve cutting down lots of trees. Furthermore, wind turbines do not produce as much energy when compared to other types of power plants.

Wind power is currently the fastest-growing renewable energy technology in Scotland. Recently,
50　the world's largest wind turbine was installed off the Scottish coast. Each of its three rotating blades is 126 meters long. Scotland has some particularly windy areas, and some of its ocean-based turbines run as much as 96 percent of the time. Scotland's Black Law Wind Farm was built on land ravaged by an open coal mine that was no longer used. The land was converted back to a wetland habitat for birds. This is possible because wind farms only utilize about one percent of the
55　land for the bases of the turbines.

It seems clear that a new era for green energy has begun. The aforementioned examples in China, Brazil, and Scotland seem to have something in common. In each case, the particular character of the location dictates the success of its experiment with green energy. In China, it is the lifestyle of the nomads. In Brazil, it is that country's abundance of ethanol. In Scotland, it is the naturally
60　windy land and sea. Perhaps the era of the dominance of fossil fuels will slowly end this way, as each individual locale chooses the green energy source that is the most suitable.

867 words　　　Time taken _____

Reading Comprehension

1 What is the author's main purpose in writing this article?
    a. to introduce several green energy sources with examples of their use
    b. to show how fossil fuel users are slow to change to green energy sources
    c. to inform the reader that new technologies are used in surprising places
    d. to convince the reader to stop using fossil fuels

2 Which negative point about fossil fuels does the author NOT make?
    a. They pollute the environment.
    b. They allow certain countries to control others.
    c. They are not renewable.
    d. They contribute to global warming.

3 Where would solar energy be least appropriate?
    a. in a satellite orbiting the Earth
    b. in the middle of the Sahara desert
    c. in an apartment in a big city
    d. on a ship in the middle of the ocean

4 Before they got solar power, how did the shepherds probably stay warm?
    a. They stayed near the power lines.
    b. They burned coal in stoves.
    c. They kept plenty of sheep in their homes.
    d. They moved to warmer places.

5 What are butanol, ethanol, and biodiesel?
    a. They are types of plants.
    b. They are types of gasoline.
    c. They are types of fuel.
    d. They are types of flex-fuel cars.

6 Why do flex-fuel cars carry a tank of gasoline?
    a. because ethanol can be hard to find
    b. in case the filling station doesn't have any
    c. to help other drivers in need
    d. to help start the engine on cold days

7 Why does the author give the example of the Black Law Wind Farm?
    a. to show that only one percent of the world's energy is wind energy
    b. to show that coal mines are no longer necessary
    c. to show that coal mines are usually windy places
    d. to show that some wind farms do little or no damage to the environment

8 Which of these statements would the author most likely agree with?
    a. Green energy sources aren't powerful enough to be useful.
    b. Green energy sources are best used in faraway places.
    c. Appropriate energy sources need to be chosen for each place.
    d. Fossil fuels will stop being used in the next few years.

Getting Ready

Discuss the following questions with a partner.

1 What civilization developed the language pictured above? Do you think it is still used today?
2 What can cause a language to "die"? Do you know any "dead" languages?
3 Is the number of people who speak your native language growing or diminishing?
4 Can you name any indigenous languages spoken today? Where are they spoken?

Chapter 1: The Exodus of Languages

Before You Read:
Lost Languages

A Answer the following questions.

1 What is the relationship between language and culture? Do you think a culture can be lost if the language spoken within that culture is lost?
2 Are you aware of any endangered languages? Where is that language spoken? Why is it endangered?

B Discuss your answers with a partner.

Reading Skill:
Identifying Cause and Effect

> Words and phrases such as "because," "due to (the fact that)," "as a result," "so," and "therefore" are used to show cause and effect relationships; in other words, they signal that one thing (the cause) makes another thing (the effect) happen. Recognizing how this language works can help you to better understand and organize the information in a reading passage.

A Read the following statement pairs. Identify which one is the cause, and which is the effect.

1 a. The Internet is an American invention.
   b. Most of the information found on it is in English.
2 a. Many people learn English so they can migrate to America.
   b. America has the world's biggest economy.
3 a. The English language is spoken differently in various parts of the world.
   b. Migration of native English speakers led to a divergence of the language.

B Look at examples of how cause and effect can be joined in a sentence. Then, with a partner, make similar sentences using the other sentence pairs from A. Use *because* and *due to (the fact that)* to talk about the cause; use *as a result, so,* and *therefore* to talk about the effect.

> • Most of the information found on the Internet is in English *because* it is an American invention.
> • The Internet is an American invention. *As a result,* most of the information found on it is in English.

C Scan through the reading passage and find the cause or effect for each sentence below. Write the information on the line. Share your answers with a partner. Then read the passage again and answer the questions that follow.

1 a. The Inuktitut dialects had a common core.
   b. _____
2 a. Languages seem to be converging to a smaller number.
   b. _____
3 a. About half the languages used worldwide are endangered or on the brink of extinction.
   b. _____
4 a. Colloquial phrases are pleasant to the ear.
   b. _____
5 a. Natural disasters, war, and famine cause people to migrate to different areas.
   b. _____

The Exodus of Languages

"I have made an impression on this first group of Inuit people. My arrival to arctic Canada was a cold one, but I'm warmed thinking of the events that will someday be stories to tell. The Inuit were surprised
5 *to see my white skin and they told rather humorous jokes about me in Inuktitut.[1] They stopped laughing though, when they heard my rebuttal in a dialect of their own tongue. I think I will enjoy this journey from Greenland to Siberia."*

10 It is doubtful that Knud Rasmussen[2] made such a diary entry on his travels, but these events did take place in the 1920s. Inuit communities throughout arctic Canada understood the Inuktitut spoken by the Greenland-born Rasmussen. Since the dialects had a common core that could be understood, the diverse dialects show a
15 common origin, or the same mother language. This **divergence** of language contrasts with the **converging** of languages today that is endangering languages worldwide.

Languages seem to be converging to a smaller number, as languages like English seem to eat up regional ones. The three languages used the most by first language speakers today are Mandarin Chinese, English, and Spanish. English is being used more and more as the main language
20 for business, science, and popular culture. Evidence suggests that the dominant languages are squeezing out[3] the local tongues of various regions in the world. Linguists estimate that of the approximately 6,500 languages worldwide, about half are endangered or on the brink of extinction. According to some linguists, the estimated rate of language extinction is one lost in the world every two weeks. If this sounds like the world is losing a species, in a way it is.

25 When a language is lost, meaning no living person can teach another, a world **perspective** is lost. Some foreign language expressions simply cannot be translated. **Colloquial** phrases are pleasant to the ear, not only because they are familiar, but also because they reflect a unique aspect of a culture. Aboriginal languages in Canada and other countries such as Australia have words that reflect a way of life that is connected closely to the Earth. There are fifty different
30 words that mean "snow" in one Canadian native language, and in the Eastern Arrernte language of Central Australia, the word *nyimpe* translates to "the smell of rain."

These various views of the world are essential for science to help create new ways of understanding and new connections between the human and the natural world. Botanists[4] have discovered new species of plants by digging deeper into the meaning of Aboriginal names
35 of flora that seemed identical. Archaeologists are also using languages to track migrations of historical cultures. University of Waterloo Professor Robert Park knows that the ancestral origins of the present Canadian Inuit communities can be partly explained by the language spoken by

the Inuit today. The Thule[5] culture spoke the same Inuktitut of present-day Inuit to a greater or lesser degree. Dr. Park knows the prehistoric Thule migrated east from Alaska and eventually to
40 Labrador and Greenland by the evidence of the mutually **intelligible**, living dialects of today.

Languages are much like living creatures that become endangered when numbers dwindle. Local natural disasters, war, and famine[6] are some of the reasons languages slip through the cracks[7] of history. The language that bore the different daughter languages for the Eskimo and Inuit was almost **wiped out** after World War II. The mother language, Proto-Eskimo Aleut,[8] was under siege[9]
45 when the Aleut people were forced to leave their land. Fortunately, some Proto-Eskimo Aleut, which originated 6,000 to 8,000 years ago, is still spoken. Languages also become endangered when they are not passed on to children or when a **metropolitan** language dominates over others.

Some groups are taking action in preserving languages. **Revival** of languages such as Irish is gaining ground. There is an Irish-language television channel and the largest age group of
50 fluent Irish speakers is now the under-twenty-fives. International organizations are mobilizing for the cause as well: UNESCO[10] has mapped the *Atlas of the World's Languages in Danger of Disappearing* in 1996. The editor of the atlas believes the preservation of moribund languages, which are spoken only by the elderly, should be a priority since they are **on the brink of** extinction.

55 Preservation can occur in two ways. First, linguists can study moribund languages and seek to preserve the components of the language: the sounds, the vocabulary, the grammar, and the traditions. The second way is to teach children the language and have linguists advise on language maintenance. An example of this latter method is the Maori language of New Zealand. It has seen a **resurgence** in the number of speakers from the 1960s and 1970s when there was
60 virtually no parent-to-child transmission. New Zealand has since set up "language nests" in early childhood centers to teach children Maori, exposing 100,000 children to their native tongue so far.

For many linguists, preserving endangered languages is vital; a loss in global languages means a loss of the diverse ideas and cultures those languages once held.

This reading was adapted from the article *The Exodus of Languages: How the loss of languages is much like the loss of a species* by Jessica Kwik © 1998. Reprinted from Imprint Online with permission from the author.

1 **Inuktitut** language of the Inuit people
2 **Knud Rasmussen** Danish explorer and ethnologist who extensively researched Inuit culture
3 **squeezing out** forcing out
4 **botanists** people who specialize in the study of plants
5 **Thule** /tʊli/ an ancestral population of today's Inuit named after a place in northern Greenland
6 **famine** extreme lack of food in a region
7 **slip through the cracks** pass by virtually unnoticed
8 **Aleut** /ælu:t/ a language spoken by natives of an island chain southwest of Alaska
9 **under siege** under attack from others
10 **UNESCO** United Nations Educational, Scientific, and Cultural Organization

A The following questions are all about the reading. Answer each one using the information you have read. Try not to look back at the reading for the answers.

1 What does the author think is happening to the number of languages in the world?
2 What are the three most widely spoken languages in the world today?
3 In addition to language, what is lost when speakers of a particular language die off?
4 What word does one Canadian language have fifty different words for?
5 What is an example of an action that can be taken to preserve a language?

B Decide if the following statements about the reading are true (T), false (F), or not given (NG). If you check (✔) false, correct the statement to make it true.

	T	F	NG
1 Knud Rasmussen was born in Canada.			
2 Language like English "eat up" smaller ones.			
3 Languages are like living creatures in that they become endangered when numbers increase.			
4 UNESCO has created a list of all the world's endangered languages.			
5 The native language of Hawaii has been lost forever.			

C Critical Thinking

Discuss these questions with a partner.
1 What do you think the advantages would be if everyone spoke the same language? What about the disadvantages?
2 Do you think that English will continue to be a globally dominant language, or will there be a resurgence in aboriginal languages?

Vocabulary Comprehension:
Odd Word Out

A For each group, circle the word that does not belong. The words in *italics* are vocabulary items from the reading.

1	*divergence*	agreement	dissimilarity	difference
2	meeting	separating	*converging*	coming together
3	conversational	*colloquial*	informal	literary
4	outlook	*perspective*	view	inspiration
5	fathomable	understandable	*intelligible*	incomprehensible
6	eradicated	eliminated	exhibited	*wiped out*
7	urban	*metropolitan*	municipal	rural
8	*revival*	reduction	rebirth	comeback
9	*on the brink of*	verging on	bordering on	hanging on
10	*resurgence*	reactivation	depletion	recovery

B Complete the sentences using the words in *italics* from A. Be sure to use the correct form of the word.

1 As Kieron and I share the same _____ on this project, we were assigned to work on it together.

2 After many years of living in a small village, Arlen wanted a more _____ way of life.

3 Contrary to what this map shows, that road sign indicates that these two roads _____ into one about five kilometers from here.

4 Josh tried everything to _____ the bugs in his kitchen. In the end, he moved to another house.

5 After months of falling sales, the company CEO finally admitted that the company was _____ bankruptcy.

6 There has been a _____ of interest in Egyptology with the screening of two excellent documentaries on the mystery of Tutankhamun's death and the discovery of Queen Hatshepsut's mummy.

7 Many years ago, overseas phone connections were so poor that only parts of a conversation were _____.

8 It seems to me that language in the United States has become very _____. Students often talk to teachers as if they were friends, without any formality at all.

9 A huge _____ in views on how the school should be run brought about the resignation of both the principal and the vice-principal.

10 Some say that peace protests in the United States are indicative of a(n) _____ of political awareness among young people.

A Read each definition below. Adapt the noun used, and add the suffix *-al* to form the adjective for each one. Use your dictionary to help you with spellings.

1 having to do with *history* _____
2 related to *tribes* _____
3 pertaining to the *tropics* _____
4 related to *geography* _____
5 having to do with *mathematics* _____
6 related to *biology* _____
7 related to *culture* _____
8 pertaining to *tradition* _____
9 having to do with *psychology* _____
10 related to *nature* _____

B Now complete the paragraph below using the words from A. Be careful to use the correct form of each word.

Before I started at the university, I was confused as to what I wanted to study. I've always been interested in medicine, so I thought that a good basic course for me would be in **(1)**_____. However, the human mind also fascinates me, so I also considered looking into some aspects of **(2)**_____ studies. In addition to my curiosity related to these fields, I enjoy reading **(3)**_____ novels about past events, and I've always loved looking at maps and studying **(4)**_____. I have always been fascinated by the earth and its **(5)**_____ peoples, and imagined myself participating in a research class where we go on some kind of expedition, exploring newfound territories in the **(6)**_____ regions of the world, discovering unknown **(7)**_____, and their **(8)**_____ ways. I've dreamed about living with the people in a remote village, learning their language, customs, and how they use their **(9)**_____ environment to their advantage, while respecting and preserving it. After all, I believe that learning about how aboriginal societies live on the earth can teach us a lot about ecological preservation and conservation. Despite this wide array of interests, I ended up studying for a degree in math. I now spend my days working on formulas and **(10)**_____ equations to produce new energy sources that I hope will one day have a positive impact on our lives.

C Think of two more examples of nouns that can be changed to adjectives by using the suffix *-al*. Write a sentence using each. Share your ideas with a partner.

1 _____

2 _____

Vocabulary Skill:
The Suffix *-al*

In this chapter, you read the adjectives "regional," "aboriginal," and "ancestral." These adjectives are formed by adapting the noun form of the word and adding the suffix "-al." Many adjectives in English are formed this way. Knowing how this suffix works can help increase your vocabulary.

Chapter 2: *Life with the Tarahumaras*

**Before You
Read:**
Indigenous
Languages

A Answer the following questions.

1 Are there any indigenous people in your country? What do you know about
   them? Where and how do they live? What language do they speak?
2 Do you think that one day these people, along with their language and
   culture, will die out? Why?
3 Look at the title of the reading and quickly skim the reading. What do you
   know about the Tarahumara people?

B Discuss your answers with a partner.

Reading Skill:
Identifying Main and
Supporting Ideas

Paragraphs often
use supporting
ideas to give more
information about
the main idea
of a paragraph.
Supporting ideas
usually follow
the main idea.
Different types of
supporting ideas
include examples,
illustrations, facts,
reasons, etc.

A Write M beside the main idea and S beside supporting ideas.

Paragraph 4
_____ Copeland is collecting stories and myths that have been passed down
        from one generation of Tarahumaras to the next.
_____ One story he has recorded is about a figure very much like the elusive
        Bigfoot, or Sasquatch, of the northwestern United States.

Paragraph 7
_____ During the winter he sleeps in his truck, and in the summer next to the
        campfire in the way of the Tarahumaras.
_____ Entering the world of the Tarahumaras has been an arduous project
        for Copeland.
_____ To reach their homeland he must drive two and a half days from
        Houston, Texas, across highways, blacktop roads, and finally a thirteen-
        mile stretch of rugged trail that takes almost a day to maneuver.

Paragraph 8
_____ He experiences the simplicity of living in nature that he would otherwise
        only be able to read about.
_____ He sees a lot of beauty in the Tarahumaras' sense of sharing and
        concern for each other.
_____ For Copeland, the experience has not only been academically
        satisfying, but it also has enriched his life in several ways.

B Skim the paragraphs and check your answers with a partner.

**C Now read the article and complete the comprehension exercises that
follow.**

Life with the Tarahumaras

In a remote area of the Sierra Madre[1] in northern Mexico, an indigenous group of people called the Tarahumaras live in almost total isolation. Aside from owning some cooking **utensils** and farming equipment, the Tarahumaras exist
5 much as they did before the Spanish arrived in the 1600s. They live in caves or in huts made of stone and wood, and they eat what little they can grow on the dry, **rugged** land.

Ten years ago, linguist James Copeland entered the world of the Tarahumaras to study their language and culture.
10 Since then, he has been visiting the Tarahumaras three or four times a year, sometimes spending as much as a month with them. Part of his strategy when he embarked on this lifetime project was to learn to speak Tarahumara so that he could deal directly with the people. Learning Tarahumara
15 is no easy task since it is not a written language. "There are no language police," Copeland says. "Children are seldom corrected by their parents. They learn by observation of speech in context and by imitation."

Copeland **acquired** the language through his frequent exposure to it and by analyzing the grammar.
20 His linguistics skills and mastery of German, Spanish, French, and Russian, plus a partial knowledge of some twenty other languages, also helped. Drawing on his research, Copeland plans to produce a Tarahumara grammar book in English and perhaps one in Spanish. He is putting together a bibliography of all the linguistic research conducted so far on the Uto-Aztecan[2] languages, the group of thirty indigenous tongues to which Tarahumara belongs.

25 Copeland also is collecting stories and myths that have been passed down from one generation to the next. Many of the stories are being lost because they are not as well remembered. One story he has recorded is about a figure very much like the **elusive** Bigfoot, or Sasquatch[3], of the northwestern United States. In the Tarahumara version, the central character is either a big bear or a large hairy man who **descends on** a valley and steals an unmarried young woman. He hides her in a cave and they have
30 a baby, who is half-human and half-bear. The Tarahumaras eventually kill the bear by tricking him into eating poisonous vegetables. They also kill the centaur[4]-like baby and rescue the woman.

In addition to his research, Copeland is consulting with a group of government officials from the state of Chihuahua about producing a literacy[5] program for the Tarahumaras. Most of the 60,000 Tarahumaras are not literate even though many, to varying degrees, are bilingual in their native tongue and Spanish.
35 Copeland hopes to convince the officials that the Tarahumaras be taught to read in their native language, and in Spanish, up to the sixth grade. The Tarahumaras, unlike other indigenous peoples, are not in danger of extinction, but Copeland is not sure what effect the literacy program will have on their culture. Back in the 1600s, contact with the literate world caused some immediate changes in the culture. Since the Spaniards could not pronounce the tribe's real name, Raramuri, they called the people
40 Tarahumaras. Raramuri means "children of the sun god."

The idea to study the Tarahumaras came to Copeland in 1984, when he discovered that very little

research had been done on their language. He made contact with a tribe member through a social worker who worked with the Tarahumaras in the border town of Juarez, Mexico. At first, the tribe member, who had taken the Spanish name of Lorenzo Gonzalez, was very reluctant to cooperate. He
45 told Copeland that no amount of money could buy his language. But after Copeland explained to him what he intended to do with his research and how it would benefit the Tarahumaras, Gonzalez agreed to help. He took Copeland to his village and served as an intermediary. "Over a period of a year our relationship became more intense, and warmer," says Copeland. "Thanks to him, the Tarahumaras started trusting us and understood what our mission was."

50 Entering the world of the Tarahumaras has been an **arduous** project for Copeland. To reach their homeland he must drive two and a half days from Houston, Texas, across highways, blacktop[6] roads, and finally a thirteen-mile stretch of rugged trail[7] that takes almost a day to **maneuver**. During the winter he sleeps in his truck, and in the summer next to the campfire in the way of the Tarahumaras. He loads up his vehicle with goods that the Tarahumaras can't easily get and gives them to the people as
55 a gesture of friendship. The Tarahumaras, who don't believe in **accumulating** wealth, take the food and share it among themselves.

For Copeland, the experience has not only been academically satisfying, but it also has **enriched** his life in several ways. "I see people rejecting technology and living a very hard, traditional life, which offers me another **notion** about the meaning of progress in the Western tradition," he says. "I
60 experience the simplicity of living in nature that I would otherwise only be able to read about. I see a lot of beauty in their sense of sharing and concern for each other."

This reading was adapted from *When Tarahumaras SPEAK . . . James Copeland Listens* by David D. Medina © 1996. Reprinted with permission from Rice News.

[1] **Sierra Madre** mountain range in northern Mexico
[2] **Uto-Aztecan** related to the group of indigenous languages of North and Central America
[3] **Bigfoot or Sasquatch** mythical hairy, manlike beast believed to have inhabited Canada and the northwestern United States
[4] **centaur** type of creature from Greek mythology having the head, arms, and trunk of a man attached to the body and legs of a horse
[5] **literacy** relating to reading and writing
[6] **blacktop** material used to pave roads
[7] **trail** a marked path through woods or dense forest

A Decide if the following statements about the reading are true (T) or false (F). If you check (✔) false, correct the statement to make it true.

		T	F
1	The article is mainly about the efforts of James Copeland to help the Tarahumaras catch up with the modern world.		
2	The Tarahumaras are descendants of the Spanish who arrived in Mexico in the 1600s.		
3	The Tarahumaras live in houses made of stone and wood.		
4	James Copeland has made his permanent home among the Tarahumaras.		
5	James Copeland found learning the language of the Tarahumaras difficult, as it is not written down.		

B How much do you remember about the reading? For each statement, choose the best answer.

1 James Copeland was well qualified for his project because _____.
   a. his mother was a Tarahumara
   b. he was a talented linguist
   c. he lived near the Tarahumaras
   d. he grew up with the Tarahumaras

2 James Copeland is working to produce a grammar book about the Tarahumara language, as well as produce written stories and myths, in order to _____.
   a. make a lot of money
   b. help preserve the language
   c. make the Tarahumaras famous
   d. finish his Ph.D. program

3 James Copeland is hoping that, as many of the Tarahumaras _____, he can convince officials to teach them using his grammar book.
   a. cannot read
   b. dislike the government
   c. have asked to study grammar
   d. would like him as a teacher

4 The Tarahumaras share all the goods that Copeland takes them as they do not believe in gaining wealth _____.
   a. by chance   **b.** in exchange for help   **c.** from outsiders   **d.** only for themselves

5 As a result of his studies of the Tarahumara culture, James Copeland has been shown _____ the meaning of progress in the Western tradition.
   a. the correctness of
   b. a different way of looking at
   c. the necessity of
   d. similar ways of looking at

C Critical Thinking

Discuss these questions with a partner.

1 Do you think the work of James Copeland will benefit the Tarahumaras? Why or why not?
2 Why do you think the Tarahumaras were so slow to trust James Copeland?
3 What ideas about progress are common in the society we live in?

Vocabulary Comprehension:
Words in Context

A Look at the following target vocabulary items from the reading. Using the context of the items within the passage, work out the meaning of each one. Then, use them to complete the paragraph below. Be sure to use the correct form of each word.

> utensils   rugged   acquired   elusive   descends on
> arduous   maneuver   accumulating   enriched   notion

Not everyone can learn a language easily. Many linguists share the **(1)**_____ that language skills, when taught at an early age, can be easier to **(2)**_____. Hence, for many monolingual adults, language learning can be a(n) **(3)**_____ journey. Many adult learners make the mistake of trying to learn a new language in isolation. Sooner or later, they discover that **(4)**_____ a large enough vocabulary to enable them to converse freely in their chosen second language is impossible.

While it's true that words are the basic **(5)**_____ of language, they alone will not make someone a good speaker, just as purchasing a fine set of golf clubs will not transform someone in to a good golfer. However, if adults change their approach to learning, what was previously **(6)**_____ to them can be achieved. In fact, there are just as many adult learners who manage to achieve a high level of literacy in their second language as those who don't. Rather than giving up, these successful learners find their lives are thoroughly **(7)**_____ by their linguistic achievements and opportunities they previously dreamed of **(8)**_____ them. Perhaps learning a new language could be compared to climbing up a steep and **(9)**_____ mountain; it's tough to **(10)**_____ your way to the top, but when you get there, your view of the world is quite amazing!

B Answer these questions. Share your answers with a partner.

1 How many different cooking and eating *utensils* can you name?
2 We talk about many things being at the end of a *rugged* road. What do you think that means?
3 If you have *acquired* the necessary skills to tackle a new language, what have you learned?

4 Some adults complain that learning a language can be *elusive*. Do you agree or disagree? Why do you think this is?

5 Have you found that new opportunities in life have *descended on* you as a result of learning English? If so, give some examples.

6 Do you find learning English to be an *arduous* task? Why? What can you do to make it easier?

7 Can you think of any ways to make *maneuvering* your way through learning English grammar easier?

8 It is said that by *accumulating* a vocabulary of 600 words in a language, you can get by using that language. Make a list of the ten words that you think would be most useful to learn.

9 Do you believe the *notion* that one's life can be *enriched* by learning another language? Explain your answer.

A Study the words below. Write the part of speech for each word; then match each one with a definition below. Use your dictionary to help you.

Vocabulary	Part of Speech	Definition
1 literature		
2 literary		
3 lectern		
4 legible		
5 lexicon		
6 lexicographer		

a. capable of being read or deciphered
b. a dictionary; a set of words used in a particular field
c. a tall desk or stand used by a speaker to rest notes or book on
d. a person who writes or compiles dictionaries
e. written works such as novels, plays, poetry; written information on a specific field
f. related to the field of books and writing

B Read each question below. Then take turns asking and answering the questions with a partner.

1 What is your favorite work of *literature*?
2 Can you name any winners of *literary* awards?
3 Do professors at universities in your country use *lecterns* during class?
4 Do you have *legible* handwriting? Do you know anyone who has *illegible* handwriting?
5 Name another word in the English *lexicon* that means "understand."
6 Do you think that being a *lexicographer* would be interesting? Why or why not?

Vocabulary Skill:
The Root Words *lit* and *lex*

Many words in the English language that are related to the subject of reading come from Latin root words. "Legere," for example, means "read," "choose," or "gather," and in modern English, it is written as "lect," "lex," or "leg." The Latin word "littera," meaning "letter," is written as "lit" in modern English. Knowing these roots and how they are used can help you build your vocabulary.

Real Life Skill:
Using a Pronunciation Key

An important function of a good dictionary is to provide the correct pronunciation of words, as well as meanings. Each dictionary uses a slightly different method of explaining exactly how the word should be pronounced. Some use special phonetic symbols, while others use normal letters of the alphabet with special symbols. Every good dictionary will have a key that explains the system of symbols it uses for pronunciation, along with basic words that give examples of usage. It's important to familiarize yourself with the system your dictionary uses so that you can get the most value out of using it.

A Read this pronunciation key from the International Phonetic Alphabet (IPA).

PRONUNCIATION KEY

The consonants /b/ as in *boy*, /d/ as in *day*, /f/ as in *fox*, /g/ as in *gate*, /h/ as in *house*, /k/ as in *car*, /l/ as in *like*, /m/ as in *mat*, /n/ as in *no*, /p/ as in *pot*, /r/ as in *rope*, /s/ as in *sit*, /t/ as in *toe*, /v/ as in *vase*, /w/ as in *water*, and /z/ as in *zebra*, are pronounced as they are spelled.

Vowels
/æ/ as in *bat*
/ɑː/ as in *father, calm*
/ɜː/ as in *girl, bird*
/eɪ/ as in *age, say*
/oʊ/ as in *home, sew*
/ɔɪ/ as in *oil, join*
/uː/ as in *soon, rule*
/aʊ/ as in *out, house*
/ʌ/ as in *up, cut*
/ʊ/ as in *book, full*
/ə/ as in *ago, pencil, lemon*
/ɪ/ as in *if, give*
/aɪ/ as in *ice, ride*
/ɒ/ as in *odd, box*
/iː/ as in *meet, seed*
/e/ as in *egg, bed*
/ɪə/ as in *here, near*
/ʊə/ as in *tour*
/eə/ as in *there, hair*
/ɔː/ as in *four, door*

Consonants
/dʒ/ as in *juice*
/ŋ/ as in *sing*
/θ/ as in *thing, path*
/ð/ as in *this, mother*
/tʃ/ as in *church*
/ʃ/ as in *shop*
/ʒ/ as in *television*
/j/ as in *yellow*

Marks are also used to show where the primary and secondary stress in a word is:
/ ' / *is used in front of a syllable to show primary stress:* /ˈmenʃən/
/ ˌ / *is used in front of a syllable to show secondary stress:* /ˌfæsəˈneɪʃən/

B Read these words aloud following the key above. Then write them out alphabetically as you would read them.

1 ɪˈspeʃəli _____
2 ˈkwestʃən _____
3 ɔːlˈredi _____
4 ˈbjuːtəfəl _____
5 kleɪm _____
6 ɪgzæməˈneɪʃən _____
7 dʒiːˈɒgrəfi _____
8 ˈdɒctər _____

C Using the pronunciation key above, write three new words you have learned in this unit using the phonetic symbols.

D Now work with a partner. Take turns reading each other's words aloud using the correct pronunciation.

What Do You Think?

1 If you could learn to speak one other language besides English, which language would you choose? Why?
2 Do you find some languages easier to understand than others? Which ones? Why?
3 Do you think that there should be one dominant language in the world? Why or why not?

Amazing Animal Survivors!

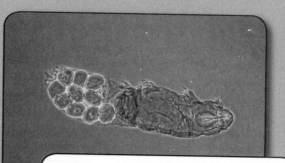

Tardigrades are microscopic creatures which can survive in temperatures from –200 to 140 degrees Celsius.

Emperor penguins can go without food for 115 days in temperatures far below zero waiting for their egg to hatch.

Cockroaches have lived at the time of the dinosaurs and witnessed their extinction. Will they outlast humans, too?

A surprising number of fish survive in the crushing pressure and near total darkness of the deep sea.

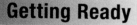

Getting Ready

Discuss the following questions with a partner.

1 Which of the animal survivors above do you think is the most amazing?
2 What are some other animals that are able to survive difficult conditions?
3 Do you think there are animals living in severe habitats that haven't been discovered yet?
4 How do humans sometimes make it difficult for animals to survive?

Chapter 1: Caught in a Melting World

Before You Read:
The Threat of Extinction

A Answer the following questions.

1 What do you know about Antarctica? Name some different animal species that can be found there.
2 Are you aware of any direct effects that global warming is having on Antarctica?
3 How do these consequences of global warming affect the wildlife found on the continent?
4 Look at the title of the reading. Name some animal species that would be threatened with extinction if the world in which they live (their habitat) were melting. In what ways would a melting habitat affect them directly?

B Discuss your answers with a partner.

Reading Skill:
Understanding Inference

Information in a reading passage can be found in two ways: by what is stated directly and written clearly on the page, or by what we can infer. When we infer, we use the information that is stated directly to draw conclusions about events, or the writer's opinion or purpose. Knowing how to infer can help you to better understand the writer's purpose and ideas. It is a useful skill to know when reading for pleasure, and can help you better understand reading passages in exams.

A Read each of the following questions carefully. As you scan through the reading passage, think about the information that each one is asking about. Answer them based on the information you read.

1 What can we infer about the weather on Antarctica the day the penguins were observed? (e.g., foggy, stormy, etc.) Which words in the passage give you clues?

2 From where do you think the writer is observing the penguins? (e.g., air, land, sea) What information tells you this?

3 Describe, in as much detail as you can infer from the passage, how Adélie penguins feed their young from the time they catch the food to the time they pass it to the baby's mouth. Underline the words or sentences in the passage that allow you to infer this information.

4 How widely can Adélie penguins be found across Antarctica? Which words or sentences in the passage tell you this?

5 What does the author think will happen in the future to other Adélie colonies on Antarctica? What information in the passage tells you this?

B Share your answers with a partner. Go over the information in the reading passage that provided you with answers to the questions.

C Now read through the passage again and complete the comprehension exercises that follow.

Caught in a Melting World

Four little heads pop up[1] **simultaneously** in a pool of blue-black water surrounded by ice as far as the eye can see. They are Adélie penguins, and the ice defines their
5 existence.

The birds—just over two feet long—leap about excitedly in tight circles, going in and out of the water, perfectly at ease in this **frigid** sea that surrounds the shores
10 of Antarctica. They are not only at ease, but at home. The seasonal freezing and thawing, spreading and shrinking, of the ocean's surface is the world they know. In recent years, as Earth's climate has warmed, it has also become a world in rapid and disturbing change.

Their food is tied, literally, to the frozen ocean. Within layers of sea ice, microscopic algae[2] bloom **in profusion** as sunlight floods in from above. When the sea ice melts with the beginning
15 of summer, the ice algae escape into the water, where they are **grazed on** by dense swarms of krill—a type of shrimplike crustacean.[3] The krill, in turn, are the Adélie penguins' primary food source. To eat them, Adélies spend their entire lives on, around, or beneath the Antarctic pack ice.

As the heads appear together at the surface, they seem to hesitate, reluctant to leave the watery world through which they swim as effortlessly as fish. Then all at once, they shoot up out of the
20 water, landing feet first on the ice. For just a few seconds they stand still. Then, as one, the little flock sets off southward across the ice, heading for the faint outline of a distant mountain range. At the base of those mountains some thirty miles away lies Cape Adare, where each year at this time some 280,000 Adélie pairs get together to raise their young—the largest such colony in all of Antarctica.

25 The four birds **recede** until they are nothing but small black dots in the bright white distance. After a feeding trip that may have covered as much as 180 miles of sea and ice, they are going back to their nests. Each will relieve a fasting[4] mate with which it has been taking turns incubating[5] two eggs for the last five or six weeks.

Within hours of hatching,[6] the tiny chicks are raising their **wobbly** heads, **begging** for food. They
30 know **innately** that growing up is urgent in a land where summer will only last a few weeks. Their squeaks are answered by their parents with ready beakfuls of krill, dutifully carried back by the bellyful from the sea far away across the ice—that ice still firmly attached to the shore.

Should the ice stay firm for too long, requiring trips in excess of sixty miles or so, the small chicks will either starve to death or grow too slowly to survive. If the ice breaks out and melts too early,
35 the ice-driven food chain will be weakened, and the chicks will be left unattended, vulnerable to predator[7] birds, and too young to **fend for themselves** while both parents are off seeking food.

Frighteningly, this has occurred ever more frequently in the last few decades, especially around the Antarctic Peninsula,[8] which is the northernmost and warmest part of the Adélies' range.

40 As the rest of the planet slides gradually into warmer climate trends—a change thought to be caused partly by human burning of fossil fuels—scientists working at the Palmer Station in this part of the Antarctic report that average temperatures there have increased by as much as three to five degrees Fahrenheit in summer over the past fifty years, and an incredible seven to nine degrees in winter. That increase is at least ten times faster than for the rest of the world.

45 The ever-increasing ozone-hole problem, a fluorocarbon[9]-induced thinning of the protective ozone layer[10] in the upper atmosphere, adds yet another unknown factor to a tricky equation. The hole is now reaching well over ten million square miles in extent. Unscreened by ozone gas, solar ultraviolet radiation strikes the surface of the Earth there and substantially reduces the productivity of the ice algae, scientists believe, and thus the krill on which the Adélies feed.

50 The combined effect of all these threats is already translating into drastic population declines in several Adélie penguin colonies. In five colonies near Palmer Station, numbers of breeding pairs have dropped from 15,200 to 9,200 in twenty-five years, while some smaller colonies have disappeared altogether. And the problem seems to be accelerating fast, with a ten percent Adélie population decline in the last two years alone. At another site farther north, a loss of about 35 percent has been measured in just ten years. It is a cruel irony that this little penguin's
55 superb adaptations to an extremely harsh environment, and its very dependence on sea ice, could cause its **undoing**. Fortunately, however, there are numerous Adélie colonies around the Antarctic continent, especially in the far south, where there is no hint of such drastic changes, at least not for the time being.

This reading was adapted from *Caught in a Melting World* by Tui de Roy © 2000.
Reprinted from *International Wildlife* with permission of the author.

[1] **pop up** thrust up suddenly or unexpectedly
[2] **algae** simple plants that live in water, e.g., seaweed
[3] **crustacean** animal with a hard outer shell, most often found living in water, e.g., crab, lobster
[4] **fasting** going without food
[5] **incubating** keeping eggs or an organism at optimal conditions to promote growth and development
[6] **hatching** emerging from, or breaking out of, a shell
[7] **predator** organism that lives by hunting for and feeding on other organisms
[8] **Antarctic Peninsula** region of Antarctica extending about 1,931 km north from the main continent toward South America
[9] **fluorocarbon** liquid or gas formed by a carbon and fluorine compound—fluorine being a highly corrosive and poisonous substance—used in aerosols, refrigerants, solvents, and the making of plastics
[10] **ozone layer** region of the upper atmosphere containing high concentrations of ozone gas (a derivative form of oxygen) that absorbs and screens the sun's harmful ultraviolet radiation

A The following questions are all about the reading. Use the information you have read to answer each one correctly.

1 What was the author's main purpose in writing this article?
2 What is the main reason that the world of the Adélie penguins is in danger?
3 What is the primary food source of the Adélie penguins?
4 How do Adélie penguins carry food back to their young?
5 How are Adélie penguins affected if ocean ice stays frozen too long?

B Decide if the following statements about the reading are true (T), false (F), or if the information is not given (NG). If you check (✔) false, correct the statement to make it true.

	T	F	NG
1 The temperature in the Antarctic is slowly increasing.			
2 Scientists believe that ultraviolet radiation helps algae grow.			
3 Adélie are starting to eat less krill and more small fish.			
4 The numbers of Adélie penguins are decreasing especially in the far south.			

C Critical Thinking

Discuss these questions with a partner.
1 Describe the food chain of the Adélie penguins. Draw a diagram to illustrate each element of the chain, and put arrows on it to show how each part of it relates to the other.
2 Do you think it's possible to prevent the extinction of the Adélie penguins? How?
3 What measures can humans take to prevent other animal extinctions in the future?

Vocabulary Comprehension:

Word Definitions

A Look at the list of words and phrases from the reading. Match each one with a definition on the right.

1 simultaneously _____
2 frigid _____
3 in profusion _____
4 grazed on _____
5 recede _____
6 wobbly _____
7 begging _____
8 innately _____
9 fend for themselves _____
10 undoing _____

a. downfall; ruin
b. look after or take care of themselves
c. asking for something (like food or money) in a very keen way
d. shaky; unsteady
e. to move further away (into the distance)
f. at the same time
g. fed on (usually by intermittently eating small amounts)
h. inborn; possessed at birth
i. in abundance
j. extremely cold

B Complete the sentences using the vocabulary from A. Be sure to use the correct form of each word.

1 Theft and fraud among his accountants led to the eventual _____ of Steve's finance company.
2 The _____ winter weather of Alaska creates a beautiful landscape, but prevents many tourists from visiting in January and February.
3 This beach is amazing. At low tide when the water _____, you can find all sorts of unusual shells and marine creatures.
4 When goats are born, they have the _____ ability to walk, even though their legs are quite _____ at first.
5 Although the offspring of many mammals cannot _____ when they are first born, unlike humans they grow to become independent very quickly.
6 A good dog owner will train his or her pet not to _____ for food.
7 Amanda's garden looks so beautiful right now. There are roses blossoming _____.
8 In order to work as a language translator for the United Nations, you must be qualified as a(n) _____ interpreter.
9 When his lawnmower broke, instead of buying a new one, Albert bought a goat to _____ the grass to keep it short.

A Study the words in the chart. What do you think they mean? Use your knowledge of prefixes, suffixes, and the roots *nat, viv, bio,* and *gen* to match each word with a definition.

> biosphere   symbiosis   nationality   vitality   genealogy   degenerate
> revive   supernatural   vivacious   convivial   biodegradable   congenital

1   lively; very cheerful _____
2   to give new energy to something _____
3   identity based on citizenship of a country _____
4   the Earth and its atmosphere in which living things exist _____
5   capable of breaking apart and being absorbed by nature through natural
    processes, without harming the environment _____
6   relationship between two or more different organisms that can be of benefit to
    each other _____
7   relating to something that exists beyond the natural world _____
8   the study of the history of one's family and ancestry _____
9   to fall into a worse condition; to deteriorate _____
10 related to a condition present at birth; not inherited _____
11 energy, strength, and health that one possesses _____
12 friendly; sociable _____

B Complete the following paragraph using some of the words from A. Be sure to use the correct form of each word. Not all the words are used.

News In Brief
Water supplies were shut off in a small coastal town yesterday after an environmental scare. It seems that a chemical powder which was thought to be **(1)**_____ was buried in soil near the source of the town's water supply. Instead of breaking down into harmless particles, the powder leaked into the water supply and contaminated it. Scientists have warned everyone in the neighborhood not to drink any tap water, especially pregnant women, as the side effects of drinking water containing the chemical can include stomach problems, skin complaints and, if consumed by pregnant women, **(2)**_____ birth defects. On a lighter note, a woman of Irish **(3)**_____ claims to have researched her family name and **(4)**_____ through **(5)**_____ methods. The woman is reported to have contacted her deceased father, grandfather, great grandfather, and great-great grandfather by using her psychic powers. In a recent interview, she told us she had made discoveries about her family history, and about characteristics of the male family members she contacted, too. She revealed that while her great-great grandfather was a very kind, **(6)**_____ man who loved to entertain, her great grandfather was the opposite—a complete introvert. And although her grandfather was an energetic, **(7)**_____ man, her father was renowned for being sickly and miserable. The woman concluded that this family characteristic explained her own son's great **(8)**_____ and spirited nature—a trait he inherited from his grandfather.

Vocabulary Skill:
The Root Words
nat/viv/bio/gen

In this chapter you read the words "innately," meaning "inborn," and "survive," meaning "to remain alive" or "to live longer than." Both words include root words that relate to life and life processes: "nat," meaning "life" or "birth," and "viv" (also written as "vit"), meaning "life." Two other root words that also mean "life" are "bio" and "gen." These roots are combined with prefixes and suffixes to form many words in English.

Chapter 2: One Legend Found, Many Still to Go

Before You Read:
Weird and Wonderful Nature

A Answer the following questions.

1 Are there any animals that especially frighten or bother you? Which ones? Why do you feel that way about them?
2 Do you know any stories about strange creatures that are reported to exist but that scientists haven't been able to find?
3 Do you believe in sea monsters? Why or why not?
4 Do you think that one day science will be able to catalog all the life on planet Earth? Explain your answer.

B Discuss your answers with a partner.

Reading Skill:
Skimming for Content

Skimming for content is a useful skill that can help you read, and comprehend, faster. You can get a good idea of the content of a passage without reading every word or sentence. By skimming quickly over the text, you can pick up on the main points of the passage, as well as the main idea of what the reading is about.

A How many of the following oddities and mysteries of nature do you know? Try to match them with the descriptions on the right. If you're not sure about any, just read the names and descriptions and think about them

1 kraken _____
2 coelacanth _____
3 okapi _____
4 yeti _____
5 Champ _____
6 sauropod _____
7 the Loch Ness monster _____

a. a large creature that reportedly lives in Lake Champlain in the state of New York
b. a furry, human-like creature occasionally sighted in the Himalayas
c. a giraffe-like animal
d. an ancient name for the giant squid
e. an odd-looking fish once thought to be extinct
f. a long-necked creature resembling a dinosaur
g. an occasionally sighted creature said to live in a lake in Scotland

B Now, spend ONE minute skimming over the passage to get a basic grasp of the content. Do NOT try to read every word. Do not hesitate or stop when you see words you do not know, or read the footnotes; just let your eyes skim quickly back and forth over the text.

C Now go back to the creatures in A and see how many of them you can confidently identify. Change any answers that you now think are incorrect. Read through the passage to confirm your answers.

One Legend Found, Many Still to Go

The human instinct to observe nature has always been mixed with a tendency to **embroider upon** it. So it is that, over the ages, societies have lived alongside not only real animals, but a shadow bestiary[1] of fantastic ones—mermaids,[2] griffins,[3] unicorns[4] and the like. None loomed larger than the giant squid, the kraken—a great, **malevolent** devil of the deep. "One of these sea monsters," Olaus Magnus wrote in 1555, "will drown easily many great ships."

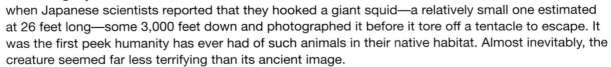

Science, of course, is in the business of **shattering** myths with facts, which it did when Japanese scientists reported that they hooked a giant squid—a relatively small one estimated at 26 feet long—some 3,000 feet down and photographed it before it tore off a tentacle to escape. It was the first peek humanity has ever had of such animals in their native habitat. Almost inevitably, the creature seemed far less terrifying than its ancient image.

Monster lovers **take heart**. Scientists argue that so much of the planet remains unexplored that new surprises are sure to show up; if not legendary beasts like the Loch Ness monster or the dinosaur-like reptile said to inhabit Lake Champlain, then animals that in their own way may be even stranger.

A **forthcoming** book by the noted naturalist Richard Ellis, *Singing Whales, Flying Squid, and Swimming Cucumbers*, reinforces that notion by cataloging recent discoveries of previously unknown whales, dolphins, and other creatures, some of which are quite **bizarre**.

"The sea being so deep and so large, I'm sure other mysteries lurk out there, unseen and unsolved," said Mr. Ellis, also the author of *Monsters of the Sea*. Explorers, he said, recently **stumbled on** an odd squid more than 20 feet long with fins like elephant ears and very skinny arms and tentacles,[5] all of which can bend at right angles, like human elbows. "We know nothing about it," Mr. Ellis said. "But we've seen it."

Historically, many unknown creatures have come to light purely by accident. In 1938, for example, a fisherman pulled up an odd, ancient-looking fish with stubby, limb-like fins. It turned out to be a coelacanth, a beast thought to have gone extinct 70 million years ago. Since then, other examples of the species have occasionally been **hauled** out of the sea.

Land, too, occasionally gives up a secret. In about 1900, acting on tips from the local population, Sir Harry H. Johnston, an English explorer, hunted through the forests of Zaire[6] (then the Belgian Congo) and found a giraffe-like animal known as the okapi. It was hailed as a living fossil.[7]

In 1982, a group of animal enthusiasts founded the International Society of Cryptozoology (literally, the study of hidden creatures) and adopted the okapi as its symbol. Today, self-described cryptozoologists range from amateur unicorn hunters to distinguished scientists.

At the website for the group, there is a list of 15 classes of unresolved claims about unusual beasts, including big cats, giant crocodiles, huge snakes, large octopuses, mammoths, biped[8] primates like the yeti in the Himalayas, and long-necked creatures resembling the gigantic dinosaurs called sauropods.

Lake Champlain, on the border between Vermont and New York, is notorious as the alleged home of Champ, a beast said to be similar to a plesiosaur, an extinct marine reptile with a small head, long neck, and four paddle-shaped flippers.

There, as at Loch Ness and elsewhere, myth-busting non-believers and believers do constant battle. "Not only is there not a single piece of convincing evidence for Champ's existence, but there are many reasons against it," Joe Nickel, a researcher who investigates claims of **paranormal** phenomena, argued in *Skeptical Inquirer*, a monthly magazine that rebuts what it considers to be scientific hokum.[9]

Then there are the blobs. For more than a century, scientists and laymen imagined that the mysterious gooey masses—some as large as a school bus—that wash ashore on beaches around the world came from great creatures with tentacles long enough to sink cruise ships. Warnings were issued. Perhaps, cryptozoologists speculated, the blobs were the remains of recently deceased living fossils more fearsome than the dinosaurs, or perhaps an entirely new sea creature unknown to science.

Then last year, a team of biologists based at the University of South Florida applied DNA analysis to the mystery. It turned out they were nothing more than old whale blubber. "To our disappointment," the scientists wrote, "we have not found any evidence that any of the blobs are the remains of gigantic octopods,[10] or sea monsters of unknown species."

Psychologists say raw nature is simply a blank slate for the expression of our subconscious fears and insecurities, a Rorschach test[11] that reveals more about the viewer than the viewed. But the giant squid is real, growing up to lengths of at least 60 feet, with eyes the size of dinner plates and a tangle of tentacles lined with long rows of sucker pads. Scientists, their appetites whetted by the first observations of the creature in the wild, are now **gearing up** to discover its remaining secrets.

[1] **bestiary** a collection of animals
[2] **mermaid** a legendary creature that is half woman, half fish
[3] **griffin** a legendary creature with the body of a lion and the head and wings of an eagle
[4] **unicorn** a legendary creature resembling a horse with one horn sprouting from its head
[5] **tentacles** the long legs of animals such as squids and octopuses
[6] **Zaire** former name of the Democratic Republic of the Congo
[7] **fossil** the remains of an animal or plant which have hardened over a long time and resemble stone
[8] **biped** a creature that walks on two legs
[9] **hokum** a quaint term meaning nonsense
[10] **octopods** relatives of the octopus that have eight legs
[11] **Rorschach test** a psychological test that uses ink shapes

A How much do you remember about the reading? For each question, choose the best answer.

1 What is the main idea of the article?
   a. Many of the myths about strange animals are true.
   b. Unusual creatures, both real and imaginary, have always fascinated humans.
   c. Scientists have shown that all monster myths are false.
   d. Most monsters are actually real animals.
2 What is the author's purpose in writing this article?
   a. to argue in favor of discovering more mysterious creatures
   b. to persuade us that mythical animals really exist
   c. to warn us that sea monsters and similar animals still threaten us
   d. to entertain and inform the reader with information about extraordinary creatures
3 Why is Richard Ellis mentioned in the article?
   a. He captured a giant squid.
   b. He is the author of two books about ocean animals.
   c. He is president of the International Society of Cryptozoology.
   d. He has doubts about the existence of the giant squid.
4 What is the symbol of the International Society of Cryptozoology?
   a. the giant squid   **b.** Champ   **c.** the okapi   **d.** the Loch Ness monster
5 What did the blobs on beaches turn out to be?
   a. whale blubber
   b. the remains of sea monsters
   c. long tentacles
   d. living fossils

B Decide if the following statements about the reading are true (T) or false (F). If you check (✔) false, correct the statement to make it true.

	T	F
1 The kraken was just a myth.		
2 Richard Ellis wrote a book entitled *Flying Whales, Swimming Squid, and Singing Cucumbers*.		
3 Lake Champlain is allegedly the home of a monster.		
4 The mystery of the blobs was solved by using DNA analysis.		
5 Scientists have completed their studies of the giant squid.		

C Critical Thinking

Discuss these questions with a partner.

1   The author asks monster lovers to take heart. Are you a monster lover? Explain your answer.
2   Would you like to join the International Society of Cryptozoology? If not, why not? If yes, what creatures would you be looking for?

Vocabulary Comprehension:
Words in Context

A **Look at the following target vocabulary items from the passage. Use the strategies outlined on pages 66 and 126 and the context for the items within the passage to work out the meaning of each one.**

> embroider upon   malevolent   shattering   take heart   forthcoming
> bizarre   stumbled on   hauled   paranormal   gearing up

B **Complete the paragraph below using the vocabulary items from A. Be sure to use the correct form of each word.**

Me and My Imagination

As a child, I was absolutely obsessed with hunting monsters. It seemed that around nearly every corner, there was a monster lurking in the shadows—not good monsters, but rather **(1)** _____ ones that were trying to "get me." I walked around my house at night in terror, jumping at every creaking door or whistling window, sure that I would **(2)** _____ a sleeping monster and be his midnight snack. When I ran to my parents for help, recounting for them in detail my encounters with monsters, they would tell me to go back to bed and stop **(3)** _____ things that had simple explanations. They thought this monster obsession was **(4)** _____, but they hoped I'd grow out of it. One day, I planned a monster hunt in our neighbor's fish pond. I **(5)** _____ by putting on my bathing suit, a mask, and borrowing my mother's biggest barbecue fork. Then I jumped in. When they **(6)** _____ me out of the pond, I was holding our neighbor's prize-winning Japanese carp. I knew that a stern lecture would be **(7)** _____ from my father. That's when he told me that there simply were no monsters—they didn't exist, and I had to forget about them. Well, I grew depressed. My fantasy world was **(8)** _____. I did my best not to think about monsters, until one day, on TV, I saw a show about UFOs, ghosts, and other **(9)** _____ phenomena. I learned that other people believed in monsters, too. No longer depressed, I **(10)** _____, and used the information I learned from that show to rebut my father's claim that monsters didn't exist.

C **Answer these questions. Share your answers with a partner.**

1 Do you know anyone who has a tendency to *embroider upon* stories and make them more interesting to listen to than they were in reality?
2 Can you think of a *malevolent* character from a movie?
3 Over the course of human history, what myths that people believed have been *shattered*?
4 When you feel afraid or lacking in confidence, what can help you *take heart*?
5 Are there any *forthcoming* movies, concerts, or exhibitions that you are looking forward to attending?
6 What animal do you think is *bizarre*?
7 What are some examples of *paranormal* phenomena?
8 What do you do to *gear up* for a job interview?

A **Look at the words below. What do you think they mean? Use your knowledge of prefixes, suffixes, and word roots to match them to the definitions.**

1 fiction _____
2 discriminatory _____
3 verbal_____
4 payment _____
5 stop _____
6 violent _____
7 flammable_____
8 existent _____
9 conformist _____

a. forcible or rough; severe
b. prejudiced; marked by unfair treatment
c. capable of burning quickly
d. someone who behaves according to a group's usual expectations and standards
e. to pause or stay in place
f. being real; present in the world
g. spoken or expressed aloud in words.
h. type of story or writing that is about imaginary characters and situations
i. money given in exchange for a service or goods

Vocabulary Skill:

The Prefix *non-*

In this chapter, you read the word "non-believers." This word begins with the prefix "non," meaning "not." This is a common negative prefix that can come before nouns, verbs, adjectives, and adverbs to form many words in English. Some of these words are hyphenated, others are not.

B **Complete the sentences below by adding the prefix *non* to the correct words from A.**

1 My favorite form of literature is _____. I especially love reading autobiographies.
2 Their landlord sued them in court for _____ of three months' rent.
3 Gregory tends to have very _____ opinions about marriage and society.
4 By taking the _____ flight to Sydney, I'll get there two hours earlier than the flight that stops in Brisbane.
5 Our company is highly regarded by others in the industry in terms of its _____ policies on gender, race, and religion.
6 Many animals use _____ ways to communicate, as sounds may alert enemies to their presence.

C **Now use the remaining words to write three sentences of your own. Share your ideas with a partner.**

1 _____
2 _____
3 _____

Real Life Skill:
Animal Terminology

English names of animals are very old, and their usage dates back hundreds of years. Many have irregular plural forms, and the names of offspring often bear little or no resemblance to those of the adult. For example, a baby penguin is called a chick (as seen in the Chapter One reading). A group of the same animal also has a special name that again, bears little or no resemblance to the name of the animal, for example, a "flock" of penguins. This vocabulary is important to know when reading about nature.

A Work with a partner to match the names of these animals with their young. Use your dictionary to check any that you are not sure of.

1 cat _____   a. fawn
2 dog _____   b. kid
3 horse_____   c. calf
4 cow _____   d. lamb
5 bird _____   e. foal
6 frog _____   f. chick
7 hen _____   g. tadpole
8 deer _____   h. puppy
9 sheep_____   i. kitten
10 goat_____   j. nestling

B Now write the plural form of each of these animals. Use your dictionary to help.

1 a mouse; two _____   4 an ox; a pair of _____
2 a goose; many _____   5 a puppy; three _____
3 a fish; ten _____   6 a wolf; several _____

C Groups of very different animals can share the same name. When we use these terms the plural form of the animal name is always used. Look at the group names below and write the plural forms of the correct animals on the appropriate line.

> kitten   wolf   bird   ox   cow   fish   horse
> seagull   puppy   shark   sheep   bat

1 A herd of _____
2 A flock of _____
3 A school of _____
4 A pack of _____
5 A litter of _____
6 A colony of _____

What Do You Think?

1 Why do you think people are fascinated with exotic and mysterious animals?
2 If you were given the opportunity to go anywhere in the world to study a species of animal, where would you go and which animal species would you study?
3 Do you think a day will come when all animal mysteries will be solved? Would you look forward to that day? Why or why not?

Music: Influence and Innovation

Beyoncé Knowles

Yo-Yo Ma

Kongar-ol Ondar

Getting Ready

Discuss the following questions with a partner.

1 Do you recognize any of the artists in the photos above? How would you describe their music and the image of each one? Would you say you are a fan of any of them?
2 How would you define your taste in music? Which musical genre or genres do you listen to the most?
3 Is there any one person or event in your life that has influenced your musical preferences? If so, what or who was it?
4 What innovations in music have taken place over the last few years? Do you think they have benefited music artists and bands, and the average music buyer? Explain your answer.

Chapter 1: Genghis Blues

Before You Read:
Ancient Sounds of Music

A Answer the following questions.

   1 Are there any types of music you have heard that sound unusual or extraordinary to you?
   2 Do you ever listen to blues music? Can you name any blues artists or bands?
   3 Are there any bands or artists in your country that produce any type of "alternative" or noncommercial genres of music? Who are the bands or artists, and what kind of music do they play?

B Discuss your answers with a partner.

Reading Skill:
Identifying Meaning from Context

You can guess the meaning of important but unfamiliar words in a reading passage by using the following strategy: 1. Think about how the new word is related to the topic of what you are reading about. 2. Identify which part of speech the new word is by looking at how it fits with the other words in its sentence. 3. Look at how the word relates to the rest of the information in the paragraph surrounding it. 4. Use your knowledge of prefixes, suffixes, and word roots to identify the basic meaning of the word.

A The following is an extract from the reading passage. As you read through it, think about the topic of the reading, and what you already know about this topic. Pay attention to the words in bold. Decide which part of speech each bold word or phrase is, and write them below.

The film follows Paul Pena, a blues musician from San Francisco, on a voyage to Central Asia, where he participates in a contest celebrating the ancient art of throat singing. Witnessing that **(1) high point** in Pena's otherwise difficult life—he's blind, in **(2) shaky** health, and prone to depression—is one of the film's major pleasures; another is encountering Pena's **(3) exuberant** friend and **(4) mentor**, the master throat singer Kongar-ol Ondar.

   1 _____   3 _____
   2 _____   4 _____

B Circle the words in the sentence that work with or affect the words in bold, and help you identify the part of speech. Look at how the word relates to the rest of the paragraph. Are there any other words or phrases that give you clues to the meaning of each word? If so, circle them.

C Now look at the parts of the words. Does each one have a recognizable prefix, root, or suffix? Use your knowledge of these word parts to try to identify the meaning of each word. Replace each one with a word or phrase, or write a definition.

   1 _____   3 _____
   2 _____   4 _____

D Use your dictionary to check whether you have interpreted the meaning of the words correctly. Share your answers with a partner.

E Now read through the passage again, and complete the comprehension exercises that follow.

Genghis Blues

Andy Warhol[1] once observed that film is, first and foremost, about personality. "People are fantastic. You can't take a bad picture," he said in the 1960s. Although some of today's television
5   calls this view into question, the documentary *Genghis Blues* proves that if you put fantastic people in front of the camera, something memorable is likely to happen.

The film follows Paul Pena, a blues musician
10   from San Francisco, on a voyage to Central Asia, where he participates in a contest celebrating the ancient art of throat singing. Witnessing that high point in Pena's otherwise difficult life—he's blind, in shaky health, and prone to depression—is one of the film's major pleasures; another is encountering Pena's exuberant friend and mentor, the master throat singer Kongar-ol Ondar.

Fiddling with his short-wave radio[2] early one morning in 1984, Pena stumbled across some strange sounds. What
15   seemed at first like electronic oscillations[3] turned out to be human voices capable of producing two or more notes at the same time. "Now that's for me," Pena said to himself. Some notes were high-pitched, twangy, and whistle-like; others had the guttural[4] quality of a bullfrog's droning, which reminded Pena of the blues singer Howlin' Wolf.[5]

It took Pena seven years to **ascertain** that the sounds he'd heard were created in Tuva, a small Russian republic
20   along the northwestern border of Mongolia.[6] Only a brief outline of the history of Tuva is supplied in the opening section of the documentary. The country was settled centuries ago by Turkic people who became allied with Genghis Khan.[7] After spending the eighteenth and nineteenth centuries under Chinese rule, Tuva was absorbed first into czarist Russia[8] (the documentary doesn't state this), and allegedly became independent before officially joining the Soviet Union in 1944.

25   Within a few weeks of purchasing a Tuvan CD, Pena was able to reproduce those sounds and had started integrating them into his music. While Ondar was greeting his fans after a concert in San Francisco during the early 1990s, Pena sidled up to the master and began vocalizing in the lower-pitched *kargyraa* style. Ondar was so impressed he invited Pena to Tuva's 1995 triennial throat singing competition.

For its first half-hour, *Genghis Blues* unfolds more or less like a conventional documentary as director, Roko Belic,
30   who produced and shot the film with his brother, Adrian, introduces Pena and the **engaging** eccentrics who either accompany him on his Asian adventure, or help make it happen. Among Pena's supporters are Ralph Leighton, a founder of the California-based Friends of Tuva, and the late Mario Casetta, a wisecracker[9] who for years played world music on Los Angeles public radio.

Shortly after the group's arrival in Tuva, however, *Genghis Blues* evolves into an intimate portrait of two **sentient**
35   artists. The **eminently** likable Pena, a Creole-American[10] who traces his familial and musical roots to Cape Verde,[11] is a spirited bundle of emotions. At various moments he's jolly, petrified,[12] confident, and despondent, though onstage he consistently wows the audience. The Tuvans call him "Earthquake" because he's from San Francisco and because he's able to hit notes so low they sound like the earth trembling. Belic told me recently that he'd been under pressure from some of the musician's friends not to show Pena's less self-assured moments—he
40   admits to despair over his blindness and becomes frantic after losing his depression medication—but the director wisely included them.

The drama in *Genghis Blues* revolves around Pena's participation in the contest, but the most **poignant** sequences occur when Ondar, who **veritably** radiates joy, takes Pena and his pals on a tour of Tuva's countryside. Though the documentary doesn't directly mention it, one **paradox** about the contest, which grew out of its founder's
45 zeal to preserve a cultural tradition, is that it presents throat singing in a wholly artificial milieu.[13] The Tuvans were nomadic herders,[14] and some still are; throat singing, which lone herdsmen did to relate to the land and to communicate with compatriots who were sometimes far away—the sounds apparently carry through the air very well—was never intended as performance per se.[15] Tuvan songs tend to be about rivers, grassland, and other aspects of nature, and it's only after the camera traces the areas that inspire the music that the connection between form
50 and content is fully made. The on-the-road footage also underscores the Tuvans' embrace of life, despite poverty and other challenges, which in turn shows how deeply **intuitive** Pena was in incorporating throat singing into blues music.

At one point, Pena stands where the Dalai Lama had stood a few years earlier, and rues[16] his inability to express the timelessness he's sensing about the place. "I don't know if you can get such a thing on camera," he says, as it focuses
55 on a nondescript monument. That the Belics left in this acknowledgment of their documentary's limitations reflects the overall **integrity** of their endeavor. Watching *Genghis Blues*, I sometimes got the feeling that there was more to the story. But Pena and Ondar are highly compelling, and the film captures the combination of sensitivity and **serendipity** that underlies artistic expression.

This reading was adapted from *Genghis Blues* by Daniel Mangin © 1999.
Reprinted from *Salon.com* with permission of the author.

[1] **Andy Warhol** (1928–1987) American artist and leader of the pop art movement
[2] **short-wave radio** a radio capable of receiving signals from all over the world
[3] **oscillations** the act of vibrating or moving back and forth with a regular, uninterrupted motion
[4] **guttural** of, or related to, a low sound produced in the throat
[5] **Howlin' Wolf** (1910–1976) American blues singer whose career peaked in the 1950s and 1960s
[6] **Mongolia** ancient region of east-central Asia inhabited by Mongol people
[7] **Genghis Khan** (c.1162–1227) tribal leader of the Mongol people who united the different tribes to form a great empire
[8] **czarist Russia** /zɑːrɪst/ Russia at the time when it was ruled by an emperor (up to 1917)
[9] **wisecracker** a person who has a tendency to be sardonic or mocking
[10] **Creole-American** a person descended from European or African settlers of the West Indies, now in the United States
[11] **Cape Verde** /keɪp vɜːrd/ an island country situated west of Senegal in the Atlantic Ocean
[12] **petrified** terrified; paralyzed with great fear
[13] **milieu** /mɪlyʊ/ environment; surroundings
[14] **nomadic herders** people who have no fixed home but continually travel around, driving and tending herds of livestock
[15] **per se** by itself
[16] **rues** feels regret or sorrow

A How much do you remember about the reading? For each question, choose the best answer.

1 Why does the writer begin with the quotation from Andy Warhol?
   a. because Warhol was also a singer
   b. in order to show that he is knowledgeable about American art
   c. to emphasize that real individuals can be fascinating on film
   d. to encourage fans of Andy Warhol to watch the film

2 What is the author's overall view of contemporary television?
   a. He thinks that some of it is not very good.
   b. He thinks that there isn't enough of it.
   c. He thinks that any television show with people in it is interesting.
   d. He thinks that it doesn't include enough music.

3 How did Paul Pena first come across the art of throat singing?
   a. He was listening to a Howlin' Wolf recording.
   b. He heard it on his short-wave radio.
   c. He saw it on a television show.
   d. He participated in a throat singing contest.

4 Where did the music Pena heard come from?
   a. San Francisco
   b. A small Russian republic
   c. Turkey
   d. Los Angeles

5 How did Pena meet Kongar-ol Ondar?
   a. Pena mailed him a recording of his own singing.
   b. Pena flew to Tuva in order to meet Ondar.
   c. Pena participated in a contest with Ondar.
   d. Pena met Ondar after a concert and sang for him.

B The following questions are all about the reading. Use the information you have read to answer each one. Try not to look back at the reading for the answers.

1 Where does most of the documentary take place?
2 Why do the Tuvans call Pena "Earthquake"?
3 For what reason does Pena feel despair?
4 For what purpose did Tuvan nomadic herders sing?
5 What are some common themes of traditional Tuvan songs?

C Critical Thinking

Discuss these questions with a partner.

1 Look back at the opening paragraph of the reading. Do you agree with Andy Warhol's point of view about film? Explain your answer giving examples.
2 Does your country or culture have any kind of unique music, or musical instruments, not widely heard of in the rest of the world? Do you like to listen to this music?
3 Do you think *Genghis Blues* would be an interesting film to watch? Why or why not?

Vocabulary Comprehension:
Odd Word Out

A For each group, circle the word or phrase that does not belong. The words in *italics* are vocabulary items from the reading.

1	come to know	divulge	discover	*ascertain*
2	fascinating	boring	*engaging*	charming
3	oblivious	sensitive	aware	*sentient*
4	*eminently*	extremely	emotionally	exceptionally
5	touching	*poignant*	dull	moving
6	questionably	doubtfully	*veritably*	dubiously
7	contradiction	parallel	*paradox*	inconsistency
8	*intuitive*	insightful	unaware	instinctive
9	fraud	*integrity*	honesty	morality
10	fortune	catastrophe	*serendipity*	luck

B Complete the sentences using the words in *italics* from A. Be sure to use the correct form of the word.

1 There may be _____ beings on other planets, but for now thinking aliens are found only in science fiction novels.

2 Jo's many years of editing experience made her _____ qualified to handle the job of publisher.

3 What makes Philippe such a talented entertainer and host is his _____ manner; people seem to be instantly drawn to him.

4 Luis likes to think of his painting of women at war as a _____ of human behavior—instead of nurturing, the women are killing off the future.

5 Many stars say that their success is nothing but _____, and that they never planned for it.

6 After seeing all the cuts and scratches on his legs, Nina quickly _____ that it was the boy next door who was climbing over her garden fence to steal her apples.

7 Though her husband passed away years ago, Margaret still wears her wedding ring as a _____ reminder of her life with him.

8 Christa's decision to quit her executive position after only two months, and take a higher paying job, shows a distinct lack of _____.

9 Although she never studied psychology, my mother knows _____ what people are thinking and what's bothering them.

10 When I saw Brad Pitt in person, my heart _____ stopped for a few seconds. I thought I was going to die!

A For each word, study the different parts. Use your knowledge of prefixes, suffixes, and word roots to write the part of speech and a simple definition for each one. Use your dictionary to check your answers. Share your ideas with a partner.

Vocabulary	Part of Speech	Definition
1 adjoining	_____	_____
2 adhere	_____	_____
3 adjacent	_____	_____
4 adverse	_____	_____
5 adverb	_____	_____
6 assimilate	_____	_____
7 assertively	_____	_____
8 assign	_____	_____
9 assistant	_____	_____
10 ascribe	_____	_____

Vocabulary Skill:
The Prefix *ad-*

In this chapter, you read the words "aspect," "ascertain," and "admits." These words all begin with the prefixes "ad-" or "as-," meaning "to," "toward," and "next to." These common prefixes are used with nouns, verbs, adjectives, and adverbs to form many words in English.

B Complete each sentence using the words from A. Be sure to use the correct form of each word.

1 As Seow Lin only returned from New York last night, I think we can _____ her bad mood to a classic case of jet lag.

2 Due to the _____ weather conditions our flight has been delayed.

3 Now that we're in senior high school, our teachers seem to be _____ us more and more homework every week. I can't keep up!

4 An _____ is a word that can be used in English to modify many other words.

5 Although Takuji is a very intelligent child, he can't seem to _____ written words as readily as other children his age do.

6 Sulinko has decided to take a job as a teaching _____ for a year to help her decide if she really wants to become a trained teacher.

7 I've heard there's a great coffee shop in the _____ building. Let's try it out later.

8 After so many years of ignoring his doctor's advice, Karl now has to _____ to a strict diet in order to maintain his health.

9 Samuel, who is usually so quiet, shocked everyone when he objected so _____ to the proposed changes in company policy.

10 Although we plan to extensively remodel our new house, every bedroom will still have an _____ bathroom, as they do now.

Chapter 2: MTV: Secrets in the Sauce

Before You Read:
Art of Music Video

A Answer the following questions.

1. Do you ever watch MTV? If so, how often? Do you watch any particular MTV shows regularly? If not, do you watch any other music programs on TV?
2. What do you like or dislike about music programs on TV?
3. Do you have a favorite contemporary song? What makes it your favorite? Have you seen the music video for this song? What do you think of it?
4. How do you think music videos have changed in the last few years?
5. How would you define "cool"? Give examples of things in the culture that you think are cool.

B Discuss your answers with a partner.

Reading Skill:
Identifying Main and Supporting Ideas

Paragraphs often use supporting ideas to give more information about the main idea of a paragraph. Supporting ideas usually follow the main idea. Different types of supporting ideas include examples, illustrations, facts, reasons, etc.

A Write M beside the main idea and S beside supporting ideas.

Paragraph 5

_____ Each program burns out and has to be replaced by something newer, cooler, funnier, and more outrageous.

_____ MTV has to keep re-inventing itself because its audience is always evolving and becoming disenchanted with what was cool last season.

_____ There is a never-ending need at MTV to stay ahead of what's happening in the world of entertainment.

Paragraph 6

_____ The list of ground-breaking MTV original programs goes on and on.

_____ 1985's *Remote Control* was the first show in which TV made fun of itself.

Paragraph 10

_____ The atmosphere at MTV encourages creativity.

_____ Senior executives have opportunities to hear from people throughout the organization.

_____ Executives want to hear what their great-looking and interesting employees have to say.

B Skim the paragraphs and check your answers with a partner.

C Now read the article and complete the comprehension exercises that follow.

http://www.asrculturelab.net/mtv

MTV:
Secrets in the Sauce

A beautiful young woman **recoils** in horror at the news she's just gotten from a fortune-teller. Her best friends have drawn cards for "success" and "wealth," but Carmen's future has even the soothsayer[1] in a funk.[2] The only thing ahead for her, he says, is "death."

Carmen, played by pop music megastar Beyoncé Knowles, runs from the fortune-teller's ornate parlor, determined to avoid her fate. In the next few hours, she'll abandon the handsome but down-and-out man she loves and hook up with Blaze, a hugely successful rap star, only to be shot dead by a **corrupt** cop. The scenes are hip, studded with music industry stars and reminiscent of Bizet's[3] famous opera, *Carmen*. Only in this production, the characters aren't singing their lines, they're rapping them.

MTV's Hiphopera, *Carmen*, topped the ratings for viewers aged twelve to thirty-four on the night of its premiere, and captured the second largest audience ever for an original film on MTV. It also typified the kind of programming left turns[4] that have kept the network out front in the art of creating new forms of TV entertainment.

MTV created its first reality show, *Real World*, a decade before the reality TV craze emerged. It also sparked a boom in bent-humored[5] animation aimed at adults and changed forever the way awards shows are presented with its annual, hugely successful showcase of the best in music video.

Behind all this innovation is a never-ending need to stay ahead of what's happening in the world of entertainment. "MTV has to keep re-inventing itself, because its audience is always evolving and becoming **disenchanted** with what was cool last season," says *TV Guide* senior critic Matt Roush. "Because each new MTV audience rebels against the previous one, each program **burns out** and has to be replaced by something newer, cooler, funnier, and more **outrageous**. MTV can never rest on its laurels,[6] because that is **antithetical** to what the network is."

The countdown of MTV's programming breakthroughs is long. Its first original program, 1985's *Remote Control*, "was the first show to **turn** TV **on its ear** and make fun of the medium itself," recalls Brian Graden who has, as programming and production president for MTV, been responsible for many of the channel's innovations since 1997. The list of **ground-breaking** MTV original programs goes on and on, while the network has launched more personalities into pop culture than any other cable outlet, including Jenny McCarthy,[7] Ben Stiller,[8] and Cindy Crawford.[9]

Yet despite such a track record, the quest to "stay fresh" and come up with new ideas has never gotten easy, says Van Toffler, president of MTV and MTV2. A big part of the way MTV operates, in fact, is geared toward keeping the entire company searching for what's next. Top executives like Toffler, and Judy McGrath, encourage department heads to identify the brightest young minds on their teams, **singling** them **out** to attend "brainstorms"—gatherings of key staff members—to address issues.

40 The brainstorm, in fact, is part of what McGrath calls "MTV secrets in the sauce." It is a gathering of people that can involve staffers from across all the MTV networks, and a dozen or so can be going on at any given time. Currently, one brainstorm is looking at interactive TV while another is examining MTV itself, its tone and attitude, and "what it tells people when making decisions about new videos, shows, or on-air talent," McGrath says.

45 An important brainstorm takes place every year in June, when sixty or so MTV executives and staffers head to a **run-down** resort on the tip of Long Island, to hole up for three days and consider new programming ideas. The event gets individuals to describe their ideas, and leads the group to build on them and agree on which projects will go forward. "We leave having greenlighted[10] fifty projects, everything we need for a year," McGrath explains.

50 The atmosphere at MTV also encourages creativity, insiders say. "The environment here is everybody talking at once and interrupting each other," McGrath says. "For me, and for a lot of us—the senior executives, if you will—it's an opportunity to hear from people deeper within the organization. You walk the halls and see these great-looking, interesting people and you want to hear what they have to say."

55 MTV staffers hit the clubs regularly, looking for what's new. A number of the network's executives make a habit of hanging out with viewers standing in line at events like the Movie Awards, or assembling daily out front of the company's Times Square headquarters.

Behind the whole process, says Toffler, is MTV Networks chairman Tom Freston, who makes it clear that creativity comes first. "The business side is important, of course," Toffler says, "but you can see his eyes light up when he hears a good idea, and you know that he knows the 60 profits don't come without the ideas." McGrath adds that what keeps the innovations coming is Freston's credo,[11] followed at MTV since almost the beginning: "Try not to let people realize that this is a business."

This reading was adapted from *Secrets in the Sauce (MTV Networks Inc's Successful Programs)* by Alan Waldman. Used by permission from *Multichannel News*, a Reed Business publication © August 2, 2002.

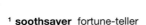

[1] **soothsayer** fortune-teller
[2] **in a funk** in a state of worry or fear
[3] **Bizet** /bizet/ classical music composer Georges Bizet (1838–1875); best known for his opera *Carmen*
[4] **left turns** moves away from the mainstream
[5] **bent-humored** comedy that has a tendency to be twisted or perverted
[6] **rest on its laurels** stop making efforts to improve as a result of being satisfied with achievements so far
[7] **Jenny McCarthy** (1972–) American ex-model turned actress, TV show host, MTV host and VJ (video jockey)
[8] **Ben Stiller** (1965–) American comedy actor best known for roles in *There's Something About Mary* and *Meet the Parents*
[9] **Cindy Crawford** (1966–) American supermodel turned MTV show host
[10] **greenlighted** approved; given the go ahead
[11] **credo** system of beliefs or principles

A Decide if the following statements about the reading are true (T), false (F), or not given (NG). If a statement is false, correct it to make it true.

	T	F	NG
1 The author thinks MTV is failing as a business.			
2 MTV's Carmen achieved very high viewer ratings on its premier night.			
3 MTV is currently planning another hiphopera.			
4 MTV's Real World was created as a response to the reality TV craze.			
5 Most of MTV's programming decisions are made at brainstorm sessions.			

B Complete the sentences about the reading with the correct answer. Then discuss your answers with a partner.

1 Some of the stars who have appeared on MTV are _____.
2 Executives at MTV are encouraged to identify the brightest _____ on their teams.
3 In June of each year, MTV executives and staffers head to a Long Island resort to consider _____.
4 The working environment at MTV encourages staff _____.
5 MTV Networks chairman Tom Freston tries not to let people realize that MTV is _____.

C Critical Thinking

Discuss these questions with a partner.
1 Name one personality who you would like to see host an MTV program. Why would you choose this person?
2 What ideas would you like to contribute to an MTV brainstorming session?
3 After the development of MTV, the invention of the CD, the MD, and the MP3, what do you think the future holds for innovations in music? Explain your answer.

Vocabulary Comprehension:
Word Definitions

A **Look at the list of words and phrases from the reading. Match each one with a definition on the right.**

1 recoils _____
2 corrupt _____
3 disenchanted _____
4 burns out _____
5 outrageous _____
6 turn on its ear _____
7 antithetical _____
8 ground-breaking _____
9 singling out _____
10 run-down _____

a. in bad condition
b. picking someone or something out from others for special attention
c. shake a situation up radically
d. original and innovative
e. shrinks back in fear or under pressure
f. totally in opposition to something
g. becomes worn out or jaded
h. disillusioned; bored
i. unrestrained or shocking; going beyond what is normally acceptable
j. dishonest and immoral

B **Complete the paragraph using most of the vocabulary from A. Be sure to use the correct form of each word. Not every word is used.**

One Eye on the Audience

As long as you don't mind the (1)_____ prices of popcorn and drinks, going to the movies is always good fun, and not only because of the movie. Sometimes watching the audience can be even more entertaining! Recently, I've become rather (2)_____ with a number of kids' movies—they just seem to recycle the same (3)_____ old plot—so I took my children to see *Spy Kids II*. Although this movie wasn't exactly (4)_____ in terms of its special effects, it was refreshingly different. However, what I enjoyed the most was watching the children. I (5)_____ a few children to our left to observe, as well as my own son and daughter. During the scary parts, they (6)_____ in joyful fear, covering their faces with candy-coated fingers. They screamed and tried desperately to bury themselves in their parents' arms. They laughed hysterically when the (7)_____ daddy was discovered, and when the Spy Kids made fun of him.

Anyway, I certainly didn't expect much from the movie. I know very well that high-quality drama and kids' movies are (8)_____. However, I was able to watch my favorite show: the audience.

C **Now write two sentences of your own using the words that are left over from A. Share your ideas with a partner.**

1 _____

2 _____

A Look at the verbs in the box below. Write them in the chart depending on whether they fit with *up*, *out*, or both prepositions. Use your dictionary to help you. Compare your answers with a partner.

take   think   draw   cheer   hurry   save   pull   split   tear
hang   burn   point   set   keep   ask   let   give   cut

Up	Both	Out
_____	_____	_____
_____	_____	_____
_____	_____	_____
_____	_____	_____
_____	_____	_____
_____	_____	_____

B Now use some of the phrasal verbs to complete the story below. Be sure to use the correct tense of each verb. Share your answers with a partner.

The Club

When I was just nine years old, my friend Noah and I **(1)**_____ a great club. We **(2)**_____ to build a place where we could **(3)**_____ by ourselves—just us, no parents, siblings, or anyone else disturbing us. When we told my mother about our plan, she **(4)**_____ that we had a big old box in the basement that we could use, if we wanted. We **(5)**_____ plans on how we could design our hangout. First we decided to paint the box, so we **(6)**_____ all our paints and decided on a color scheme. We **(7)**_____ and Noah went back to his house to look for things to put on the outside of the box. We **(8)**_____ pictures from lots of different magazines—photos of our favorite pop stars, actors, and actresses, pictures of animals, and photos of our favorite foods. We **(9)**_____ two flaps on the box for an entrance so that we could easily go in and out. We also **(10)**_____ our pocket money to buy things for our little hideaway. Needless to say, the club was a great success. In summer, we would **(11)**_____ the box and put it in the back yard, and in winter we would bring it indoors to the basement. We would invite friends over, and many of our most long-lasting friendships were formed in that box. To this day, my father keeps threatening to **(12)**_____ the box and throw it in the garbage, but my mom, knowing how much it still means to me, always persuades him to leave it right where it is—in a cozy corner of our basement.

Vocabulary Skill:
Phrasal Verbs with *up* and *out*

In this chapter, you read the phrasal verbs "hook up," "hole up," "single out," and "burn out." In English, many verbs can be combined with the prepositions "up" and "out" to form phrasal verbs that are used in a wide variety of contexts.

Real Life Skill:
The Orchestra

Advertising for an orchestra concert generally gives information about the music that will be performed, and the conductor or musicians. Often, the descriptions refer to the different sections (or types) of instruments in the orchestra. If you are looking for a concert in which you will hear a particular type of instrument, you need to be familiar with these terms.

A Read the following definitions of the sections of instruments in an orchestra.

> **strings**—instruments with strings that create sound
> **brass**—instruments that are usually made of metal and played by blowing into a mouthpiece; the sound is created by the vibration of the player's lips
> **woodwind**—instruments that are or used to be made of wood, or that are played by blowing through a mouthpiece containing a small piece of wood that vibrates to create sound
> **percussion**—instruments that are played by striking or hitting them

B Match these orchestra instruments to the correct category by writing them on the appropriate line. Use your dictionary to help you as necessary. Add any other instruments that you know.

> French horn   cymbals   cello   violin   trumpet   clarinet   tuba
> drum   piano   oboe   double bass   harp   trombone

strings: _viola,_

brass: _euphonium,_

woodwind: _flute,_

percussion: _kettledrum,_

C Discuss these questions with a partner.

1 Which of these types of instruments do you enjoy listening to? Are there any that you dislike? Explain your answers.
2 Can you play any of these instruments? Are there any that you would like to learn to play?
3 Which instrument do you think is the easiest to learn to play? Which do you think is the most difficult?

What Do You Think?

1 Do you generally have a taste for traditional art forms or cutting-edge ones? Explain your answer.
2 Should children be encouraged to appreciate traditional art forms?
3 Which TV shows or channels are considered to be the "coolest" these days?
4 Which ancient musical practices are in danger of disappearing?

Fluency Strategy: Reading *ACTIVEly*

In order to become a more fluent reader, remember to follow the six points of the **ACTIVE** approach—before, while, and after you read. See the inside front cover for more information on the **ACTIVE** approach.

Activate Prior Knowledge

Before you read, it's important to think about what you already know about the topic, and what you want to get out of the text.

A **Look at the passage on the next page. Read only the title and look at the pictures. What do you think the article is about? What do you think a "language survivor" is?**

B **Now read the first paragraph of the passage. Do you know of a language that is extinct? What do you think are some factors that cause a language to become extinct? Discuss with a partner.**

Currently, linguists estimate that there are between 6,000 and 7,000 languages in the world. Some experts have sounded the alarm that, by the year 2100, at least 3,000 of those languages could be wiped out forever. With so many languages on the brink of extinction, the efforts of social activists, educators, government officials, and many others have converged to try and solve this difficult problem. From their accumulated experiences, it has become clear that easy answers are elusive, and the unique and complex situation of each language has to be taken into consideration if a language is to experience a revival.

Cultivate Vocabulary

As you read, you may come across unknown words. Remember, you don't need to understand all the words in a passage to understand the meaning of the passage. Skip the unknown words for now, or guess at their meaning and come back to them later. Note useful new vocabulary in your vocabulary notebook—see page 6 for more advice on vocabulary.

A Now read the first paragraph of the passage again. Circle any words or phrases you don't know. Can you understand the rest of the paragraph even if you don't understand those items?

Currently, linguists estimate that there are between 6,000 and 7,000 languages in the world. Some experts have sounded the alarm that, by the year 2100, at least 3,000 of those languages could be wiped out forever. With so many languages on the brink of extinction, the efforts of social activists, educators, government officials, and many others have converged to try and solve this difficult problem. From their accumulated experiences, it has become clear that easy answers are elusive, and the unique and complex situation of each language has to be taken into consideration if a language is to experience a revival.

B Write the unknown words here. Without using a dictionary, try to guess their meaning. Use the words around the unknown word and any prefixes, suffixes, or word roots to help you.

New word/phrase

_____

_____

I think it means:

_____

_____

Think About Meaning

As you read, think about what you can infer, or "read between the lines," for example about the author's intention, attitudes, and purpose for writing.

Read the opening paragraph again and discuss these questions with a partner.

Where do you think you might see this piece of writing? Who do you think it was written for? Who do you think might join with social activists, educators, and government officials to solve the problem of disappearing languages? Do you think the author believes that a language can return from near extinction?

Increase Reading Fluency

To increase your reading fluency, it's important to monitor your own reading habits as you read. Look again at the tips on page 8. As you read, follow these tips.

Now read the whole passage "Language Survivors." As you read, check your predictions from "Think About Meaning."

Verify Strategies

To build your reading fluency, it's important to be aware of how you use strategies to read, and to consider how successfully you are using them.

Use the questions in the Self Check on page 219 and 220 to think about your use of reading strategies.

Language Survivors

Currently, linguists estimate that there are between 6,000 and 7,000 languages in the world. Some experts have sounded the alarm that, by the year 2100, at least 3,000 of those languages could be wiped out forever. With so many languages on the brink of extinction, the efforts of social activists, educators, government officials, and many others have converged to try and solve this difficult
5   problem. From their accumulated experiences, it has become clear that easy answers are elusive, and the unique and complex situation of each language has to be taken into consideration if a language is to experience a revival.

The Hawaiian Language

The Hawaiian language belongs to a related but not
10   mutually intelligible group of languages spoken by Pacific islanders. It was the only language spoken in Hawaii from A.D.1000 until Captain Cook's ships descended on the islands in 1778 and disturbed their peaceful isolation. The Hawaiian language was
15   thereafter enriched with a writing system, and it flourished under the Kingdom of Hawaii, which existed from 1795 to 1894. It is shocking to think that the number of native speakers of Hawaiian has declined from about 500,000 when Captain Cook
20   arrived to a mere 1,000 today.

There is good news, however. Hawaiians have adopted an idea from the Maori people called a "language nest." This is a preschool where children spend time with native speakers of the language. There has been a distinct resurgence in second language speakers of Hawaiian: from 8,000 in 1993 to 27,000 in 2003.

25   The Tjapukai Language

The Tjapukai language is spoken by the Tjapukai people. They inhabited the Kuranda region of northern Queensland, Australia, for 10,000 years. When white settlers attempted to build a railroad
30   through their land to connect the metropolitan areas of Cairns and Herberton, the Tjapukai people fought back. For this, they were forced to move off their land, to give up their way of life, and to do rugged farm work. Their culture destroyed, their language soon followed,
35   until only a few Tjapukai speakers remained.

In 1987, an educator named Michael Quinn and one of the last Tjapukai speakers named Roy Banning got the notion to revive the Tjapukai language. With the help of an artist, they created materials for language teaching, and while older Tjapukai began to remember their forgotten language, younger people became more interested and acquired the language. Then, in 2004, the
40   Tjapukai were given land in a national park to live on. The resurgence of their language and culture has since been an extraordinary success.

Evaluate Progress

Evaluating your progress means thinking about how much you understood from the passage, and how fluently you were able to read the passage to get the information you needed.

Check how well you understood the passage by answering the following questions.

1 Why did the author decide to write about the Hawaiian and Tjapukai languages?
   a. because they are both examples of successful language revival
   b. because they both very old languages
   c. because they are both taught in the same way
   d. because they are both probably going to become extinct

2 How many languages could be wiped out this century?
   a. 2,100
   b. 3,000
   c. 6,000
   d. 7,000

3 Why are there no easy answers to the problem of language revival?
   a. because there are too many opinions
   b. because there aren't enough language teachers
   c. because it's a complex problem, different for each language
   d. because there isn't enough money

4 Before Captain Cook arrived in Hawaii, which of these statements was true?
   a. There was an independent Kingdom of Hawaii.
   b. The Hawaiian people already spoke a little English.
   c. There were only about 1,000 speakers of the Hawaiian language.
   d. There was no writing system for the Hawaiian language.

5 Why is a "language nest" probably effective?
   a. because it is a Maori idea
   b. because young children can learn from native speakers
   c. because language nests use excellent textbooks
   d. because both English and Hawaiian are used together

6 At first, why did the white settlers want the Tjapukai land?
   a. to do rugged farm work
   b. to build schools for the Tjapukai
   c. to make a national park
   d. to build a railroad

7 What did Michael Quinn and Roy Banning do to help the Tjapukai language?
   a. They created language teaching materials.
   b. They made a writing system for the Tjapukai language.
   c. They gave the Tjapukai land to live on.
   d. They created a Tjapukai language nest.

Self Check

A Write a short answer to each of the following questions.

1. Will you use ACTIVE reading strategy outside of English class?

    Yes   No   I'm not sure

2. Do you think the ACTIVE strategy is helpful? Why or why not?

    Yes   No   I'm not sure

    _____

3. Which of the six reading passages in units 10–12 did you enjoy most? Why?

    _____

    _____

4. Which of the six reading pasages in units 10–12 was easiest? Which was most difficult? Why?

    _____

5. What do you know now that you didn't before studying units 10–12?

    _____

    _____

6. What else would you like to know about any of those topics?

    _____

    _____

7. How will you try to improve your reading fluency from now on?

    _____

    _____

    _____

B Here is a list of all the reading skills in Active Skills for Reading Book 4. For each skill, say whether you found the skill useful, not useful, or if you need more work with it. Check (✔) the appropriate box.

Reading skill	Useful	Not useful	Needs work
Arguing For and Against a Topic			
Identifying Cause and Effect			
Identifying Chronological Events			
Identifying Fact Versus Opinion			
Identifying Main and Supporting Ideas			
Identifying Meaning from Context			
Previewing			
Recognizing Sequence Markers			
Recognizing Simile and Metaphor			
Scanning			
Skimming for Content			
Understanding Inference			

C Here are the four fluency strategies covered in the Review Units. For each strategy, say whether you found it useful, not useful, or if you need more work with it. Check (✔) the appropriate box.

Fluency strategy	Useful	Not useful	Needs work
Muscle Reading			
SQ5R			
PARCER			
Reading ACTIVEly			

D Look again at the *Are You an Active Reader?* quiz on page 10 and complete your answers again. How has your reading fluency improved since you started this course?

Review Reading 7: *Sea Monsters*

Fluency Practice

Time yourself as you read through the passage. Try to read as fluently as you can. Record your time in the Reading Rate Chart on page 240. Then answer the questions on page 223.

Sea Monsters

Sea monsters are mysterious and generally large or giant sea animals whose existence is difficult to prove or to disprove. In the days of wooden ships, sea monsters were feared as malevolent
5 creatures that shattered ships at sea. Sea monster sightings have been claimed in nearly every country bordering the sea from the past through the present. Here are a few examples:

Whale Fat and Basking Sharks
10 In the recent past, a profusion of bizarre and mysterious items have been hauled out of the sea or have washed up on shore. These items have included strange blobs, some as large as a bus. They were often believed to be parts of
15 sea monsters. Recently, however, scientists have determined that these wobbly masses are simply the fat of sperm whales, not monsters. Another surprising item was found by a Japanese fishing boat in 1977. It was thought to be the body of a dead plesiosaur, a dinosaur long thought to be extinct. In fact, it was a dead basking shark, the second largest shark in the world. After their death, these sharks take on an unusual
20 shape, which can be mistaken for that of a plesiosaur.

The Bloop
The bloop is the name of a sound heard by scientists using listening equipment off the coast of South America in 1997. The sound indicated some type of animal lurking in the deep—an animal much larger than any known whale. Some scientists have suggested that the sound was made by
25 a new species of squid or octopus. Others have suggested that the sound could have been a hoax, created by a machine. Still others believe that the bloop could have been made by a number of sea creatures simultaneously. Unfortunately, since 1997 no further bloops have been forthcoming, so further research has not been possible.

Kraken
30 Kraken was the name given to sea monsters up to 13 meters long that were feared by fishermen fishing in the frigid waters off the coasts of Iceland and Norway. It is thought that kraken were quite possibly giant squid. Kraken were thought to attack ships on the surface.

The stories of kraken were later exaggerated in written accounts. They became as big as islands and capable of pulling large warships to the bottom. The British poet Tennyson wrote a poem entitled "The Kraken," which is why *the* is often used before *kraken* to this day, as if it were only one creature. An actual giant squid was discovered in 1857, but a live one was not seen until one was hooked on a line and filmed by Japanese scientists in 2005.

Trunko

Trunko is the name of a South African sea monster which reportedly washed up on shore near the city of Margate on October 25, 1924. According to witnesses, the dead body of the monster was covered in white fur eight inches long. Reportedly, the monster was about 15 meters long and three meters wide, with a long nose like an elephant's trunk. A witness, Hugh Ballance, said that he had seen the monster before it died. He claimed that it had been fighting for its life with two whales for three hours, using its tail to attack the whales. He claimed that it looked like "a giant polar bear" at one point. Evidently, the whales were the monster's undoing, and its body washed up on shore.

Even thought this story was indeed printed in a newspaper in December of that year, one has the innate sense that it could well be a hoax. Some people have offered the explanation that Trunko was the dead body of a basking or whale shark which began to look furry as it decayed. Others feel that Trunko may have been a kind of sea elephant. It has even been suggested that a Trunko creature might have been responsible for the aforementioned bloop!

Caddy

Caddy is the nickname for cadborosaurus, a type of creature reportedly living in some numbers off the Pacific coasts of California and Canada. It gets its name from Cadboro Bay, which is where the monster is most often seen. A Caddy is reported to be from five to 15 meters long. It is said to look like a snake with a head resembling a horse's. Caddies are reported to be very fast swimmers.

Here are three examples of Caddy sightings:
- In 1937, a ten-foot Caddy was found in the belly of a whale. Photographs were taken, and they match eyewitness accounts.
- In 1968, a small Caddy was caught in British Columbia.
- In 1991, a two-foot baby Caddy was found and returned to the water.

The evidence for the existence of the cadborosaurus seems fairly convincing, with actual baby Caddies supposedly kept by various people and more than 100 documented sightings.

To conclude, the various accounts of sea monsters include examples that are more believable and less believable. Some seem to be a mixture of truth and legend; others are very difficult to explain; still others seem quite plausible; while some are simply begging to be called hoaxes. In time, perhaps the truth will become clear.

851 words   Time taken _____

Reading Comprehension

1 What was the author's purpose in writing this article?
   a. to prove that most sea monsters are actually hoaxes
   b. to convince the reader to believe in sea monsters
   c. to inform the reader about several sea monsters
   d. to show the similarities between different sea monsters

2 What does the author tell us about whale fat?
   a. It shows that sea monsters sometimes kill whales.
   b. It is sometimes mistaken for a sea monster.
   c. It is often found by Japanese fishermen.
   d. It is usually found with basking sharks.

3 Which theory about the bloop was NOT mentioned in the article?
   a. It could have been created by a machine.
   b. It might have been made by an octopus or squid.
   c. It could have been made by more than one sea creature.
   d. It might have been made by a submarine.

4 Which sea monster was once believed to pull ships to the bottom of the ocean?
   a. kraken
   b. the bloop
   c. Trunko
   d. Caddy

5 Which sea monster does the author seem to believe in the least?
   a. kraken
   b. the bloop
   c. Trunko
   d. Caddy

6 According to Hugh Ballance, how did Trunko likely die?
   a. A polar bear killed Trunko.
   b. Trunko died of old age.
   c. Trunko was killed by whales.
   d. Trunko was killed by the bloop.

7 Which of these sea monsters has never been seen by an eyewitness?
   a. the bloop
   b. kraken
   c. Trunko
   d. Caddy

8 What does the author think about the evidence for Caddy?
   a. It's not believable.
   b. There's not enough of it.
   c. It definitely proves the existence of Caddy.
   d. It is quite convincing.

Review Reading 8: Music and Advertising

Fluency Practice

Time yourself as you read through the passage. Try to read as fluently as you can. Record your time in the Reading Rate Chart on page 240. Then answer the questions on page 226.

Music and Advertising

Advertisers know that music has the power to enhance advertisements through its ability to entertain the audience. Music can also make advertisements more engaging and memorable.
5 Furthermore, music can be used to help target advertisements to specific groups within the larger population. From the early days of stage performances to modern television commercials, music has played an essential role in selling
10 products and services of all kinds. Over time, recording artists have slowly been drawn into the business of advertising, and today some music programming on music networks seems to have blurred the line between what is
15 advertising and what is the content of the show.

Secrets of Advertising with Music

It might seem outrageous for advertisers to spend the large amounts of money they do for recording artists and their songs. After all, the direct connection between the music in a commercial and the amount of money the company will make from it is difficult to
20 ascertain. But, advertisers know that a thrilling or poignant song will do a much better job of catching and keeping people's attention than will a commercial that offers just information about a product. Intuitively it may seem strange, but catching people's attention can be more important to sales than trying to get any particular information across about the product or service being advertised.

25 Another reason that advertisers are willing to pay top dollar for music is because it sticks in the memory. Music has the quality of staying in a person's mind long after it has been heard. We've all had the experience of trying to get a catchy song out of our head. Advertisers make use of this quality of the human mind to "get inside the head" of their customers.

30 A third and very important reason for using popular music and musical artists in commercials is in order to target or direct a message at a particular group within the general population. For example, it isn't simply serendipity that leads advertisers of soft

drinks to choose recording artists who are popular with young people to utilize in their advertisements. They know that most soft drinks are drunk by younger people, and they
35 want to get their message to their best customers. In the same way, popular musicians and styles of music from the 1970s might be used to sell luxury cars or other luxury items, as those are things that middle-aged customers might be more likely to buy.

Highlights in the History of Music and Advertising

It was during World War II that the first advertising jingle—a short, catchy advertising
40 message in the form of a song—was broadcast over the radio in the United States. It was for a soda called Pepsi-Cola, and it was entitled "Pepsi-Cola hits the spot." Soon after that, the jingle for Chiquita bananas was declared to be number one by Time magazine. It was being played nearly 400 times a day on the radio, but it was so catchy that people never seemed to tire of it or get burnt out on it. It was even recorded by several famous singers of the time.

45 By the 1960s, the connection between popular songs and commercials had gotten even closer. In 1964, a song entitled "Little GTO" was a big hit in the United States. It was a song about a type of car, and the song was reportedly written at the request of that very car company. In 1966, a famous car rental company managed to have its jingle played by over 30 college marching bands. The jingle was heard by over 3.5 million fans at college football
50 games across the United States. While some people may recoil at these seemingly corrupt connections between music and advertising, it was becoming more and more "business as usual."

The next groundbreaking step for advertisers was to move beyond jingles and to obtain rights and control over eminent artists and their work in order to use these freely in
55 advertisements. In the 1980s, the Rolling Stones, Michael Jackson, and Madonna all formed close relationships with advertisers. The Beatles' song "Revolution" was used to sell sports shoes. Some people questioned the integrity of these performers, who were so quick to "sell out" for money. Nonetheless, these relationships were successful, and advertisers continued to approach artists for their help. Certain artists, disenchanted with commercialism,
60 refused to allow their songs to be used, but many have chosen to involve themselves with advertisers.

To conclude, it is important to mention a trend in music and advertising that has purists and critics up in arms. This is the paradoxical idea that advertising is programming, and programming can veritably be advertising. We are all familiar with infomercials—television
65 shows that are actually long commercials. Now, new programs are produced through the cooperation of television producers, advertisers, and retailers that have appeared on certain music television networks. These shows further confuse the difference between advertising and content. I wonder if one day we may watch TV shows which seem to have no commercials, because in fact they are full of commercial messages side by side with content
70 that keeps us entertained.

855 words   Time taken _____

Reading Comprehension

1 What is the main message about music and advertising?
   a. Music should remain separate from advertising.
   b. Music and advertising work together and help each other.
   c. Music needs advertising in order to entertain us.
   d. Music has always wanted to join advertising.

2 According to the passage, why might some people think that it is outrageous to pay lots of money to a famous recording artist for music used in an advertisement?
   a. because recording artists don't deserve so much money
   b. because the commercial should only contain product information
   c. because it's not clear that it will result in more sales
   d. because it's not right to mix music and advertising

3 Which of the following secrets of advertising with music is NOT mentioned in the passage?
   a. Music makes an advertisement memorable.
   b. Music helps with the targeting of customers.
   c. Music catches people's attention.
   d. Music brings different parts of a television advertisement together.

4 To target particular customers, what suggestion about music does the passage make?
   a. Choose music that creates a visual image of the product.
   b. Choose music from younger recording artists.
   c. Choose dynamic music that attracts attention.
   d. Choose a style of music that is popular with those customers.

5 Which of the following best describes an advertising *jingle*?
   a. a short, catchy song that sells a product
   b. a bell that is used in television commercials
   c. a song by a famous recording artist
   d. music that is played a great many times on the radio

6 What is significant about the song, "Little GTO"?
   a. It was the first radio advertising song.
   b. It was a very popular jingle.
   c. It was written at the request of a car company.
   d. It was an advertisement for a car rental company.

7 In the 1980s, who did advertisers try to gain more control over?
   a. competing advertising firms
   b. television networks
   c. customers
   d. eminent recording artists

8 Which surprising idea is part of a recent trend?
   a. Advertising is programming.
   b. Music is advertising.
   c. Commercials are music.
   d. Infomercials use music.

Vocabulary Index

Unit 1
Chapter 1

a handful of /ə ˈhændfʊl əv/ *exp.* a few: *There are a handful of people who believe that war is necessary.*

compelling /kəmˈpelɪŋ/ *adj.* forceful and persuasive: *She gave us compelling reasons to accept her proposal.*

cynicism /ˈsɪnəsɪzəm/ *noun* negativity; thinking that people only do things for money or pleasure: *There is a lot of cynicism about politics and politicians.*

in conjunction with /ɪn kənˈʤʌŋkʃn wɪð/ *exp.* together with: *Tough competition, in conjunction with outdated products, led to the company's downfall.*

legacy /ˈlegəsi/ *noun* something passed on or left by an earlier generation, event, etc.: *We must not let destruction of the environment be our legacy to the next generation.*

ploy /plɔɪ/ *noun* a trick, a maneuver to gain advantage or to disguise one's true intent: *He said on the telephone that he was conducting a survey, but that was just a ploy to sell me life insurance.*

tenacity /təˈnæsəti/ *noun* determination, or resolve: *She works on her project with tenacity.*

ulterior motive /ʌlˈtɪriə(r) ˈmoʊtɪv/ *noun* a hidden reason: *She has an ulterior motive for visiting her parents: she wants to move back in with them.*

venture /ˈventʃə(r)/ *noun* an act, especially a business deal, with risk: *Two companies made a joint venture to send a rocket to the moon.*

volatile /ˈvɒlətaɪl/ *adj.* unstable, likely to produce change or harm: *The situation is very volatile; rioters may try to overthrow the government.*

Chapter 2

clarification /ˌklærəfəˈkeɪʃn/ *noun* an explanation or correction: *Government officials often issue clarifications of their earlier statements.*

complement /ˈkɒmpləmənt/ *verb & noun* to make up a whole, or bring to perfection; something that completes: *The new lamps are a beautiful complement to the living room.*

concise /kənˈsaɪs/ *adj.* said in few words with much meaning; succinct: *The speaker made a concise statement of his ideas.*

deliberate /dəˈlɪbərət/ *adj.* done on purpose: *That was no accident; it was deliberate!*

inconsistency /ˌɪnkənˈsɪstənsi/ *noun* a thing that is not matching, different from: *There are many inconsistencies in her statements given to the police.*

rapport /rəˈpɔː(r)/ *noun* a friendly, sympathetic relationship between people: *Our teacher has a good rapport with her students.*

resume /rɪˈzuːm/ *verb* to begin again; restart: *The TV show will resume after this commercial.*

sarcastic /sɑːrˈkæstɪk/ *adj.* unkind, critical (comments, attitude): *Your sarcastic tone of voice shows that you don't respect your father.*

tact /tækt/ *noun* consideration, care in dealing with others, especially not to offend or shock: *She is a psychologist who uses tact in her relationships with her patients.*

think on your feet /θɪŋk ɒn jɔː(r) fiːt/ *exp.* react quickly: *Paramedics need to think on their feet while on the job to make the right diagnoses and treatment plans.*

Unit 2
Chapter 1

assert /əˈsɜːt/ *verb* to put oneself forth forcefully, become aggressive: *She finally asserted herself and gained the attention of her superiors.*

code /koʊd/ *noun* a way of hiding the true meaning of communications from all except those people who have the keys to understand it: *Spies use secret codes.*

dominate /ˈdɒmɪneɪt/ *verb* to have or use power or command over: *He dominates his company with an iron hand.*

intimate /ˈɪntɪmət/ *adj.* close: *We have had an intimate friendship since we were young.*

malicious /məˈlɪʃəs/ *adj.* evil, malevolent: *The malicious virus destroyed the computer.*

perpetrator /ˈpɜː(r)pətreɪtə(r)/ *noun* a person who commits a crime: *Police arrested the perpetrator right after he stole the watch.*

predominately /prɪˈdɒmɪnətli/ *adv.* the majority: *There are pine trees growing predominately in this area with some spruce.*

rationale /ˌræʃəˈnæl/ *noun* reason(s) to do something, the purpose for an action: *The rationale for buying* a house instead of renting is to build personal riches.

relinquish /rɪˈlɪŋkwɪʃ/ *verb* to give up, hand over, to surrender: *The author relinquished all rights to the book in exchange for a million dollars.*

replicate /ˈreplɪkeɪt/ *verb* to make a copy of something, to reproduce: *An art student replicated a famous artwork by painting a copy of it herself.*

Chapter 2

cordial /ˈkɔː(r)dʒəl/ *adj.* warm, friendly: *Everyone at the party was cordial to each other.*

cunning /ˈkʌnɪŋ/ *adj.* sly, shrewd: *The cunning spy was able to find out secrets.*

decline /dɪˈklaɪn/ *verb* to refuse, usually politely: *He declined our invitation to dinner.*

graffiti /grəˈfiːti/ *noun* words and drawings on walls, often rude, funny, or political: *The walls of those buildings are covered in graffiti.*

groom /gruːm/ *verb* to keep tidy: *They hired a gardener who kept the garden beautifully groomed.*

immaculate /ɪˈmækjələt/ *adj.* clean, spotless: *She wore an immaculate white dress.*

mangle /ˈmæŋgl/ *verb* to damage badly, to mutilate or deform: *Our photocopy machine mangles pieces of paper when it is not working correctly.*

play along /pleɪ əˈlɔːŋ/ *exp.* pretend to agree: *She knew it was a scam so she played along with it.*

prodigy /ˈprɒdədʒi/ *noun* a genius, someone of great ability: *She was a child prodigy on the violin.*

stand up for /stænd ʌp fə(r)/ *exp.* speak for or to support: *When she was bullied, he stood up for her and protected her from the bullies.*

Unit 3
Chapter 1

decipher /dɪˈsaɪfə(r)/ *verb* to puzzle out, figure out the meaning of something: *His handwriting is so bad that I can't decipher his note.*

emerge /ɪˈmɜː(r)dʒ/ *verb* to appear: *The hunter emerged from the forest and walked toward us.*

exclaim /ɪkˈskleɪm/ *verb* to cry out or shout: *"I'm insulted!" he exclaimed.*

giggle /ˈgɪgl/ *verb* to laugh in a silly, uncontrolled way, usually when nervous, amused, or embarrassed; titter: *The schoolchildren giggled when the famous football player walked into their classroom.*

heartily /ˈhɑː(r)təli/ *adv.* strongly, earnestly: *I heartily agree with what you say.*

inquire /ɪnˈkwaɪə(r)/ *verb* to ask about something: *My friend inquired about my health because I was sneezing.*

jaded /ˈdʒeɪdɪd/ *adj.* tired, worn-out: *She is jaded from working too much.*

lapse /læps/ *verb* to fall gradually: *The patient lapsed into unconsciousness.*

pristine /ˈprɪstiːn/ *adj.* pure, especially in nature, unspoiled: *We hiked through pristine wilderness in Alaska.*

radiant /ˈreɪdɪənt/ *adj.* having a bright shine, glowing: *The faces of the bride and groom were radiant at their wedding.*

Chapter 2

averse to /əˈvɜː(r)s tuː/ *exp.* to be against, or not fond of: *If you want to get far, you should not be averse to hard work and failures.*

awe-inspiring /ɔː ɪnˈspaɪərɪŋ/ *adj.* spectacular, amazing: *The landscapes depicted in his paintings are truly awe-inspiring.*

behold /bɪˈhoʊld/ *verb* to see, or look at: *Behold the beauty of the sunset!*

decked out /dekt aʊt/ *exp.* be dressed up in: *The girls were decked out in their best for the prom.*

eerie /ˈɪəri/ *adj.* strange and frightening, weird: *That old house is an eerie place at night.*

endemic /enˈdemɪk/ *adj.* often found within a particular area or group of people: *Ill health is endemic to the poor.*

exhilarating /ɪgˈzɪləreɪtɪŋ/ *adj.* invigorating, enlivening: *The cold autumn air is exhilarating.*

gracious /ˈgreɪʃəs/ *adj.* kind and polite: *She is a gracious hostess who provides her guests with everything they need.*

lucid /ˈluːsɪd/ *adj.* clear and easily understood: *She wrote a lucid explanation of the problem.*

plummet /ˈplʌmɪt/ *verb* to plunge; to go downward rapidly and far: *An airplane caught fire and plummeted to earth.*

Unit 4
Chapter 1

indifferent /ɪnˈdɪfrənt/ *adj.* not caring, without feeling; apathetic: *His indifferent attitude toward food made him lose weight.*

inspiration /ˌɪnspəˈreɪʃn/ *noun* someone or something that makes a person work hard or be creative; motivation: *She is a writer who gets her* *inspiration from the novels of Hemingway.*

nerve-racking /nɜː(r)v ˈrækɪŋ/ *adj.* stressful; causing fear and tiredness: *The flight was nerve-racking because of the storm.*

prevailing /prɪˈveɪlɪŋ/ *adj.* usual, frequent: *The prevailing wind is from the west in this area.*

rouse /raʊz/ *verb* to awaken and get up: *He rouses himself out of bed every morning at 6:30 A.M.*

summon /ˈsʌmən/ *verb* to call or send for: *My partner summoned me over to talk with him.*

swear /sweə(r)/ *verb* to declare or promise when taking an oath: *We swore to be loyal forever.*

taunt /tɔːnt/ *verb* to tease with unkind remarks; to mock: *Older boys taunted a little one, "Hey, Shorty, when are you going to grow up?"*

torment /ˈtɔː(r)ment/ *verb* to make someone miserable, inflict cruelty: *The little boy tormented insects by pulling off their legs.*

vengeance /ˈvendʒəns/ *noun* bitter retaliation; a harmful act against someone who has done something wrong to you: *He is seeking vengeance for the murder of his brother.*

Chapter 2

account /əˈkaʊnt/ *noun* a description, narrative: *The police wrote an account of the accident.*

chilling /ˈtʃɪlɪŋ/ *adj.* scary or frightening: *All throughout the night, we heard chilling coyote cries.*

despite the fact /dɪˈspaɪt ðə fækt/ *exp.* in spite of, notwithstanding: *Despite the fact that she was tired, she continued to work late into the night.*

disconcerting /ˌdɪskənˈsɜː(r)tɪŋ/ *adj.* disturbing: *The sight of a strange man at my door was disconcerting.*

engrossed /ɪnˈɡroʊst/ *adj.* have your attention kept completely; to be captivated: *He engrossed himself in his writing for many months.*

fear the worst /fɪə(r) ðə wɜː(r)st/ *exp.* expect the worst or something bad: *We have not heard from him in months. We fear the worst for his safety.*

mortals /ˈmɔː(r)tlz/ *noun* living beings: *All of us are mortals and will die one day.*

puzzle /ˈpʌzl/ *verb* to confuse: *The location of the sunken city puzzled explorers.*

vanishing /ˈvænɪʃɪŋ/ *adj.* disappearing: *The story of the vanishing man in the taxi is an urban myth.*

verify /ˈverɪfaɪ/ *verb* to prove something is true; to confirm: *I verified the store's address by calling to check it.*

Unit 5
Chapter 1

anecdotes /ˈænɪkdoʊts/ *noun* short stories, especially about one's own experiences: *The sailor tells amusing anecdotes about his travels.*

arbitrary /ˈɑː(r)bətreri/ *adj.* unwilling to use reason or listen to others; high-handed: *He made an arbitrary decision to sell the house without asking his wife.*

confinement /kənˈfaɪnmənt/ *noun* the state of being kept within certain limits: *When a prisoner is kept in solitary confinement, he or she is the only one in a prison cell.*

exquisite /ɪkˈskwɪzɪt/ *adj.* very great feeling of pleasure or pain; beautiful: *Nothing can compare with the exquisite joy of knowing your mother is proud of you.*

facet /ˈfæsɪt/ *noun* part, aspect: *The problem that we face now has many legal and financial facets.*

miniature /ˈmɪnətʃʊr/ *adj. & noun* very small; a small original or copy of something: *She paints miniatures of people.*

profound /prəˈfaʊnd/ *adj.* intellectually deep, insightful: *A philosopher's profound insights into life inspire his readers.*

reinforce /ˌriːɪnˈfɔː(r)s/ *verb* to add strength to something, make it stronger: *Having steel rods in the concrete structures helps reinforce the building.*

sparse /spɑː(r)s/ *adj.* scanty or scattered; not having a lot of substance: *The sparse vegetation will not support much wildlife.*

unity /ˈjuːnəti/ *noun* two or more things made into one: *Playing a sport requires a unity of body and mind.*

Chapter 2

consciously /ˈkɒnʃəsli/ *adv.* with deliberate intention: *She was consciously making an effort to annoy her mother.*

creep in /kriːp ɪn/ *exp.* sneak in; build up gradually: *When they realized that they were lost, fear slowly crept in.*

diagrams /ˈdaɪəɡræms/ *noun* drawings with markings to show how something is put together or works: *The engineer drew a diagram of a telephone circuit (a machine, ventilation system, etc.).*

draft /dræft/ *noun* a less than finished version of something written: *the first draft of a letter, the final draft of a report*

exaggerated /ɪɡˈzædʒəreɪtɪd/ *adj.* overstated: *The*

exaggerated version of the story is more interesting than the original.

grab me /græb miː/ *exp.* be enthusiastic about or attracted by something: *The photo in the magazine grabbed me as it was so beautifully taken.*

infant /ˈɪnfənt/ *noun* a baby: *The mother held an infant in her arms.*

settled on /ˈsetld ɒn/ *exp.* decide on something: *After looking through many designs, we finally settled on the one which was quite reasonably priced.*

watertight /ˈwɔːtə(r) ˈtaɪt/ *adj.* made so that water cannot pass through; impervious: *The wooden boat was made watertight with special sealants.*

wrinkle /ˈrɪŋkl/ *noun* a line or fold in something; a crease: *The old lady has wrinkles in her face.*

Unit 6
Chapter 1

across the board /əˈkrɔːs ðe bɔː(r)d/ *exp.* applies to everyone; unanimously: *The feelings of loss were felt across the board.*

astute /əˈstuːt/ *adj.* intelligent, keen in judgment: *She is an astute investor in the stock market and always knows which stocks to avoid.*

bypass /ˈbaɪpɑːs/ *verb* to go past or to find a way around: *The problem is so difficult that we must find a way to bypass it.*

empathy /ˈempəθi/ *noun* the ability to share or understand another person's feelings (attitudes, reasons, etc.): *I have empathy for you in your fear about speaking in front of a group.*

endow /ɪnˈdaʊ/ *verb* to give a good quality or ability: *Her parents endowed their daughter with high intelligence.*

malaise /mæˈleɪz/ *noun* a feeling of illness; unhappiness: *He suffers from a general malaise with pains and depression.*

prone to /proʊn tə/ *exp.* inclined toward, likely to do something: *He is prone to forgetting his car keys.*

restraint /rɪˈstreɪnt/ *noun* not acting with full force, and in control of emotions or power; moderation: *Even though the mother was very angry, she acted with restraint and didn't yell at her child.*

stability /stəˈbɪləti/ *noun* a state of very little change or upset: *There is political stability in the country, now that the war is over.*

track down /træk daʊn/ *exp.* find by following a trail; follow up on: *Paul tracked down his long lost*

friend and finally found him.

Chapter 2

allude to /əˈluːd tə/ *exp.* talk or write about something indirectly, to hint: *The politician alluded to the idea that she might not run for office again.*

conceive /kənˈsiːv/ *verb* to think of something: *I can't conceive of why he did such a stupid thing!*

crave /kreɪv/ *verb* to desire greatly or uncontrollably: *She craves chocolate and will do anything to get it.*

criteria /kraɪˈtɪrɪə/ *noun* rule used to judge something; standard of measurement: *Our company must make a 10% profit in the first quarter and another in the subsequent quarters; that is the criteria of success that we use.*

dynamics /daɪˈnæmɪks/ *noun* the factors that shape a personal relationship: *Their love and devotion are the key dynamics in their marriage.*

gifted /ˈgɪftɪd/ *adj.* having a special natural ability: *She is a gifted violinist.*

hypothesis /haɪˈpɒθəsɪs/ *noun* a working theory: *Scientists do experiments to see if their hypotheses work.*

novelty /ˈnɒvəlti/ *noun* something new and unusual: *It is a novelty to visit an amusement park for the first time.*

postulate /ˈpɒstʃəleɪt/ *verb* to state something as true without proof: *Scientists postulated the existence of Pluto more than 30 years before it was finally discovered in 1930.*

take the plunge /teɪk ðe plʌndʒ/ *exp.* immerse oneself in a potentially risky situation: *She took the plunge and invested all her money in that fund.*

Unit 7
Chapter 1

alert /əˈlɜː(r)t/ *verb* to bring to the attention: *We alerted the hotel staff to the suspicious package in the hall.*

ambiguity /ˌæmbɪˈgjuːəti/ *noun* something that is not clear and having more than one meaning: *The ambiguity of the case made it hard for all to understand.*

attributed to /əˈtrɪbjuːtɪd tə/ *exp.* to be credited for; be the reason for: *His success can be attributed to his talent and hard work.*

compositionally /ˌkɒmpəˈzɪʃnəli/ *adv.* the way how something is put together, its makeup: *Compositionally, this medicine uses traditional* herbs in a modern form.

fuss /fʌs/ *noun* a show of great concern over something unimportant: *What a fuss over such a small mistake!*

generate /ˈʤenəreɪt/ *verb* to make something happen; to produce; to initiate: *Advertising has generated a big increase in demand for the product.*

mandatory /ˈmændətɔːri/ *adj.* required; dictated by law; compulsory: *The law makes it mandatory for children to go to school until they reach the age of 16.*

proponents /prəˈpoʊnənts/ *noun* a supporter; someone who favors something: *That senator is a proponent of lowering taxes.*

revolve around /rɪvɒlv əˈraʊnd/ *exp.* to have as a focus: *His life revolves around his family.*

texture /ˈtekstʃər/ *noun* the visual pattern and degree of smoothness or roughness to touch produced by a material, through the placement of fibers in the fabric: *Wool flannel has a smooth, soft texture.*

Chapter 2

abundant /əˈbʌndənt/ *adj.* plentiful, profuse: *Food is in abundant supply in this country.*

account for /əˈkaʊnt fɔː(r)/ *exp.* to explain: *Stress and lack of nutrition accounted for his ill health.*

adhere to /ədˈhɪə(r) tə/ *exp.* to obey; to follow strictly: *Car drivers must adhere to the rules of driving or be punished.*

analysis /əˈnæləsɪs/ *noun* work done to find facts and solutions to problems; a careful study: *We did an analysis of the problem and proposed solutions to it.*

correlating /ˈkɒrəleɪtɪŋ/ *adj.* the state of how one thing relates meaningfully to another: *Because of our successful marketing campaign, we will be able to see the correlating increase in profits in months to come.*

restrict /rɪˈstrɪkt/ *verb* to restrain or control: *Restaurants restrict the use of their toilets to customers only.*

rule out /ruːl aʊt/ *exp.* to decide something is not possible: *Since we have ruled out the possibility of buying a new car, we must get the old one fixed.*

staple /ˈsteɪpl/ *noun* common or important item: *Olive oil is a staple of the Greek diet.*

therapeutic /ˌθerəˈpjuːtɪk/ *adj.* healing, curative: *The mineral waters of the spa have a therapeutic effect on people with arthritis.*

validate /ˈvælɪdeɪt/ *verb* to confirm; to learn whether something is true or not: *The police officer*

validated the man's story about the robbery.

Unit 8
Chapter 1

coagulate /koʊˈægjuleɪt/ *verb* to change from liquid to firm or solid form: *Blood coagulates and closes a cut.*

coalesce /ˌkoʊəˈles/ *verb* to come together and form a whole: *Our plans for a long trip finally coalesced when we mapped out exactly where to go.*

contemplate /ˈkɒntəmpleɪt/ *verb* to think about something seriously: *The manager contemplated the results of the report for hours.*

dreary /ˈdrɪri/ *adj.* dark and sad, gloomy: *That old house has such a dreary look.*

nudge /nʌʤ/ *verb* to push in a gentle manner: *I nudge him to get his attention.*

perilously /peˈrələsli/ *adv.* something that is in the way of becoming dangerous or harmful: *They came perilously close to death.*

plunge /plʌnʤ/ *verb* to plummet, dive, or fall fast and far: *A diver plunged into the water from a cliff.*

remnants /ˈremnənts/ *noun* leftover bits or something that remains, especially of cloth: *I made a colorful blanket from remnants of cloth.*

spine-chilling /spaɪn ˈtʃɪlɪŋ/ *adj.* frightening: *We heard a spine-chilling account of how the village was wiped out.*

testify /ˈtestɪfaɪ/ *verb* fig. to demonstrate or provide proof for something: *Her success testifies to much hard work.*

Chapter 2

deduce /dɪˈduːs/ *verb* to reach a conclusion by reasoning from the general to the specific: *Tom becomes quiet when his girlfriend is angry with him; today he is quiet and so I deduce she is angry.*

dispatch /dɪˈspætʃ/ *verb* to send (someone or something): *The Ministry dispatched a message (representative, car, etc.).*

dormant /ˈdɔː(r)mənt/ *adj.* inactive: *In winter, the plants are dormant; then they come to life again in the spring.*

laden with /ˈleɪdn wɪð/ *exp.* full of: *The truck is laden with goods for the market.*

lurk /ˈlɜː(r)k/ *verb* to wait in hiding: *The robbers lurked in the woods near the house as they waited for darkness to fall.*

moisture /ˈmɔɪstʃər/ *noun* dampness, small amount of liquid on something: *The moisture in the air makes it humid today.*

peruse /pəˈruːz/ *verb* to read or examine something carefully: *He perused the newspaper, looking for news of his hometown.*

residue /ˈrezɪduː/ *noun* something left over after a process, remainder: *My dishwasher is leaving soap residue on my glasses.*

teasing /ˈtiːzɪŋ/ *adj.* desirable or enticing: *Teasing offers of free merchandise at that store are just to get you to come in and buy.*

untenable /ʌnˈtenəbl/ *adj.* describing something (an opinion, lawsuit, etc.) which cannot be defended; indefensible: *The army is located in an untenable place and must retreat or be killed.*

Unit 9
Chapter 1

blip /blɪp/ *noun* a short electronic signal (sound, picture, etc.); an occurrence: *An airplane makes a blip on a radar screen.*

devote /dɪˈvoʊt/ *verb* to put aside or use for a special purpose: *The town council devoted an area to housing for the poor.*

extract /ˈekstrækt/ *verb* to remove or pull out (something firmly fixed): *The dentist extracted a bad tooth.*

fiscal /ˈfɪskəl/ *adj.* related to taxation and spending of government money: *The country's fiscal policy is to lower taxes and increase spending in order to stimulate the economy.*

fossil fuels /ˈfɒsəl ˈfjuːəlz/ *noun* fuel, such as coal and oil, produced by the changing of ancient plant and animal life into carbon: *Fossil fuels produce substantial air pollution.*

intermittent /ˌɪntə(r)ˈmɪtənt/ *adj.* happening with stops and starts, periodic: *There will be intermittent rain showers today in Los Angeles.*

measure up to /ˈmeʒər ʌp tə/ *exp.* to meet standards: *The new student's work measures up to the level of the other students.*

ravaged /ˈrævɪdʒd/ *adj.* something that has been attacked violently and/or destroyed: *His body was ravaged with sickness and pain.*

scarcity /ˈskersəti/ *noun* very small or limited amount of something: *There is a scarcity of water in the desert.*

swift /swɪft/ *adj.* quick, rapid: *The artist drew my portrait with a few swift movements of his pencil.*

Chapter 2

aforementioned /əˈfɔː(r)ˌmenʃənd/ *adj.* stated before; said earlier in writing or speech: *The aforementioned person was at the scene of the accident.*

better off /ˈbetər ɒf/ *exp.* live more comfortably compared to before: *Despite being better off than before, they were not happier.*

compress /kəmˈpres/ *verb* to press together, or make compact: *That big garbage truck compresses cartons and tin cans until they are flat.*

in reserve /ɪn rɪˈzɜː(r)v/ *exp.* keep something for later use: *I keep a small radio in reserve, so I can listen to music if my stereo system breaks.*

literally /ˈlɪtərəli/ *adv.* according to the exact words: *I know he told you to get lost, but he didn't mean it literally; he just wanted you not to bother him.*

mass-produce /mæs proʊˈduːs/ *verb* to manufacture products in large amounts using modern machinery: *Mass producing automobiles will enable almost everyone to own a car.*

muck up /ˈmʌk ʌp/ *exp.* pollute: *Pollutants that muck up the atmosphere contribute to environmental damage in the long run.*

obstacle /ˈɒbstəkəl/ *noun* something that gets in the way and stops action or progress; hurdle: *A tree fell across the road and became an obstacle for cars and trucks.*

reach a peak /riːtʃ ə piːk/ *exp.* to reach the highest point: *The price of gas has reached a peak and will stay high for some time.*

side effect /saɪd ɪˈfekt/ *noun* an additional and possibly unexpected result of an action: *If we buy over that company, the side effects will be a large bank loan and the need to fire many people.*

Unit 10
Chapter 1

colloquial /kəˈloʊkwiəl/ *adj.* typical of informal spoken language: *We use colloquial language when talking among friends.*

converge /kənˈvɜː(r)dʒ/ *verb* to meet at a common point: *On hot days, people converge on the beach to cool off.*

divergence /daɪˈvɜː(r)dʒens/ *noun* the state of being separated and going off in different directions, especially in conflict: *Because of divergence* in political opinions, several political parties were formed.

intelligible /ɪnˈtelɪdʒəbəl/ *adj.* able to be heard and understood: *There were loud noises from the burning building, but the firefighters' shouts were still intelligible.*

metropolitan /ˌmetrəˈpɒlɪtən/ *adj.* related to a city and its suburbs: *Metropolitan Miami covers a much larger area than the city of Miami itself.*

on the brink of /ɒn ðə brɪŋk əv/ *exp.* very close to: *The economy is in such bad shape that it is on the brink of disaster.*

perspective /pə(r)ˈspektɪv/ *noun* the set of beliefs, interests, attitudes, etc., that contribute to one's judgment on issues and events: *She has a unique perspective on the economic problems of Southeast Asia.*

resurgence /rɪˈsɜː(r)dʒəns/ *noun* a rise or increase that happens after a time of no or slow movement; an upward trend: *A resurgence of growth in the economy is always good news.*

revival /rɪˈvaɪvəl/ *noun* a reawakening, a new consciousness: *A religious revival swept the nation.*

wiped out /waɪpt aʊt/ *exp.* completely destroyed or devastated: *The flood wiped out all roads and houses in the area.*

Chapter 2

accumulate /əˈkjuːmjəleɪt/ *verb* to add up, increase: *Interest accumulates in my savings account month by month.*

acquire /əˈkwaɪə(r)/ *verb* to gain: *She acquired a knowledge of Spanish while living in Latin America.*

arduous /ˈɑː(r)dʒuəs/ *adj.* difficult, tiring: *The refugees made an arduous journey through the mountains.*

descend on /dɪˈsend ɒn/ *exp.* arrive suddenly, as in an attack: *The opera star's fans descended on him, begging for autographs.*

elusive /ɪˈluːsɪv/ *adj.* hard to see or get a hold of: *He is an elusive man. We never know what he is doing or where he is going.*

enrich /ɪnˈrɪtʃ/ *verb* to add good things to: *The farmer enriched the soil with fertilizer.*

maneuver /məˈnuːvə(r)/ *verb* to move or turn with skill: *It was difficult to maneuver our car over the rugged terrain.*

notion /ˈnoʊʃn/ *noun* an idea or belief: *He has a silly notion about making a million dollars without working.*

rugged /ˈrʌgɪd/ *adj.* hilly, referring to land that is

difficult to travel over: *The Rockies have rugged mountains and winding roads.*

utensil /juːˈtensəl/ *noun* a tool or implement, especially for eating food: *Utensils for eating include knives, forks, and spoons.*

Unit 11
Chapter 1

beg /beg/ *verb* to ask strongly, to plead: *He begged her to stay with him, but she left any how.*

fend for oneself /fend fɔːr wʌnˈself/ *exp.* take care of oneself without anybody's help: *When her parents died, she had to fend for herself.*

frigid /ˈfrɪdʒɪd/ *adj.* freezing, very cold: *Dress warmly; it's frigid out there.*

graze on /greɪz ɒn/ *exp.* feed on grass: *The sheep grazed on the grass in the fields and on the hills.*

in profusion /ɪn prəˈfjuːʒn/ *exp.* in a great amount, in abundance: *Leaves burst out in profusion on trees in the springtime.*

innately /ɪˈneɪtli/ *adv.* inborn, being part of someone from birth; naturally: *He knows innately that he has to work hard to make a difference.*

recede /rɪˈsiːd/ *verb* to move back, to retreat: *Sea water recedes when the tide goes out.*

simultaneous /ˌsaɪmlˈteɪniəs/ *adj.* things or events happening at the same time: *The final trumpet blast was simultaneous with the loud crash from the drums.*

undoing /ʌnˈduːɪŋ/ *noun* downfall, defeat: *He spent too much money, which was his undoing.*

wobbly /ˈwɒbli/ *adj.* something that is not steady, shaky: *One of the legs of the chair is wobbly. We should fix it soon.*

Chapter 2

bizarre /bɪˈzɑː(r)/ *adj.* odd, weird: *She died under bizarre circumstances no one could explain.*

embroider upon /ɪmˈbrɔɪdər əˈpɒn/ *exp.* exaggerate or dress up with fanciful ideas: *The urban myth was embroidered upon with many fanciful details.*

forthcoming /ˌfɔː(r)θˈkʌmɪŋ/ *adj.* arriving in the future, due to be delivered: *More information will be forthcoming shortly.*

gear up /gɪər ʌp/ *exp.* to prepare, put on equipment: *Let's gear up for our adventure into the jungle.*

haul /hɔːl/ *verb* to carry a load: *Trucks haul sand to build a new road.*

malevolent /məˈlevələnt/ *adj.* evil or harmful: *The malevolent leaders inflicted a lot of grief on the people.*

paranormal /ˌpærəˈnɔː(r)ml/ *adj.* a supernatural occurrence or something that has no scientific explanation: *Paranormal sightings in the area are common.*

shatter /ˈʃætə(r)/ *verb* to expose or to reveal the truth: *His exaggerated story was shattered by the truth.*

stumble on /ˈstʌmbəl ɒn/ *exp.* find or reach accidentally or unexpectedly: *She stumbled on an interesting book café on her daily walk last week.*

take heart /teɪk hɑːrt/ *exp.* regain faith or be encouraged: *Fans took heart when they heard that their retired idol would stage a comeback concert.*

Unit 12
Chapter 1

ascertain /ˌæsəˈteɪn/ *verb* to determine, find out (facts, a situation, etc.): *The lawyer ascertained the facts about the accident.*

eminent /ˈemɪnənt/ *adj.* widely recognized as important; distinguished: *She is eminent in the field of linguistics*

engaging /ɪnˈɡeɪdʒɪŋ/ *adj.* charming, captivating: *She has an engaging personality.*

integrity /ɪnˈteɡrəti/ *noun* completeness; moral strength and honesty: *The integrity of our nation depends on working together.*

intuitive /ɪnˈtuːɪtɪv/ *adj.* related to feeling, not learned knowledge: *He never took lessons, but he has an intuitive knack for playing the piano.*

paradox /ˈpærədɒks/ *noun* a puzzling statement that states two opposing truths; an impossible state of affairs: *He tried to explain the paradox that on his vacation, he had the best and the worst time of his life.*

poignant /ˈpɔɪnjənt/ *adj.* deeply moving, highly emotional: *The sudden death of the little girl was a poignant experience for the entire community.*

sentient /ˈsentɪənt/ *adj.* conscious or having sense perception: *Even though he was young, he was sentient of his surroundings.*

serendipity /ˌserənˈdɪpəti/ *noun* something good that happens by chance or luck: *It was by serendipity that I found a ten-dollar bill on the street.*

veritably /ˈverɪtəbli/ *adv.* truly, really: *He veritably*

enjoys learning interesting facts from the encyclopedias.

Chapter 2

antithetical /ˌæntɪˈθetɪkəl/ *adj.* opposite or in direct contrast to: *His actions are antithetical to the company's beliefs.*

burn out /bɜː(r)n aʊt/ *exp.* run its course of popularity; suffer a breakdown: *New trends come and go. Old ones burn out and make way for new ones.*

corrupt /kəˈrʌpt/ *adj.* dishonest: *That official is corrupt because he takes bribes.*

disenchanted /ˈdɪsɪntʃæntɪd/ *adj.* no longer believing in something that was valued; disillusioned: *Her boss made her promises but didn't keep them; now she is disenchanted with him.*

ground-breaking /ɡraʊnd breɪkɪŋ/ *adj.* something that is original and innovative: *The scientist who came up with the ground-breaking insight became famous overnight.*

outrageous /aʊtˈreɪdʒəs/ *adj.* ridiculous, shocking: *That hotel charges outrageous prices.*

recoil /rɪˈkɔɪl/ *verb* to move back quickly from something, especially in horror, fear, etc.: *The hunter recoiled when he saw a poisonous snake in front of him.*

run-down /rʌn daʊn/ *adj.* in poor condition, needing to be fixed; dilapidated: *That old house is run-down and needs repairs and painting.*

single out /sɪŋɡl aʊt/ *exp.* to choose or point out one person from a group: *The professor singled out the only person who answered the question correctly.*

turn something on its ear /tɜː(r)n ˈsʌmθɪŋ ɒn ɪts eə(r)/ *exp.* to radically change something, for example, to make it more exciting: *The new manager was able to turn the shop's image on its ear.*

Maps: North & South America

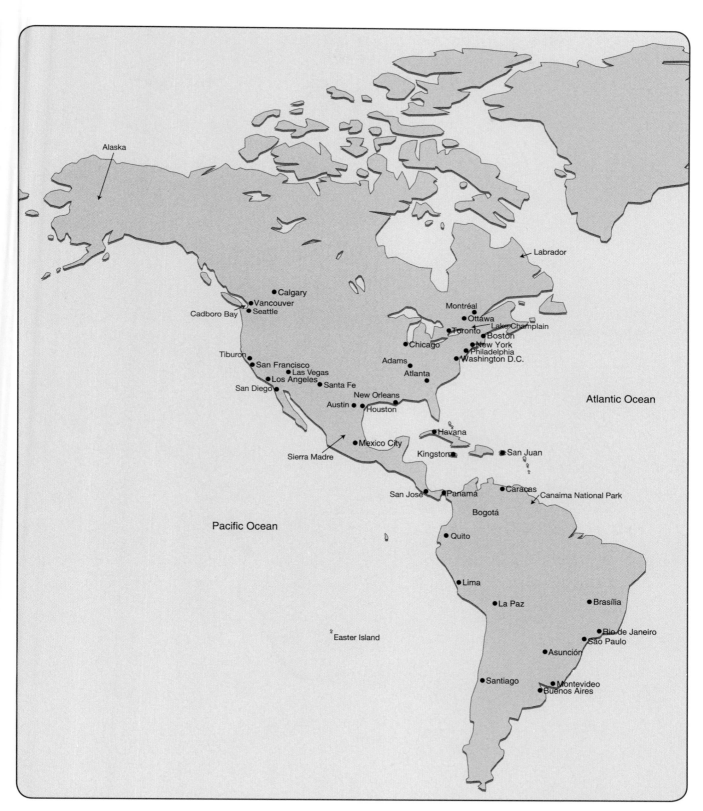

Alaska

Labrador

Calgary
Vancouver
Cadboro Bay
Seattle

Montréal
Ottawa
Lake Champlain
Toronto
Boston
Chicago
New York
Philadelphia
Washington D.C.

Tiburon
San Francisco
Las Vegas
Los Angeles
Santa Fe
San Diego

Adams
Atlanta

New Orleans
Austin
Houston

Atlantic Ocean

Havana
Kingston
San Juan

Mexico City

Sierra Madre

San Jose
Panamá
Caracas
Canaima National Park

Bogotá

Pacific Ocean

Quito

Lima

Easter Island

La Paz
Brasília

Rio de Janeiro
São Paulo
Asunción

Santiago
Montevideo
Buenos Aires

Maps: *Europe & Africa*

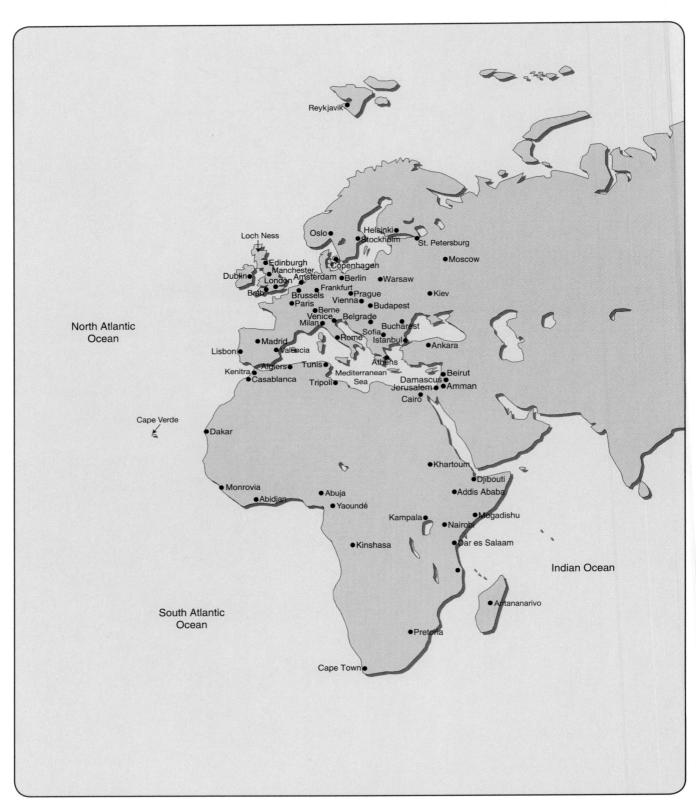

North Atlantic Ocean

South Atlantic Ocean

Indian Ocean

Mediterranean Sea

Reykjavik

Loch Ness
Oslo
Helsinki
Stockholm
St. Petersburg
Moscow
Edinburgh
Copenhagen
Manchester
Dublin
Amsterdam
London
Berlin
Warsaw
Bath
Frankfurt
Kiev
Brussels
Prague
Paris
Vienna
Berne
Budapest
Venice
Belgrade
Milan
Bucharest
Rome
Sofia
Madrid
Istanbul
Lisbon
Ankara
Valencia
Athens
Kenitra
Algiers
Tunis
Beirut
Casablanca
Tripoli
Damascus
Jerusalem
Amman
Cairo

Cape Verde

Dakar

Khartoum
Djibouti
Monrovia
Addis Ababa
Abidjan
Abuja
Yaoundé
Mogadishu
Kampala
Nairobi
Kinshasa
Dar es Salaam

Antananarivo

Pretoria

Cape Town

Maps: Asia & Oceania

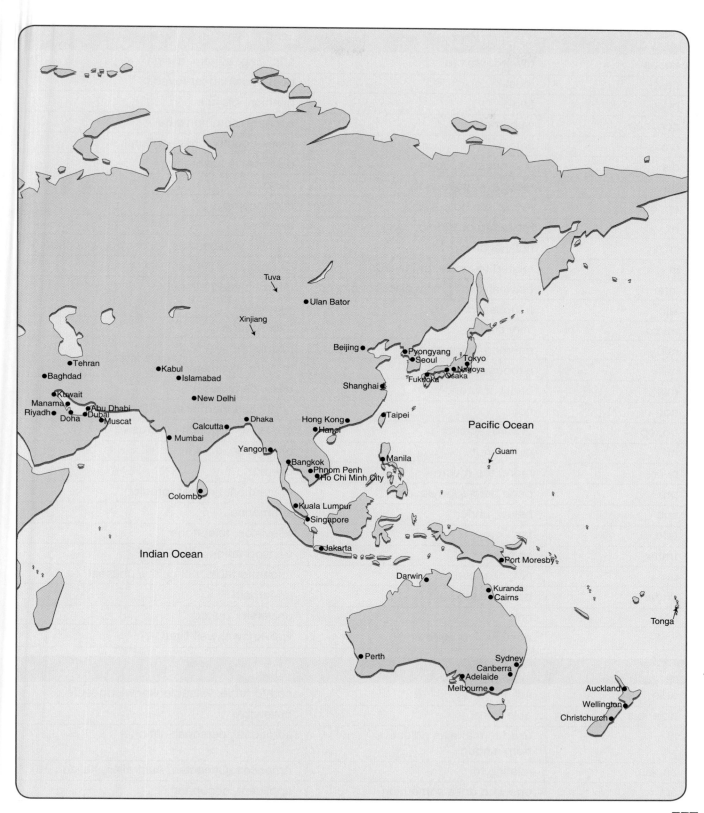

Tuva

● Ulan Bator

Xinjiang

Beijing ● ● Pyongyang
● Seoul   Tokyo ●
● Tehran   ● Nagoya
● Baghdad   ● Kabul   Fukuoka ● ● Osaka
● Islamabad   Shanghai ●
● Kuwait
Manama ● ● New Delhi
Riyadh ● ● Abu Dhabi   Hong Kong ●   ● Taipei   Pacific Ocean
● Doha ● Dubai   ● Hanoi
● Muscat   Calcutta ● ● Dhaka
● Mumbai
Yangon ●   ● Manila   ● Guam
● Bangkok
● Phnom Penh
● Ho Chi Minh City
Colombo ●
● Kuala Lumpur
● Singapore
Indian Ocean   ● Jakarta
                                                        ● Port Moresby
                          Darwin ●
                                        ● Kuranda
                                        ● Cairns
                                                                        Tonga
● Perth   Sydney ●
                        Canberra ●
                    ● Adelaide   Auckland ●
        Melbourne ●   Wellington ●
                                        Christchurch ●

Prefixes and Suffixes

Here is a list of prefixes and suffixes that appear in the reading passages of this book.

Prefix	Meaning	Example
ad, as	toward, next to	adjoining, adhere, assign
best-	most	best-known, best-loved
bi	two	biathlon, bicycle
con, com	with, together	connect, communicate
cross-	across	cross-country, cross-cultural
dis	not, negative, apart	disapprove, disorder
de	reduce, remove, not	deprive
en, em	to put into, to cover	endangered
ex	related to outside or away	expense
im, in	not, negative	impolite, independent, insensitive, inconsistent
in	related to inside, or inwards	income
inter	between two or more places or groups	Internet, international
kilo	a thousand	kilometer
micro	very small	microphone
mid	referring to the middle	midnight
milli	a thousandth	milliliter, millimeter
mis	badly or wrongly	misunderstood
non	not	nonfiction, nonbeliever, non-verbal
ob, op	toward, against	obstacle, opponent, obtrusive
off	out of, not	off-season, off-limits
over	more, too much	overeat
pre	done before / in advance	precaution, prepaid, predict
sub	below, under	submarine
tele	far	television, telephone
trans	across	transportation
un	not, negative	uncomfortable, unhealthy, unusual
under	beneath, too little	underpaid
uni	one	university, united
well-	done well, or a lot	well-known, well-liked

Suffix	Meaning	Example
able	full of	comfortable, valuable, knowledgeable
able/ible	able to be	believable
al	used to make an adjective from a noun	additional, personal, national
an, ian	relating to	American, Canadian, Australian, Italian
ant	one who does something	applicant, occupant

Suffix	Meaning	Example
ant/ent	indicating an adjective	important, independent
ate	used to make a verb from a noun	originate
ation/ution/ition	used to make a noun from a verb	combination, resolution, competition
dom	state of being	freedom
eer	one who does something	engineer
en	used to form verbs meaning to increase a quality	harden, threaten, frighten
ence	added to some adjectives to make a noun	excellence
ent	used to make an adjective from a verb	excellent
ent	one who does something	student
er, or	someone or something that does something	computer, air conditioner, ringer, reporter, competitor, learner, teacher
er	(after an adjective) more	faster, safer
ese	relating to	Taiwanese, Japanese
est	(after an adjective) most	closest, earliest, thinnest
ever	any	whatever
ful	filled with	harmful, useful, beautiful, colorful, forgetful
hood	state or condition	adulthood, childhood
ion, sion, tion	indicating a noun	permission, discussion, education, invention
ine	indicating a verb	combine
ish	relating to	British, Irish, foolish
ist	one who does something	terrorist
ity	used to make a noun from an adjective	personality, celebrity
ive	indicating an adjective	expensive, sensitive
ize	used to make a verb from an adjective	socialize
less	without, not having	hopeless
logy	the study of	biology, psychology, geology
ly	used to form an adverb from an adjective	carefully, frequently
mate	companion	roommate, classmate
ment	used to make a noun from a verb	movement, excitement, government
ness	used to make a noun from an adjective	foolishness
ous, ious	relating to	adventurous, dangerous, delicious, curious
-shaped	in the shape of	moon-shaped
some	full of	awesome, handsome
th	indicating an order	fifteenth, eighteenth
un	not, negative	unhealthy, unfortunate
ure	indicating some nouns	culture, temperature, candidature
y	indicating an adjective	healthy, flashy

Reading Rate Chart

Time (minutes)	Review Reading 1	2	3	4	5	6	7	8	Rate (words per minute)
1:00									850
1:15									680
1:30									567
1:45									486
2:00									425
2:15									378
2:30									340
2:45									309
3:00									283
3:15									262
3:30									243
3:45									227
4:00									213
4:15									200
4:30									189
4:45									179
5:00									170
5:15									162
5:30									155
5:45									148
6:00									142
6:15									136
6:30									131
6:45									126
7:00									121

Reading Comprehension Chart

Score	Review Reading 1	2	3	4	5	6	7	8
7								
6								
5								
4								
3								
2								
1								
0								